OCEANIA

45 KONA, Hawaii
46 HAWAII
47 CHRISTMAS
   ISLAND, Kiribati
48 TAHITI
49 MICRONESIA
50 DARWIN,
   Australia
51 CAIRNS, LIZARD
   ISLAND, Australia
52 CAPE BOWLING
   GREEN, Australia
53 BRISBANE, CAPE
   MORETON,
   Australia
54 BAY OF
   ISLANDS, NORTH
   CAPE, New
   Zealand
55 WHAKATANE,
   BAY OF PLENTY,
   New Zealand

THE
WORLD ATLAS OF
SPORT FISHING

THE
WORLD ATLAS OF
SPORT FISHING

KEN SCHULTZ

HAMLYN

DEDICATION

To Roger Tucker

Picture Acknowledgments

The publishers would like to thank the following organisations and individuals for their kind permission to reproduce the photographs in the book:

All photographs by the author Ken Schultz, except: Bermuda Department of Tourism pages 28, 29; Larry Dunmire pages 104, 105, 106, 110, 113, 151, 152, 153, 154, 187, 189, 206; Chuck Garrison pages 47, 48, 49, 50, 53, 55, 108, 109, 111; Richard Gibson pages 10, 43, 78, 79, 92, 95, 98, 99, 100, 101; Jim Hendricks pages 159, 163, 164, 165, 171, 177; Darrel Jones pages 20, 76, 115, 117, 122, 125, 169, 171, 173; Don Mann pages 24, 31, 32, 34, 35, 39, 52, 80, 81, 93, 96, 103, 128, 130, 132, 133, 134, 135, 136, 137, 140, 141, 142, 144, 145, 146, 156, 167, 186, 197, 198, 204; Mariner Outboards page 15; Mauritius Government Tourism pages 200, 201, 202; Mike Millman page 193; Bill Munro pages 37, 114, 129, 131; Northern Territory Tourist Commission page 166; Penn Reels page 25; Queensland Travel and Tourist Corporation page 168; Bob Stearns pages 46, 70; Walter Stearns pages 2, 36, 67, 69, 127; Stephen Weitzen page 38; Walker Agency page 41; and Russell Wilson page 107.

All diagrams by Oxford Illustrators.

Published in 1990
by The Hamlyn Publishing Group Limited
a division of The Octopus Publishing Group,
Michelin House, 81 Fulham Road, London SW3 6RB

ISBN 0 600 56807 5

Produced by Mandarin Offset
Printed in Hong Kong

Acknowledgments

A project such as THE WORLD ATLAS OF SPORT FISHING requires various forms of assistance. I want to extend special thanks to:

Paul Merzig, President, Paul Merzig's Adventure Safaris, Chicago, for advice, encouragement, technical support, and locational assistance.

Melita Thorpe, President, Grouptrav National, Santa Cruz, California, for consultation and especially moral support and encouragement.

Roger Tucker, for invaluable research assistance.

Julian Brown, Editor, Octopus Publishing, for being easy to work with, for doing a great job of pulling this and other projects together, for smoothing out wrinkles, and for graciously enduring my idiosyncracies and whining.

Stephen Weitzen, President, BDD Promotional Book Co., for his interest in the marriage of sportfishing and publishing.

My daughters Kristen, Alyson, and Megan, for putting up with a writer's moods and deadlines.

At the risk of possibly leaving someone out, and for which I apologize, I would like to acknowledge the assistance of the following: Lois Gerber, Canadian Consulate General; LaVerne Barnes, British Columbia Tourism; Barbara Kelly and Marty Dowling, Rivers Inlet Sportsmans Lodge, B.C.; Eric Petersen, April Point Lodge, B.C.; Judy Loring, United Touring Company; Bruce Holt, G. Loomis, Inc.; Lisa Weisbord, Hill and Knowlton; the Bermuda Department of Tourism; Gabriel Huerta, the Mexican Government Tourist Office, Los Angeles; Peggy Bendell, Development Counselors International; J. Pask Associates; Mauritius Government Tourism, New York; Victoria Bonavita. Australia's Northern Territory Tourist Commission, New York; Queensland Tourist and Travel Corp., Los Angeles; Virginia Schultz, Direct Response Marketing Corp.; Carolyn Speidal, Manning, Selvage & Lee; New Zealand Tourist and Publicity Office, New York; Linda Jacobson, Peter Martin Associates; Mike Walker and John Mazurkewicz, The Walker Agency; Jim Kalkofen, Mercury Outboards; Bill Munro, Mako Marine; Jim Hendricks, Bear Advertising; and Walker's Cay Resort, Bahamas.

Finally, thanks to the many people who allowed me to take their photographs and who appear in this book, and to the following photographers whose excellent work graces these pages: Larry Dunmire; Chuck Garrison; Richard Gibson; Jim Hendricks; Darrell Jones; Don Mann; Bill Munro; Bob Stearns; Walter Stearns; and Russell Wilson.

Ken Schultz

CONTENTS

INTRODUCTION

Producing this book gave me a severe case of wanderlust. There was more than one occasion when I sat at the computer with fingers not making any motion on the keyboard because my thoughts were out in blue water. Out where the breeze was warm. Where I had to put sunblock on to keep from being fried. Where screeching birds were diving for baitfish that were being pummeled by frenzied predators. Where a big, angry fish tethered to my rod was tailwalking across the ocean. Where a strong speedy torpedo was pulling line off my reel at the speed of light. Where the air was fresh, the scenery compelling, the fishing too good to be true.

It happens. Not all the time, of course. If it did we wouldn't appreciate it enough. But somewhere right now a fisherman has found what Zane Grey called his El Dorado. Chances are good that it is a locale mentioned in this book.

I have to confess that when I finished writing this book, I impressed myself with just how many good places there were to go saltwater fishing (there are even more in freshwater, but that's another story). If I was handed an open checkbook right now and told to go to the best saltwater angling hole in the world, I'd have to think long and hard about *many* of the locations that you are going to read about.

To me a great fishing location isn't one that just has terrific angling, or the potential for same. That's the main ingredient, but the quality of the setting, the manner of fishing, the distance to productive areas, and other factors, are all part of the equation that subjectively makes any place a great one for saltwater sportfishing.

I've tried to take a lot of things into consideration when compiling this information and writing about these locations. Much of what is said here is relatively general, both out of practicality and design. I did not, for instance, note that if you leave a certain inlet, head north till your boat lines up with the lighthouse, then take a 65 degree bearing until your sonar reads 150 feet, that you would be over a certain wreck that was sure to produce. That's not the function of this book. The function is to whet your appetite, give you an idea what might be, how some places look, provide a "feel" about the sport and the locations.

Another thing I didn't do here was include information on places to stay, expenses, travel arrangements, and the like. Some of that information is outdated before the printer's ink has dried. Camps change hands, lodges go out of business or deteriorate, new ones pop up, the fishing turns poor. You can find out about these matters by checking advertisements in sporting magazines, by contacting the appropriate tourism agency, and by dealing with a booking agent.

I also didn't try to let non-angling matters influence the choice or level of coverage here. Panama, for example, was not a particularly good place to be in the late 80s; one of the best and most renowned Central American fishing lodges closed abruptly as a result at the same time that articles appeared in major magazines about the good fishing nearby. With recent political changes there, perhaps that will soon change. Weather has, and will, affect the fishing, or at least the ability to fish, in certain places. In September 1989, Hurricane Hugo did severe property damage in the Caribbean, damaging St. Thomas, crippling Puerto Rico, and devastating St. Croix. These things happen, and in time they'll recover. The fishing will have to wait.

It should be noted that the fishing in many locales is great precisely because it has been hard to access. There are a fair number of places in the world right now that could be tomorrow's discoveries and hotspots . . . if. If a few good boats with knowledgeable anglers were able to spend enough time exploring and divining the patterns of the local fish and the places and techniques. Sounds easier than it is. The oceans are vast and one boat in a distant locale can only cover so much ground in a day, a month, a season. Discoveries are often born out of accident or necessity. Many a good place today was discovered when the fishing at yesterday's good place declined and anglers sought other horizons. If you're looking for a new hotspot, keep an eye out for such opportunities.

At the risk of being accused of preaching, I want to note that you can – and I think should – do your part to see that the good angling in these places remains good. By releasing (and in some cases tagging, too) most of your fish, carefully and quickly, you will be giving and not just taking. It is encouraging to see that the number of big-game fishing tournaments that are release events is increasing; more people are realizing that many fish are too valuable to be caught only once.

Surely, the greater threat to good sportfishing comes from sophisticated and highly efficient commercial fishing operations, via long liners, drift netters, and purse seiners. Some of

the good fishing areas in this book are on the rebound because commercial fishing was restricted or abolished, allowing local and migratory populations to recover.

The good news is that there are a lot of excellent fishing locales around the world to be enjoyed, a lot that have withstood the years, and probably a lot more that we haven't learned about just yet.

Ken Schultz

THE AMERICAS

From the deep offshore canyons to the mangrove flats; from cobalt blue water to a murky, frothing surf; from fish that must be muscled to fish that must be finessed, the Americas possess the most diverse and most widely pursued saltwater angling to be had in any section of the world.

The peculiarities of their Atlantic, Pacific, and Caribbean environments, including currents and tradewinds, make them rich with many types of gamefish. These species support the most intensive angling efforts, from all sizes of boats and with all types of equipment and manner of technique, that can be found. Much of the history of modern sportfishing has its roots in these waters, and the legends of many skippers, guides, and even some literary giants have been established here.

Legends may be a bit harder to establish these days, but the possibility of experiencing great sport for any number of gamefish is just as real.

NORTH LAKE

PRINCE EDWARD ISLAND

Scientists say that only two creatures in the sea outswim the bluefin tuna, those being mako sharks and killer whales. How they came to determine this puzzles me, but no angler who has been awed by the strength and swiftness of these bruisers would argue. Bluefin tuna, it is said, are capable of bursts of up to 55 miles an hour. Imagine such a locomotive on a fishing rod! Perhaps not surprisingly, to those who know their big game, the large bluefin tuna – the ones that are referred to simply as giants – are the penultimate catch on a rod and reel.

But what rods and reels these fish are pursued with: 130-pound-test I.G.F.A. outfits, weighing so much that the ordinary angler would get tired of

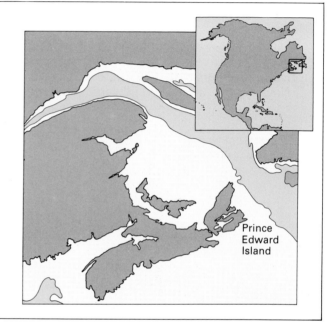

On Prince Edward Island, most of the giant bluefin tuna are caught out of North Lake, or from ports to the west. The fish here migrate westerly into the Gulf of St. Lawrence and wind up in the Bay of Chaleur in the early part of autumn, then come back out again later in the fall. The biggest fish usually don't arrive off Prince Edward Island until about the middle of September, but in late-arriving years, they have not shown up until October.

Prince Edward Island

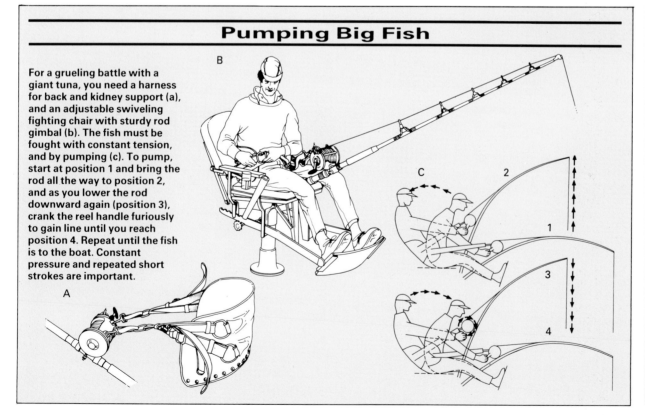

Pumping Big Fish

For a grueling battle with a giant tuna, you need a harness for back and kidney support (a), and an adjustable swiveling fighting chair with sturdy rod gimbal (b). The fish must be fought with constant tension, and by pumping (c). To pump, start at position 1 and bring the rod all the way to position 2, and as you lower the rod downward again (position 3), crank the reel handle furiously to gain line until you reach position 4. Repeat until the fish is to the boat. Constant pressure and repeated short strokes are important.

The largest bluefin tuna in the world have come from the waters off Prince Edward Island. Giants, including fish weighing over a ton, migrate from southerly waters to the food-rich North Atlantic each year.

holding them after just a few minutes. No ordinary tackle will do for such an extraordinary fish. A fish that can reach 35 years of age, grow to weigh over 1,000 pounds, be more than 11 feet long, and gain 200 pounds in a season in the North Atlantic.

Each fall, the largest bluefin tuna in the world appear in the North Atlantic after making one of this planet's greatest long- distance migration marathons. They are, or have been, historically prominent off Newfoundland, Nova Scotia, and Prince Edward Island. But overfishing by commercial interests (for sale in the Japanese market for consumption as sashimi and sushi dishes among other uses) have drastically depleted their numbers and quotas are now established each year for commercial and recreational catches in the North Atlantic.

Nevertheless, the place to be for giant bluefin tuna angling come September, October, and sometimes into November, is at North Lake, Prince Edward Island. Everything in the town of North Lake, it seems, is labeled the "Bluefin" something-or-other, and the area proudly claims itself to be the "Tuna Capital of the World".

Part of that claim is based on its standing in the record book. There, three big fish from North Lake, including two over 1,100 pounds, are line-class world records. And part of that claim is based on the fact that every year, giants swim in these waters. A few years ago, for example, the first eight tuna weighed in for the fall season had an average weight of 1,054 pounds. Those are giants in anyone's estimation.

Amazingly, these fish are pursued here by visual observation, with anglers waiting to sight one before going into prime action. This usually means trying to intercept them and put a daisy chain of mackerel in front of their nose.

When tuna are feeding on schools of bait (which includes such species as mackerel, herring, and squid), they cruise near the surface. The giant tuna bulge a great deal of water, and sometimes actually clear the surface, splashing into the water in a tumultuous crash.

CAPE COD
MASSACHUSETTS

We've taken some liberty here and referred to this section as Cape Cod, but the intention is to talk about the great sportfishing action that can be had in the vicinity of Cape Cod. This includes not only the Cape proper, but Massachusetts Bay to the north, Narragansett Bay to the south in Rhode Island, Martha's Vineyard and Nantucket Islands, and the waters extending to Block Island. While this encompasses two states and seems like a lot of territory, it is all relatively close, and the entire region is renowned along the East Coast.

This Massachusetts-Rhode Island area of New England has one of the longest histories of fishing to be found in North America, dating to the colonial days when pilgrims discovered the abundance of bluefish and stripers in area waters.

Until the recent demise of East Coast striped bass stocks, that species was the foremost catch in this region, and Yankee blood still boils for stripers even though the scenario is vastly different today. Stripers seem to be making a comeback through strict management provisions, so it is mostly small bass that are caught in area waters now, beginning in May in Rhode Island and the southern Bay State waters, and lasting through fall. However, trophies in the 40- to 50-pound class and better are still occasionally taken, mostly in October and sometimes in November. Key locales include Cuttyhunk, Block Island, and Martha's Vineyard.

Bluefish have taken up the slack, however. Bluefish numbers have been riding a high crest for many years and while there is some suspicion that a crash is in the offing, that does not seem to be materializing. The num-

There is no lack of opportunity or places in the Rhode Island-Massachusetts region. Cape Cod has the distinction of being a surf fisherman's haven, and well it is at such locales as Race Point at Provincetown, Nauset Beach in Orleans, and also at several other locations. Martha's Vineyard, Nantucket, and Cuttyhunk Islands, which lie south of the Cape, are good locales, as is Plum Island. In Rhode Island waters, Narragansett Bay, Pt. Judith, and Block Island are the most notable locations.

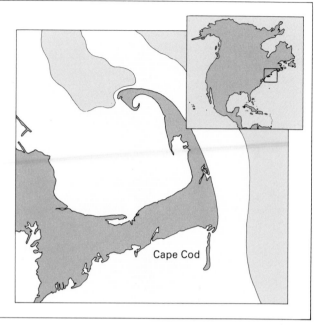

Cape Cod

Left: Some of the best action on Cape bluefish is had when the cool, brisk weather of fall arrives. Boaters troll for these fish, but also find them chasing schools of bait and cast to them. Bluefish put up a strong battle when hooked.

Right: Bluefish have been a staple for New England saltwater anglers for years, being available in large numbers each season through the fall. When they are found in schools, a good number of fish can be taken.

bers in area waters do not support this, and bluefish are the main draw in the Rhode Island-Massachusetts region, rivalling the New York-New Jersey area and North Carolina as prime U.S. locations for catching this species.

Bluefish arrive in early May, much like stripers do, and in many of the same locales. Fishing really heats up as the summer progresses, with bluefish being the main quarry locally from July through October. Fish range in the 8- to 15-pound class, although some bigger blues are caught occasionally. A 26½-pound bluefish caught in 1984 in Buzzard's Bay still reigns as the 30-pound line-class world record.

Bluefish used to migrate southerly in September but now linger into October and sometimes beyond. The last blues are usually caught in early- to mid-November from Narragansett Bay to Block Island. In the fall, there is often action close to shore, including in the surf. Surf fishermen have their moments in the summer, too, unless a sizzling summer sends the fish out deeper. The Plum Island vicinity is noted for surf fishing.

This area has many good bluefish locations throughout the year. Cape Cod, the vacation haven for Bostonians and others throughout the Northeast, is especially notable, with excellent opportunities available at Nauset Beach in Orleans, and at Provincetown.

Provincetown, or P'Town, as it is known locally, is at the end of Cape Cod, and is a foremost fishing locale, especially with surf fishermen. There, at Race Point, current and surf help wash baitfish such as squid, mackerel, and sand eels in, and they are followed by larger game. The flats out beyond Race Point Light are considered best, but action can be had for several miles along the beach. Anglers fish from the beach, using four-wheel-drive vehicles to get around, or from boats leaving the ports of Wellfleet or Provincetown.

Birds Mean Fish

Very often, the business of catching fish in saltwater, especially in offshore environs, has to do with how well you see. Looking for, and finding, a school of birds is often the way to find game fish (singly or in schools) that are marauding baitfish. Some birds, by the manner in which they are flying, can tell you that something is up somewhere, or down below. Birds working one area, for example, but staying high, can mean that there are baitfish below, but deep. A frigate bird, or Man-O-War, is a bird to watch closely; when it dives, get to the spot, because deep-feeding fish have come to the surface. Frigate birds cannot land in the water, and must stay airborne and follow fish, so following them can be a good idea. The most obvious sign, of course, is a group of birds, often seagulls, which are madly diving into the water to scoop up bait which is being plundered by fish below. Big

game creatures, such as tuna and the various billfishes, are often caught by trollers who spot working birds (sometimes at great distances) and then troll their natural or artificial offerings around the edge of the activity, without driving the boat over the quarry and putting the action down.

On the bigger-game front, the historically notable bluefin tuna fishery is not what it once was, due in large part to commercial operations. However, bluefins are still caught and giants are around in the late summer and fall, though not in the concentrations of years past. August and September are prime, with some fish in October.

Yellowfin tuna runs have been good in recent years, with some of these fish showing up in June or July and the better fishing being had in late August and September. The best yellowfin action takes place off Rhode Island, with anglers running offshore to the canyons.

Block and Atlantis are the two canyons fished from this area, with Veatch, which is further out, also being worked. Although yellowfin are prime targets here, some large bigeye tuna, in the 125- to 200-pound class, are caught, as well as the occasional blue marlin. Although not a lot of blue marlin are caught in these distant waters, 600-pounders are produced every season, and fish to 900 have

Tuna, such as the small bluefin being placed in the floor well of this boat, are caught in the offshore waters although not in the size and numbers of the past.

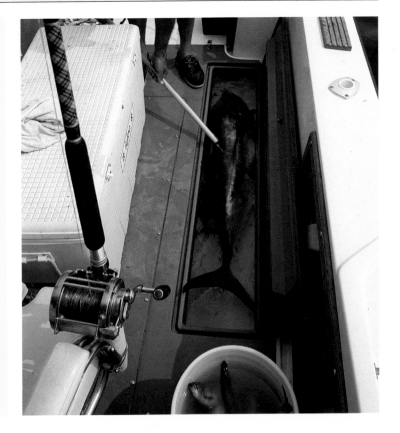

FLOUNDER

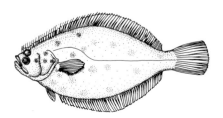

Summer and winter flounder are the two most abundant members of the flounder clan, and are found along the Atlantic coast only, with winter flounder having the more northerly range. Winter flounder are primarily a coldwater species, predominant in late winter and early spring and in the fall. Summer flounder, which are also widely referred to as "fluke", are a warmer water species and grow larger. They are primarily found on a sand or mud bottom, or a mixture of both, in bays, harbors, estuaries, creeks, canals, and in the proximity of piers and bridges.

been landed. Dolphin and albacore are among the incidental catch here while trolling for other species.

White marlin have been a pleasant surprise in recent years, especially off Nantucket, which currently claims four line-class world records for this species. Here, too, boats are running well offshore from Nantucket for these fish, from mid-July through early September, although some of the action takes place south of the Elizabeth Islands in Massachusetts.

Other species of note at various times here include false albacore, bonito, weakfish (now scarce and

known as squeteague in New England), sharks, and swordfish.

Swordfish are infrequently seen and hard to tempt, but occasionally an offshore angler fights one in the 200- to 300-pound range. July has historically produced some of these fish in Block Island Sound and southward, but highly efficient commercial operations are making this less and less likely.

Shark fishing has become a much more popular activity here in recent years, as it has in other Northeastern locales. There are plenty of sharks to be had in these waters, with mako in

the 150- to 400-pound class possible and most revered.

As if all this wasn't enough to choose from, there are a host of popular inshore fish to be had in these waters as well, plus the deep dwellers. The assorted bottom fish in the area provide a great deal of recreational fishing throughout the season. Flounder and fluke are among the staples; Quincy Bay flounder, for instance, are a draw for anglers from throughout the Northeast. Cod are a bread-and-butter fish, too, from Rhode Island all the way north, with haddock another mainstay in good times.

Many bottom-dwelling species of fish, from cod to flounder, are popular with New England anglers. Quincy Bay in Massachusetts, in particular, is renowned for its flounder fishery.

MONTAUK
NEW YORK

To the uninitiated it is hard to imagine that there could be fishing within sight of New York City that ranks with such exotic and far-away waters as Cabo San Lucas, Cairns, Bimini, and so forth. Well, we exaggerate a bit. Montauk Point, being roughly 100 miles from Manhattan, is not quite within sight of the Empire State Building.

But, when fishing in the New York Bight, one can range within sight of the skyline on a clear day, and especially at night, and the fishing, both inshore and offshore, is truly exceptional. There is hardly a time in the season when an angler can't be satisfied here with some manner of angling, from surf casting to rip jigging to tuna chunking to billfish trolling.

Take the inshore fishing, for example. For years the striped bass fishing here was the mainstay of angling efforts, as Montauk Point was a key site in the migratory path of the great Chesapeake Bay populations. It was always a reliable summer fishery, but was most noted for the availability of 40- and 50-plus-pounders in the fall. Monstrous stripers were caught here then, particularly at night around the full moon period, both by surf casters and boaters, the latter trolling, jigging, casting, and fishing with live bunkers (menhaden). They occasionally still are caught, although striped bass populations everywhere in North America have undergone a drastic decline.

In 1976 a 76-pound striper was taken off the heavily fished Shagwong Reef, located within minutes of the Montauk Marine Basin. This broke a revered and long-standing all-tackle world record for this species, only to be surpassed the following year by a

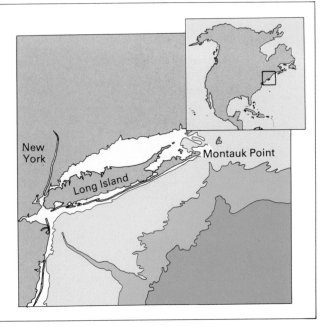

Jutting into the Atlantic at the eastern tip of New York's heavily populated Long Island, Montauk and its environs are like a magnet for migrating gamefish, which find the many rips, reefs, and banks in the area conducive to foraging. The availability of some species is dependent on currents and water temperatures as much as on fish stocks and bait. Area anglers are easily able to head offshore to the deep-water canyons, or to north or south attractions, as well as find productive fishing inshore and in close proximity to the Point, which, incidentally, was the site of the first lighthouse ever built in the United States.

New Jersey catch that still stands. If, and when the striped bass, which are the most prized of all saltwater fish along the Eastern Seaboard, return to abundance, Montauk will likely shine again for these fish.

In the meantime, bluefish, which have taken over the popularity crown from stripers, are abundant throughout the season, not only off Montauk, but in the entire metropolitan New York-New Jersey area (referred to as the New York Bight), and are key to most small-boat fishing efforts. Of course, assorted other, less glamorous species are highly sought after by private boaters as well as the party boat fleet.

Bluefish are usually available for the entire season at Montauk, generally from the middle of May through November, making it the most consistent of all locales for this species. From the Point to Block Island is especially notable, and there are many rips and ledges that regularly produce. Jigging and trolling are popular techniques, and cut bait is also widely used. Some casting is done as well, when bluefish are working a school on the surface, or when they roam the shallows and become the target of surf pluggers.

With the advent of better boats and increasingly greater horsepower outboard motors, fishermen ventured further and further offshore and a variety of pelagic species were encountered at Montauk. In the past two decades, and especially recently, the Montauk area and its offshore waters have become the site of good tuna action, and this fishery has grown in stature and importance every year.

Both bluefin and yellowfin tuna are caught here, and although the bluefin don't rival those of Prince Edward Island in size, there are giants in these waters. More than a few are caught each year, and a lot of fish in the sub-giant size, not to mention the school tuna and hard-fighting fish under 150 pounds. Tuna fishing at Montauk used to be a trolling proposition, but chunking – chumming at anchor with chunks rather than

ground-up, fish – is the mainstay now, with butterfish, bunker, and herring the preferred baits.

Yellowfins are primarily a summer proposition, with the fish disappearing when the water gets cold. Sizes vary; in some years there has been an abundance of 50- to 70-pound fish, and in others fish in the 100- to 120-pound class. They are mainly caught on the top of banks where bait is abundant, some being 10 to 12 miles from the Point. Truly outstanding yellowfin angling is frequently had well offshore, out in Block Canyon and at the spot known as Fish Tales, usually on overnight expeditions. Here there can be good action well into the fall.

Yellowfin range widely off Montauk; sometimes the hotspots remain the same for several days, but often they vary daily and certainly weekly. As many as 300 boats may be anchored on a bank out here on a summer day when the action is hot, so it is seldom a secret where to go. For these fish, long parabolic trolling rods have given

Left: Striped bass have been the fish of historical importance to Montauk fishermen; although not presently abundant, some large stripers are still caught in area waters.

Right: With the Montauk shoreline in the distance, anglers bring a bluefish aboard. Bluefish are abundant off Montauk and are eagerly sought by private boaters, charter boaters, and the party boat fleet here.

way to shorter (5½-foot) stand-up tackle, and this is saving a lot of backaches.

With bluefin tuna, there have been some giants caught hereabouts, with those fish most likely to be in the 500-pound class. Sometimes the big bluefins show up briefly in the summer, with the odd giant or two taken by someone fishing for yellowfins, Fall is when larger fish are usually more reliable.

The best bluefin action doesn't actually take place right at Montauk proper, but off in the distant canyon grounds. Most Montauk tuna anglers head to the Butterfish Hole and the Texas Tower, trolling with mackerel spreader rigs. The distant canyon grounds offer bluefin opportunities.

Certainly other fish are caught offshore, including bigeye tuna, albacore, bonito, dolphin, swordfish, and marlin. Although blues had occasionally been caught in Montauk's offshore waters, this fishery was generally neglected until recently. Earlier in this decade, when anglers started paying greater attention to

On the Ball for Tuna

The sportfishing tuna fleet at Montauk predominantly anchors, ladling out chunks of fish to draw tuna close to the boat, where they will hopefully take a whole or chunked bait with a hook in it. To fish, a long length (depths can exceed 200 feet) of anchor rope is attached to a heavy-duty chain and anchor. The rope is usually coiled into a garbage pail when not in use. When the anchor is set out, the rope end is clipped to a large (usually bright red) floating ball at the boat. When a boat hooks up with a big fish, the line is detached from the boat and the ball is quickly thrown over so the boat can move off. This way you can fight the fish and then later come back to your anchoring location. When another boat fighting a big fish comes by, a nearby boat should get off its ball quickly if asked to do so, and move out of the way of the angler. Unfortunately, not all anglers do this, or do so quickly enough. If the taut line of the fisherman rubs the anchor rope or chain, it will either break or fray, leading perhaps to breakage later on.

Above: When bluefin are relatively close to the Point, fishermen anchor and chum, breaking away from the anchor and the fleet of other anglers when a large fish is hooked.

Right: When thermal currents are particularly warm, bluefin may be caught within a few miles of shore, but most angling is done well offshore, and in the canyons.

thermal currents and trolling at fast speeds, they found out that there was more here than was thought. Since then, a number of fish in the 800- to 1,000-pound range have been caught, with a 1,174-pound blue taken in July several years ago. These monsters have come from waters in the 65 to 80 fathom curve, which is well offshore but still inside the deep shelf that

canyon tuna anglers work. Trolling with artificials is the preferred method.

The other giant species that Montauk is noted for is shark. In particular the biggest fish ever caught on rod and reel: the 3,427-pound great white shark boated in August a few years ago. Shark fishing was slow to take off here, but it has become extremely

Striped bass are an anadromous fish, living in the ocean and migrating into estuaries and brackish or freshwater environs, usually rivers, to spawn. They are native to the Atlantic, and were introduced to Pacific environs a century ago, where they prospered. They have also been very successfully introduced into inland freshwater environs. Stripers, which are also called rockfish in some locales, are a schooling species in saltwater, and usually group by size. They are large-mouthed, and are opportunistic feeders, consuming various smaller fish and eels.

popular since the *Jaws* movies. Those thrillers were set in a town modeled after a village not far from Montauk, and the character Quint was modeled after one of Montauk's most famous skippers, who was the captain of the boat that took the aforementioned great white.

In any event, Montauk has been a hotbed for pursuing various toothy creatures, with blue sharks being most abundant, followed by brown sharks and hammerheads. Most preferred, however, is the mako, which is a strong (sometimes leaping) fighter and also good table fare. The current all-tackle world record mako, a 1,080-pounder, was caught off Montauk in 1979.

While it is too far north or too cold to offer such great saltwater species as bonefish, tarpon, and permit, or black or striped marlin, Montauk nevertheless ranks so highly in so many other categories that many saltwater fishing authorities rate it tops in North America for overall fishing, and that makes it one of the best sportfishing areas of the world.

OCEAN CITY
MARYLAND

The commerce types bill Ocean City, Maryland, as the white marlin capital of the American Atlantic coast, and while the folks to the south in North Carolina might dispute this claim, it is a fact that plenty of white marlin seasonably inhabit the various canyons offshore from Maryland.

It is true that during the summer months, Ocean City is a better locale for white marlin adventures than North Carolina, in part due to the fact that these fish range farther north along the continental shelf. Of course, Carolina ports like Hatteras and Oregon Inlets offer big blue marlin as well, while Ocean City is not a prime blue marlin locale. But then the yellowfin tuna action is better off Maryland, not to mention the availability of wahoo and dolphin. Such choices!

The white marlin catch in these waters, although still good and better than most other places, has been off in recent years, and not up to the standards of the past. However, catch records here have shown great fluctuation since the late 30s, and while the explanation isn't clear, it does seem that the varying movement of the Gulf Stream is an important influence on the abundance (or lack thereof) of these highly nomadic fish.

More sportfishing is done in the canyons now than ever used to be, in part because of the development of better, faster boats, but also because the prime inshore areas – such as Jackspot, which is about 22 miles offshore – have not continued to be white marlin magnets.

So the fishing is concentrated at such places as Baltimore, Wilmington, Washington, Poorman's, and Norfolk Canyons. The hotspots vary over the years; Baltimore had been the

In addition to providing good fishing for various species, Ocean City is attractive because of its proximity to major population centers, being just over 100 miles from Washington, D.C., 230 miles from New York City, and 120 miles from Norfolk, Virginia. A lot of people, therefore, visit annually, with the premier attraction lying in the Canyons well offshore. Baltimore Canyon, which has been of historical fishing significance, is over 50 miles from Ocean City, and requires a run of several hours.

White marlin have been the prime catch off Ocean City, with most trolling activities taking place between the 50- and 100-fathom curves.

prime one but was superseded by Washington and Poorman's. In any event, most fishing takes place over at least the 50-fathom curve, and more often than not out at the 100-fathom curve. The edges of the canyons, with the blue water, warmer temperature, and bait, are where one usually finds the whites.

The best concentration of fish is in this neighborhood from mid-August through mid-September, although whites show up as early as the beginning of June. The major tournaments here are scheduled in early September to coincide with peak fishing, as the marlin are migrating southward. The fish average in the 55- to 70-pound range, which will break no records, but, if pursued with light tackle, provide the best of sport. Trolling is the ticket here, of course, with both baits and lures used, and most of the fish being released.

Not too many of the tuna caught here are released, understandably. Yellowfins, which are abundant at times, are found in the 30- to 90-pound class. But some monster bigeyes have come into Ocean City ports. The latter include four world records, the best of which is the all-tackle and 50-pound line-class Atlantic bigeye, which weighed a mammoth 375½ pounds. Bluefin are also caught in these waters during their migratory expeditions, and Ocean City has the 30-pound line-class record for the bluefin tuna as well.

Fish Tagging

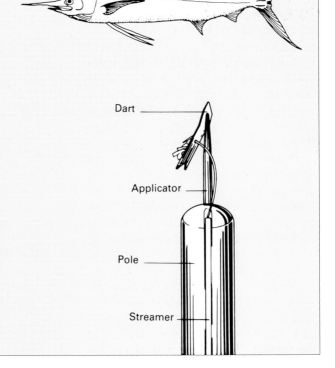

Gamefish tagging for conservation purposes and species migration information has been increasing in acceptance as more fishermen realize the impact that sport and commercial anglers alike have on gamefish populations. Using tagging sticks (which can be purchased in many tackle shops or from some mail order suppliers) and tags supplied by various organizations, anglers are able to tag many large species of fish at boatside, without harming the fish and without having to boat it. This is especially important for billfish and tunas and is often accomplished without handling the fish by keeping the boat in slow forward gear and holding onto the leader. Insert the tag 2 inches into the fish; the proper spot is just below the forward part of the dorsal fin on billfish, below the second dorsal fin for tuna, and below and behind the first dorsal fin for other fish. Try to incline the tag dart toward the fish's head. Jab the fish and quickly withdraw the stick; the dart will stay in the flesh of the fish.

Dart

Applicator

Pole

Streamer

OUTER BANKS

NORTH CAROLINA

Record books don't tell everything, but a glance at the bluefish category in the International Game Fish Association record listings says an awful lot about North Carolina, specifically about the Outer Banks. What it says is that the locale there must be one heck of a place to catch bluefish, which it is. But then, the offshore waters here are a mighty fine place to catch white marlin and blue marlin, too, although there is only one indication of that in the record books.

Inshore, offshore, this is one of the best places to fish on the Atlantic Seaboard of North America, whether one is a boater or a wader. Actually, while boaters have great reason to ply the inshore and offshore waters, they do so at considerable risk in this area at times. For this section of the coast is commonly known as the "graveyard of the Atlantic," because of the many vessels that have met their demise in these turbulent waters. Oregon and Hatteras Inlets, in particular, can be treacherous.

Here, shifting shoals stretch for many miles into the ocean beyond the banks that separate Pamlico Sound from the Atlantic. The banks act as a natural sandbar and protect the mainland; from these narrow banks, or in the near-shore waters, were taken 10 out of a possible 17 world-record bluefish, including the 50-pound line-class and all-tackle record of 31 pounds 12 ounces. That particular trophy was garnered in 1972, when bluefish reappeared here in great numbers. They had been missing for several decades prior to that.

All of those record fish were taken between November and January in their respective years, which is fitting. The bluefish blitzkrieg in the fall on

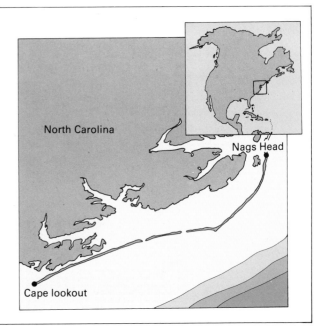

The Outer Banks are a 140-mile-long narrow strip of barrier islands. The marlin fishery is centered from 12 to 70 miles or so offshore in the warm waters of the Gulf Stream, with Oregon Inlet and Hatteras Inlet being the prime ports of departure for blue water. Bluefishing action is notable inshore as well as in the surf. Key locales for shore fishing are where the bluefish become concentrated, which occurs at the various inlets, plus Nag's Head, Rodanthe, Cape Point, and Cape Lookout.

the Outer Banks is renowned, and as long as the bluefish population – thought by some to be cyclical – remains at a high level, the fall action will be excellent.

Nevertheless, small blues are available here all season long. Bluefish provide surf casters and inshore boaters with a good level of action in the fall, so good, in fact, that using light tackle, including a fly rod, is feasible. However, the bigger blues do not always migrate into the surf for the shore fishermen, nor do they necessarily stay long when they come in, so sometimes there will be light action off the beach while a good mass of fish is offshore.

Outer Banks blues average about 12 pounds in the spring prior to their northward migration, and 15 in the fall. They winter off the various capes and generally provide the best fishing in the months of May and November. The Nag's Head-Oregon Inlet area is

one of the better locales, as is Cape Hatteras. Surf fishermen drive their vehicles along the beaches here in search of diving birds, which indicate bluefish in the surf chasing bait. This is restricted because much of the Banks is in the Cape Hatteras National Seashore.

When the blues aren't the quarry, big red drum can fill the void. As with bluefish, North Carolina waters have produced a lot of record fish, filling 10 of 19 categories, including the all-tackle and 50-pound line-class record with a 94-pound 2-ounce monster. The hottest fishing is in November, with action all along the banks, but great activity in the surf at Cape Hatteras.

Cape Hatteras, which lent its name to one of the foremost line of sport-fishing boats, and Oregon Inlet are two ports of renown where billfishing is concerned. They provide anglers with access to the offshore grounds and the Gulf Stream, the edge of which

Bluefish are caught all season long off the Outer Banks, with great action encountered in the fall. Some especially large bluefish, including the current all-tackle world record, have been caught in North Carolina.

Long-distance surf casting

To execute a pendulum cast while surf fishing: start by swinging the sinker in the opposite direction to the intended cast (1). The pendulum movement of the sinker brings it back in the direction of the cast (2). When the sinker reaches its highest point, the caster pivots in the direction of the cast (3) and whips the rod in a baseball-like swing, bringing the sinker around and behind him. As the sinker nears its highest point behind the caster (4), he leans forward as he brings the rod upward, ready to release the cast. With the rod pointing skyward at a 45-degree angle, the cast is released. The caster holds this position until the sinker reaches its destination.

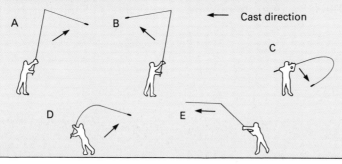

White marlin are abundant at times, especially in the fall, in the offshore waters of the Outer Banks; these spectacular fighters are frequently found balling schools of bait, resulting in multiple hookups.

is about 12 miles from Cape Hatteras. The Stream is closer to land here than at any other spot north of Florida's Cape Canaveral. This proximity means that the offshore waters harbor lots of white marlin and record-size blue marlin. In fact, the waters off North Carolina can lay claim to having the best potential in the coastal U.S. for catching a grander, if not the all-tackle record.

Oregon Inlet has been the port of record for three Atlantic blue marlin granders (including the first, in 1974). Others have been registered at Hatteras and Morehead City (a mainland port). These five fish comprise half the total number of granders caught in the U.S. The most recent catch was in August 1989, a fish that was taken at the 80-fathom mark northeast of Cape Lookout; the largest was 1,142 pounds, which was a former all-tackle world- record holder.

North Carolina blue marlin have held various world records over the years, and still possess the 80-pound line-class mark with a 1,128-pound fish. Near-granders are caught virtually

BLUEFISH

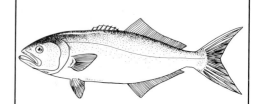

Named for their bluish-green back, bluefish range widely throughout the world, but in North America are found only in Atlantic waters, although they are distributed from Nova Scotia to Florida. These fish roam widely, marauding schools of baitfish, and are most abundant in the western Atlantic in spring and fall, although lately through summer months as well. Bluefish are strong fighters, putting up a long vigorous battle. They are typically caught in the 5- to 12-pound range, although fall fish are usually at the upper end of that range and bigger.

each season here, and fish estimated as granders have been lost each season as well.

While there is opportunity for large blue marlin out of any of the four ports along the Banks, Oregon Inlet in particular has been the hot port. The area to the northeast has been especially productive in recent years. Published reports say that during the three-day span of the full moon in August 1987, there were four blue marlin caught off Oregon Inlet that each weighed over 800 pounds.

The marlin season here begins earlier than it does further north, thanks to the warm Gulf Stream influence, and this brings northern boats down for the June and July action. Hatteras, in particular, produces well in the beginning of the summer, and then the attention in August and September shifts more to the Oregon Inlet waters.

The blue marlin trolling fishery here, incidentally, is one of few that is almost exclusively bait-oriented. Lures may have caught on, in the rest of the billfish grounds, but here the sentiment is overwhelmingly traditional, for swimming or skipping bait.

As for white marlin, the offshore waters have plenty in season. It has been called the best white marlin fishery in North America, and the action can border on the unbelievable at times. Locals still talk about the phenomenal catch and release of 108 white marlin made in a single day in 1983 by one sportfishing boat, and that during a tournament.

Certainly that was a blitz but in a good day a boat here might see upwards of 15 fish. Pods of white marlin are a frequent sighting, especially when they are "balling bait" in the fall. The 100- to 600-fathom water off Oregon Inlet is noted for white marlin, with the summer months being good, but the months mid-August to October being prime.

These fish aren't large, with 45 to 60 pounds being average size. There are no record-makers here, but they provide good light-tackle action, as well as opportunities for casting a fly or using spinning tackle.

However, a problem with white marlin fishing here is that it occurs offshore where the big blue marlin roam as well. This means that there are many times when the bigger blues hit a small bait meant for whites and a great tackle mismatch can occur. Such a problem, right?

Other notable fishing action in these waters, incidentally, includes wahoo, dolphin, and yellowfin tuna. Yellowfin have been fairly abundant in recent years.

The offshore waters from North Carolina's Outer Bank are also known for their rough conditions, and sometimes it is too rough to make distant expeditions. This frequently happens in the fall.

Yellowfin tuna have been abundant in North Carolina in recent years. The closeness of the warm Gulf Stream brings these and other pelagic species within easy reach of boaters.

BERMUDA

At one time Bermuda was frequently placed on maps in the British West Indies, and even now a great many people associate this place with the Caribbean, which is 1,000 miles to the south. In a sense it is the northernmost tropical island in the western Atlantic. Actually, Bermuda is a chain of about 150 small islands that cover less territory than the city of New York, and which lie in the shape of a fish hook.

This is appropriate, for although Bermuda is an extremely popular general tourist attraction and one of the world's foremost honeymoon destinations, it also offers some fine angling, both inshore and offshore. Sportfishermen have had a light-tackle angling love affair with many of the species to be encountered here.

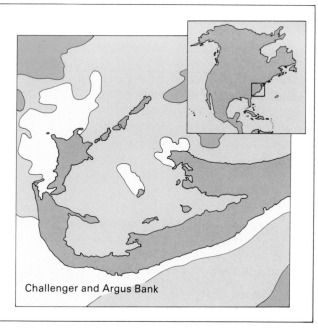

The islands of Bermuda lie like a small fish hook in the western Atlantic. The Challenger and Argus Banks, which are 15 and 25 miles respectively from the southwestern corner, are the major offshore tuna spots, with trolling for various species accomplished between the banks and the mainland. Inshore, opportunities abound for various species.

Challenger and Argus Bank

Chumming

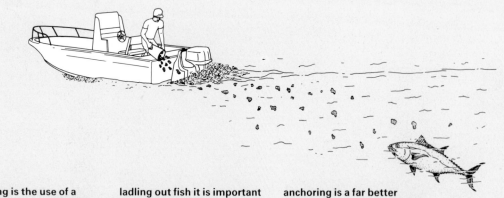

Chumming is the use of a stream of bait to attract fish to a particular spot. Chum may be parts of freshly caught fish ladled overboard piece by piece, or it may be a ground-up mixture of assorted small fish that is ladled overboard by the cupful or left hanging in the water by the boat. When ladling out fish it is important not to chum excessively, and also to keep an uninterrupted flow in the line in order to attract, and hold, fish in the area. This means continuing to chum even when someone in the boat is fighting a hooked fish. When anchoring isn't possible, boats drift, although anchoring is a far better solution. Hooked bait, or pieces of bait, are drifted with the chum, preferably falling at the same rate as the chum, and drifting in the same manner. Fish are remarkably astute at detecting hooked bait that differs in some way from unhooked bait.

Fishing offshore at the Challenger Banks in Bermuda, an angler battles one of many hard-fighting species to be encountered here, where a lot of fish are chummed while at anchor.

Oddly enough, although Bermuda sits alone in the western Atlantic with so much water in any direction, it has not been known for consistent outstanding catches of any species of fish. The course of the Gulf Stream may have something to do with that. It snakes between the United States coast and Bermuda, which are themselves separated by a minimum of 600 miles, and veers away to the northeast, carrying its fertile waters and fish around this former British colony.

Yet it is variety which makes Bermuda shine as a fishing spot, and this includes the pelagic species as well as the inshore and reef dwellers.

The Bermuda islands are rather amazing, geologically speaking, and an appreciation of this leads to an understanding of why the area is attractive piscatorially. In the 16th and 17th centuries, Bermuda was known as the Isle of Devils because of its isolation and treacherous coral reefs that had produced numerous shipwrecks (one of which inspired Shakespeare's play, *The Tempest*). Those reefs exist because Bermuda is literally the top of a mountain that rises 15,000 feet from the bottom of the Atlantic. The islands and neighboring reefs are the tip of an extinct volcano of eons ago, which is further evidenced in the craggy bluffs and pink-tinted sand onshore.

Offshore, the bottom gives way to great depths in between crags, and it is these features that are plied for such roaming species as marlin, tuna, and wahoo. No less than two "grand" marlin have been caught here, the first being a 1,130-pound blue in June 1983, and the second being a 1,190-pounder in July 1989. That both were caught by the same boat and same captain is especially impressive, as only 20 Atlantic blue marlin over 1,000 pounds have ever been recorded. Nevertheless, Bermuda is not really known as a billfish hotspot, although opportunities obviously exist and comparatively few people really go after the blues.

Blue marlin first show up in Bermuda with warmer water in June, and they are caught up to September.

While two or three hookups may happen in a day, there are many days without action. This is true in marlin fishing everywhere, of course, and in Bermuda, since demand is light, many marlin are caught either trolling to or from the offshore banks to pursue other types of fishing. In other words, with more effort, who knows what might be possible? Besides the recent grander, blue marlin up to 900 pounds have been caught in Bermuda in recent years and white marlin enter the catch as well.

The primary fishing adventure in Bermuda, however, is with yellowfin tuna, which are one of the hardest fighting brutes in the sea. Bermuda's yellowfin, which are also known as Allison tuna, don't run large on average, with 25- to 40-pounders the norm. But sometimes there are schools of bigger fish, including those in the 100-pound class, to be had.

Most tuna fishing in Bermuda nowadays is done with relatively light tackle. Outfits with 12- to 20-pound line are employed in stand-up fishing, using bait that has been dropped into a chum slick and fighting the tuna from a stationary boat. In tournament fishing here, more points are awarded for light tackle use, and some fishing is done with 8-pound line. The author once boated a 72-pound yellowfin in Bermuda using freshwater fishing tackle, and it took a full hour and several trips around the anchored boat to overcome it.

The yellowfin are primarily caught while chumming on the Challenger Bank, which is 15 miles offshore, or the Argus Bank, which is 25 miles offshore. These are pinnacles that are over 150 feet deep, and which take a lot of anchor rope to get positioned on. Chum is ladled out and cut or whole bait is fished amidst the chum.

In Bermuda this chumming is particularly exciting because fish are hooked close to the boat and are often spotted as they cruise through the chum slick. A wide range of fish are caught by this method, including yel-

lowfin tuna, blackfin tuna, rainbow runner, dolphin, mackerel, and wahoo.

Wahoo are one of Bermuda's foremost fish. Bermuda holds several line-class world records for this species (and also for blackfin tuna) and there is usually an abundance of wahoo on the banks in September and October. Wahoo are found, however, from May on, and many are taken by trolling.

Still another notable offshore quarry here is amberjack. The Challenger

Banks yielded the all-tackle and 80-pound line-class world record amberjack, which weighed 155 pounds 10 ounces, as well as the previous world best, a 149-pounder. Reportedly, a 168-pounder was caught here in 1985 but disqualified for record purposes.

Inshore, there may not be any records, but there is plenty of opportunity. On the numerous inshore reefs, there is no lack of such species as yellowtail snapper, gray snapper, little tunny (bonito), and various jacks.

Bermuda has yielded two blue marlin over 1,000 pounds, although marlin are not pursued with great intensity here or by many anglers.

Right: Yellowfin tuna are one of the major angling targets in Bermuda, with most fishing taking place on deep banks offshore.

Below: Pompano and small inshore species, including barracuda and bonefish, are available for the angler who wanders the beaches and bays of Bermuda.

BLACKFIN TUNA

Blackfin tuna are only found in Atlantic waters, ranging from Massachusetts to Brazil and into the Gulf of Mexico. They are a small, football-shaped tuna, but a spunky fish good for light-tackle angling. They generally feed close to the surface on small fish, squid, and crustaceans. Many blackfins are caught by trolling feathers, bait, and spoons; by casting with plugs or jigs; and by fishing with live or cut bait offshore.

These are caught by chumming and fishing bait, or by jigging.

Along the shoreline shallows, there is a potpourri of species available to shore-based casters and to small boaters. Barracuda are one of the most abundant, and palometa perhaps the most popular. The latter, which are a pompano, are highly sought table fare, and are caught on small jigs and spoons, and flies, plus bait.

Bonefish and tarpon inhabit the inshore waters of Bermuda, too, though the latter are extremely rare and not very large, while the former are difficult for the unguided angler to locate, since there are not many traditional tidal flats areas. Thus, the water is deeper than flats anglers are accustomed to, and spotting and stalking tailing bonefish is seldom possible. Bonefish are caught in Whitney, Long, and Shelly Bays, and at Castle Point, with small jigs as the favored offering.

Although Bermuda is thought of as a tropical destination, it does not provide significant fishing opportunity in the winter months, so most angling is centered from mid-May through November. Bermuda is often a windy place, too, it should be noted, with hard blow days to be experienced at times even during the warmer months.

FLORIDA GULF STREAM

The offshore fishery on the east coast of Florida can be very good for species ranging from dolphin to billfish. The Gulf Stream is the major reason, for here it veers close to shore near Palm Beach and gradually tapers away up the coast. Actually, this is the Florida Current, which is a branch of the Gulf Stream, coming from the Gulf of Mexico through the Straits of Florida. It meets with the Antilles Current from the east somewhere about or above Cape Canaveral, forming what is universally referred to as the Gulf Stream here, and is so-marked on most maps.

In the north, the Jacksonville-St. Augustine region is the farthest from the deep blue water. From St. Augustine, for example, it is over 50 miles to the edge of the Continental Shelf and 100-fathom water. So boats from that port make the run to the 28-fathom curve, where the bottom drops off and steadily declines to the shelf, for wahoo, dolphin, sailfish, blue marlin, yellowfin tuna, and sometimes swordfish.

King mackerel are a foremost quarry for the closer-to-shore crowd, although they have not been as abundant in recent years as they formerly were. And, of course, an assortment of bottom fish are found here and further south, including the Daytona to Cape Canaveral region. It is not quite as far to the Gulf Stream from these locales, but still far enough. Some blue marlin are caught by the long-distance runners, but on the inside edge of the Stream, dolphin and sailfish are the primary targets.

Stuart to Palm Beach, further south, is the region where sailfish reigns king, especially from Jupiter south through Palm Beach County. The Gulf

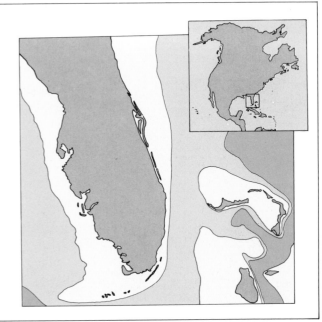

Florida is a much larger state than many people realize: it takes about eight hours of highway driving to get from the northern border to Miami. Clearly there are a lot of east coast shoreline fishing possibilities, including pier, surf, and inshore bottom fishing. The decline of some species, the relative nearness of the Gulf Stream, and the surging interest in sportfishing boats has lead to an increase in offshore fishing in the northerly areas as well as in the more traditional billfishery off Palm Beach and Stuart.

Kite Fishing

Fishing kites, of sturdy construction and with easy takedown features for storage, are used for sailfishing. The technique is one that has been around for years and is used in other places besides Florida. Live bait is primarily used and the kite serves to bring the bait away from the boat, to keep it high in the water and struggling, and so allow you to see a striking fish. Fishing line extends from rod to hooked bait, and is clipped in a release on the kite line. When a fish takes the bait the fishing line pops out of the release. Although most baits are live and fished near the surface, dead baits can be used, and depths can be adjusted via weights to get live or dead bait deeper.

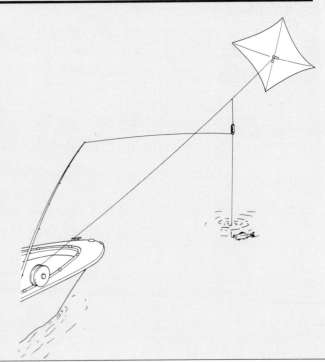

King mackerel, or kingfish, have been one of the main angling species along the east coast of Florida. Large specimens, such as this one, provide a good fight, especially on light tackle.

Stream comes within a few miles of shore here, and that blue water is referred to by many as "Sailfish Alley". Stuart calls itself the "Sailfish Capital of the World", but that appellation could be hung on the entire region.

Sailfishing here is largely a matter of live bait fishing, using fishing kites. (Further north, the sailfishing is a mixture of this and trolling, while it is all trolling in more northerly waters still, where the search is on for a variety of pelagic fish.) Sailfish are a reliable fish all year long off Palm Beach, through good weather and bad, and this is probably the foremost area in North America to visit for one's first chance at this acrobatic billfish.

Using light tackle, in the 12- to 30-pound range, is standard here, and makes for a good matchup with fish that run up to 100 pounds. Six or eight fish in a day is possible in prime time, which is January through April, and white marlin and occasionally blue marlin make the catch headlines here, too. Wahoo, dolphin, and king mackerel (kingfish) get some play as well (especially dolphin).

Probably the most significant inshore fishing is at Stuart, where the St. Lucie River meets the Intracoastal Waterway. There, many snook inhabit the canals, creeks, and backwater sloughs, some up to 20 pounds. Small tarpon roam the area as well.

SOUTH FLORIDA

A person would be hard-pressed to find a place with more notable, diverse, and entertaining fishing opportunities than South Florida. In fact, you'd probably have to go as far as the northern coast of Australia to be competitive in the look-what-I've-got-to-offer realm, the major difference being that South Florida is half a century or more ahead in land development and population. Also in fishing exploration. And if the fishing is good enough to be recommended today after so many years of utilization, then it must be something special indeed. Not only that, but there's still plenty of room for more anglers.

South Florida – for this book's purpose that area from the Everglades Parkway (Alligator Alley) south to Flamingo, but excluding the Keys (which is covered separately) – is home to the superstars of the flats, the billed bruisers of the Gulf Stream, and an assortment of hard-pulling creatures in between. Not everywhere, of course, nor at all times. In fact, the area has some distinctly different opportunities.

In the western section of South Florida, the Ten Thousand Islands beckon the inshore angler with snook, tarpon, and assorted other species in a myriad of cuts, creeks, and mangrove-lined shores. Naples, Port of the Islands, and Marco Island are the jump-off spots for brackish water wild-country fishing southward in and along the Everglades.

This is relatively unspoiled territory as yet, described by some as Florida's last frontier. A fisherman can easily get lost here, way back in channels and creeks, and never explore all of it. It's a primitive area noted for its beauty and wildlife, including many species

Right: Snook are one of the prime targets of coastal anglers in South Florida, especially in the Everglades and along the west coast, where boaters travel far into the back country.

Left: South Florida has diverse fishing from Gulf Stream waters on the east, which produce dolphin such as this, to inshore flats and creek fishing.

grove islands. In some areas the redfish are found tailing, and one can cast to moving fish, but in others casting is done blindly around various holes and bars.

Baby tarpon are common in the far reaches of creeks, but larger tarpon aren't found until migration brings them through. February and March offers potential for fish from baby to 100-pound size in the western region.

The same species are found in the southern tip of Florida, along the northern reaches of Florida Bay. Flamingo is the main departure point here, with anglers heading west to Cape Sable or east toward the Florida Keys. As with the Gulf Coast section of the Everglades, this region has many creeks, small bays, and mangrove-lined islets and channels.

Redfish are making a strong comeback throughout this region as the result of a ban on commercial netting and more stringent regulations; angling for these species is looking quite promising. Smaller fish are often found in large schools in Florida Bay, and 3- to 5-pounders are common. The region around Flamingo is one of the better locales for redfish.

Seatrout are very popular here, and virtually provide a year-round fishery

of birds and waterfowl, as well as many snakes and the ever-abundant (throughout this state) alligator. Snook, spotted seatrout, redfish, and tarpon are the angler's main attractions, but various other creatures swim these waters.

Snook are the foremost quarry for many anglers, especially in the area of Chokoloskee. Some real giants, up to 30 pounds, are caught on shallow-running or surface plugs here by those in-the-know, but the average is more like 3 to 8 pounds.

Trout and redfish are caught throughout the Everglades, which serve as a nursery for both of these species. Both are found in deep channel holes and redfish are also attracted to oyster bars along man-

The Everglades take in all of South Florida, but for saltwater anglers, they stretch from the Ten Thousand Islands region on the west near Everglades City all the way down the coast and around Cape Sable virtually to the bridge connecting the mainland to the Keys. Untold numbers of creeks, channels, bays, inlets, and other fishable locales are found there, with key departure points being Marco, Port of the Islands, and Flamingo. Biscayne Bay on the east coast, just south of Miami, provides excellent fishing, and the run to offshore waters from Miami and Fort Lauderdale is literally just a few miles.

except for severe winter cold spells. The better fishing is usually from March through May.

Along the western portion of South Florida, from the Overseas Highway to Miami, the emphasis begins to shift. The Miami to Fort Lauderdale section has produced nice snook, including fish up to 20 pounds, in various inlets and around bridges, as well as tarpon, although this is nothing like the desolate-country fishing in the Everglades. Various other inshore species provide action as well, but the big ticket is running offshore from this region, where the Gulf Stream is just a few miles out.

Sailfishing is very popular here, in part because spindlebeaks can be taken with some predictability. Kite fishing with live bait is the forerunner in techniques, and efforts are usually directed in 80 to 150 feet of water. Blue marlin are caught in these waters, mainly in the 300-pound and less class, but for these fish, all of the big boats berthed in Ft. Lauderdale or Miami simply run out to the Bahamas.

Other Gulf Stream denizens include the occasional wahoo, bonito, king mackerel, and dolphin. Dolphin are

Above: Sailfish are a mainstay of the South Florida fishery along the Gulf Stream; they are especially sought by anglers using kites to drift bait away from the boat.

Right: Large bonefish are found in Biscayne Bay, being caught by anglers who wade or fish from a poled boat.

A Traveling Rod Case

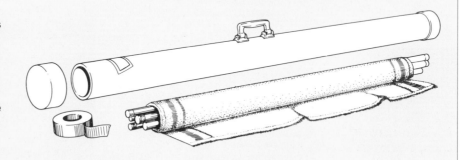

When traveling by plane the best way to transport long rods is to secure them in an indestructible container that will be checked as baggage. Between four and a dozen rods can be packed in either a 6-foot case or a 7-footer made of 4-inch (inside diameter) Schedule 40 PVC tubing. Caps are fastened to each end, with one epoxied firmly and the other secured tightly with duct tape. A small carrying handle is attached to the tube. Rods are alternately laid butt to tip and taped together, then wrapped in two towels, before being placed in the tube. The tube is also padded at each end so the rods can't move in any direction. There are commercially available tubes, and some are satisfactory for a few trips. You should, however, pad your rods in these so they cannot move, and tape the latches so they don't break or snap open. Airlines check rod cases as fragile merchandise at the traveler's risk, and therefore you usually are not eligible to make a damage claim. The greatest worry, however, is likely to be that your rod arrives with you and in the appropriate place for your use. Unfortunately, that sometimes doesn't happen.

Known throughout Florida and the Gulf of Mexico as redfish, the red drum is a highly sought inshore saltwater species, respected both for its fight and for its culinary attributes. It was this species (blackened redfish) that helped launch the blackened style of Cajun fish cookery that has been popular in the U.S. in recent years. Redfish are bottom feeders and schooling fish, commonly caught near breakwaters, jetties, pilings, channels, sandy and muddy shorelines, inlets, and shellfish beds.

individual fish, although schools might be encountered in the summer. These fish are found year-round here, although in the winter a severe cold snap will make them scarce. April is generally thought to be prime. Six-pounders are average, slightly greater in spring and fall, and much larger bones are possible. Good numbers exist on the flats along Key Biscayne, too, as well as permit.

Permit are more elusive, of course, here. They turn up sometime in March, becoming more abundant as the season wears on, with summer months offering the most potential. Tarpon migrate through here from spring through early summer, and the potential exists for all three species in a given outing, which locally constitutes a grand slam.

Considering that this review hasn't touched on such other opportunities as fishing for various jacks and bottom fish inshore, bluefish inshore or out in deep water, offshore fishing in the Gulf of Mexico, or the entire (and nearby) Florida Keys, you'd have to say that South Florida truly has a range of excellent saltwater angling.

always here it seems, and in the summer are the most reliable offshore catch. Angling for these fish, plus sailfish and miscellaneous inshore and bottom species, can be pretty crowded at times.

Casting anglers, small boaters, and wade-fishermen head for the expansive waters of Biscayne Bay, which has gained an increasing reputation in recent years for its flats fishing oppor-

tunities, including its potential for large bonefish. The fact that some of this takes place within sight of Miami comes as a surprise to unknowing visitors. Bonefish, permit, and tarpon, however, are all on the itinerary here, as well as sharks, mutton snapper, ladyfish, and barracuda.

Bonefishing in Biscayne Bay is done by wading and by casting from a poled boat, sightfishing in the shallows for

FLORIDA KEYS

FLORIDA

There is probably no saltwater fishing destination of renown that has been written about more than the Florida Keys. Such places as Key Largo, Islamorada, Marathon, and Key West are legendary for fishing, and the last locale for its attraction to Ernest Hemingway, the jet setters, assorted writers and celebrities, and those trying to lose themselves in a place that is warm and distant but still in the United States. Islamorada has gained additional recent fame as the place that President George Bush visits periodically – doing so right after his 1988 election – to go fishing.

Most anglers know the Keys for flats fishing for bonefish, permit, and tarpon, and many think of it as a winter getaway spot. But the Florida Keys are a great year-round angling destination (with some of the best action in the heat of summer), and a place with tremendous angling diversity. From snappers to tarpon to marlin, there is something here to suit any interest.

Tarpon, of course, are a main quarry for visitors, and fly fishing for these bruisers is a specialty in the Keys, although not the only technique or necessarily the best. However, two of the I.G.F.A.'s five fly rod tippet classes for tarpon were established in the Keys (both at Marathon), and also nine of its line-class world records. Most of those were at Key West, including a phenomenal 243-pounder on 20-pound line in 1975, which, though a long time ago, indicates the upper range of Keys fish.

The tarpon are mostly in the 50- to 100-pound class, but there are plenty of them seasonally, as well as some fish over 100 pounds. Tarpon are very sensitive to cold weather, and while they may be present during warm

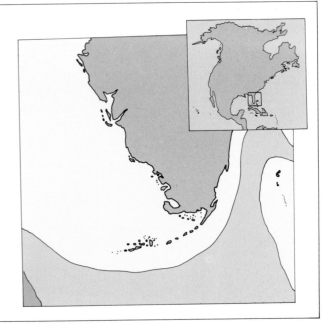

The Florida Keys stretch for 160 miles south and west, bordering Florida Bay toward the mainland and tucking into the Gulf of Mexico. North of Key West, shallow flats extend well into the Gulf; to the south, the Gulf Stream is just a short distance away, sweeping by the Keys into the Florida Straits. Reefs, wrecks, and extensive shallow water areas offer diverse fishing opportunities in all seasons, while the blue water beckons billfishermen. Some boaters venture out to the Marquesas or to the Dry Tortugas as well.

Right: Permit are one of the most elusive but coveted fish of the Keys, and many records for these fish have been established in and near Key West.

Left: Tarpon are perhaps the most spectacular fish of the Florida Keys, and a species that is especially associated with the shallow flats of this region.

appearance in the winter and early spring. Angling for bonefish is good from April through the end of the year, though the larger bonefish are often caught from late summer through fall.

The last, and less-often caught, glamor fish of the skinny water is the permit. Many of the things that hold true for bonefish also hold true for this species, except that it is less prominent in Florida Bay waters, and more numerous at the far end of the Keys. Spring and early summer are good times. The Keys hold 12 out of 16 line-class world records for permit and all five fly rod tippet-class records, with most coming from Key West and surrounding waters.

Though popularly sought on the flats – where it is difficult to approach within casting range and where it is hard to land on the fly rod or light spinning tackle – permit are also caught in deeper waters around reefs and shipwrecks in the Florida Keys. Wrecks are, in fact, abundant, and the fishing there for various species is

---

spells in the winter months, they don't regularly appear until the water temperature hits 75 degrees or better. May and June, therefore, are prime months in the Keys for tarpon, and migratory schools of fish become numerous. April may be very good, too, if the weather has been favorable. By summer, most fish are migrating northward, although some tarpon may be had throughout the year in canals, harbors, and bridge areas.

Tarpon are found in many locales throughout the Keys, including the backwaters of Florida Bay and over toward Flamingo, as well as in the Marquesa Islands out in the Gulf. Key West has a heralded run of big tarpon in the winter in the harbor area.

Bonefish are the other most-venerated flats quarry in the Keys. They, too, are widely available, although the upper Keys and Florida Bay have greater concentrations and somewhat larger fish, particularly from Islamorada to Marathon. Bonefish of 6 pounds are common, and heavyweights of 10 pounds and more do get caught. Eight line-class world records have been set in the Keys, including six out of Islamorada, the largest being a 14-pound 10-ounce fish caught on 8-pound line in 1988, as well as several fly rod records.

The speedy bonefish is caught all-year long on the ocean flats of the Keys and in Florida Bay, but cold fronts cause their temporary dis-

---

TARPON

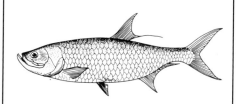

Tarpon are primarily an inshore coastal fish ideally pursued in warm shallow water. Habitat in which they are commonly found includes slow rivers, bays, lagoons, shallow flats, passes between islands, mangrove-lined banks, and the like. Small, or "baby" tarpon – those up to 20 pounds or so – are usually located in estuaries and river mouths, even considerable distances up freshwater rivers and in sloughs and canals. They feed on crabs, shrimp, and assorted small fishes, and often patrol shallow water in small groups and in a daisy chain arrangement. The high, frequent jumps out of the water that tarpon make, and their stamina, endear them to all anglers.

Left: Although the Keys flats get a great deal of attention, there is good fishing throughout this region for various species, on wrecks and offshore; these big king mackerel were caught off Islamorada.

Dead Bait Rig

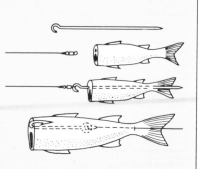

This is a very effective dead-bait rig for bottom fishing for tarpon. Use a 10/0 hook at one end of a 6-foot 120-pound-test monofilament leader, and a barrel swivel at the other end. Insert a bait needle the full length of a beheaded mullet, attach the swivel to it, and pull the entire leader through the mullet and out the tail.

Right: Sailfish are quite popular in the upper and lower Keys seasonally.

racuda, mackerel, and others, plus the occasional pelagic fish.

In the offshore realm, the Keys have plenty of entertainment as well, especially for dolphin and sailfish, but also for marlin, tuna, wahoo, king mackerel, and the like.

Sailfishing is very popular in the upper Keys early in the year, and in the lower Keys from November through winter. Fish are quite plentiful, although small (30 to 70 pounds on average), which makes them a great target for light-tackle fishing and fly-rodding. Here, a lot of searching is done, particularly looking for a school of bait that is being plundered by sailfish and visibly evident. When found, a rigged live bait is tossed out. Kites, popular off mainland Florida, are only occasionally used in the Keys, usually when anchored and chumming for bottom fish, to pick up a straying sailfish.

Blue marlin are an important quarry in the lower Keys, especially out of the lower Keys where a sharp drop exists, and in fall months, with sizes ranging up to 400 pounds. They are caught in spring and summer, too, and spring has potential for white marlin as well. The Gulf of Mexico contributes a lot of water to the Gulf Stream at Key West, and the mixing has a beneficial influence on billfish.

Dolphin are a possibility all season long, but come on strong in spring and last through the summer. June, July, and August are particularly good for large dolphin offshore. Various tuna are among the catch here, incidentally, including yellowfins in the 100-pound range in early fall off Key West, and blackfins. Four current fly rod world record blackfin tuna are Keys fish.

Another fish that is very prominent in the Keys is cobia. These are most abundant throughout the winter, and provide considerable light-tackle action. Cobia from the Keys dominate the line-class and fly rod world record listings, the biggest of these being a 98-pounder.

quite popular with many fishermen who bring their own boats.

Key West is a popular port for wreck fishing, exploring both Gulf and Atlantic waters. In the Gulf, wrecks are fairly shallow, in 50 to 100 feet of water, but in the Atlantic they can be much deeper. Jigging, plugging, trolling, and bait fishing are all done here, although

using bait and chumming with fresh bait obtained in the morning from commercial shrimp boats receives hands-down local approval.

Much of the good wreck fishing takes place throughout the winter. In addition to permit, popularly sought species include amberjack, various groupers, mutton snapper, cobia, bar-

WEST FLORIDA

Many people are familiar with fishermen's maps, the kind commonly found in bait and tackle shops with the many silhouettes of fish on them to designate the places where certain species are abundant and where there is good angling. If you were to look at such a map for the section of western Florida that borders the Gulf of Mexico, it would be full of fish symbols from Fort Myers Beach on up to Crystal River.

Because the Gulf's blue water is a long way offshore, and because there is so much going on closer to shore, most angling is centered inshore and in the bays, passes, and inlets that are abundant throughout this area. The exception to this would be reef fishing for various bottom fish, especially groupers and jewfish, which takes place from 5 to 20 miles out depending on where you start from. Inshore, however, the opportunities are broad for such species as tarpon, snook, seatrout, redfish, bluefish, snappers, pompano, and ladyfish, with the first four of these being the mainstays.

Seatrout are perhaps the most abundant of the major species, and are avidly pursued all along the coast, in rivers and creeks, from bays and bridges, over grass beds, and along oyster bars. Snook, too, are highly esteemed, likewise being found in diverse locales. Shallow mangrove edges are the typical habitat, but inlets and passes, as well as bridges and piers, and assorted local holes, also produce.

In actuality, tarpon is the king here, at least as far as many sportsmen with boats are concerned, and constitute the big-game fish of this region. Such places as Boca Grande and Homosassa are world-renowned for their tarpon

The western coast of Florida is replete with the types of habitat that favor both resident and migratory fish. Among the latter, tarpon are most renowned in the waters off Homosassa and Boca Grande, although they are also found all along the coast, in bays and many passes and shorelines. The area above St. Petersburg through Homosassa to Crystal River, is shallower near shore than it is to the south, and the northern portion near Crystal River has many keys, passes, and fish-laden hideaways. To the south, the Boca Grande to Fort Myers region sports many locales that have prime fishing, particularly around Boca Grande and Captiva Passes.

Temperature Charts

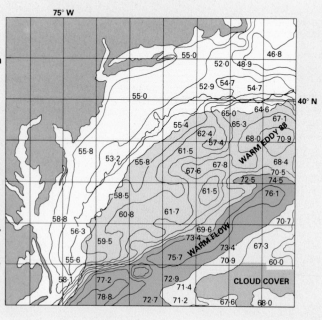

For a long time now, anglers have been using sonar and loran to help them find fish, locate structures, and navigate well. Now, satellite-generated ocean temperature information is playing a more important role in offshore fishing for pelagic species that are very temperature sensitive. Anglers are obtaining surface temperature charts and studying them over a period of time to pinpoint the location of warm water edges, eddies, and patterns of movement to lead them to productive areas to fish. The impending changes in warm water locales or current direction help in the short term, but are most useful when studied over a period of time to forecast areas to fish. These are most useful when anglers are equipped with surface temperature gauges on their boats.

fishery, in particular the possibility of giant tarpon.

Homosassa, just south of Crystal River, has become famous for its spring monster tarpon fishing, and is the locale where expert fly fishermen annually pursue giants, looking to be the first to land a 200-pounder on the light wand. While fish of this size have been hooked and played, none have been landed yet, although the biggest record-book tarpon on a fly, a 188-pounder on 16-pound tippet, was caught at Homosassa.

The Boca Grande Pass is perhaps even more famous, and is billed as the "Tarpon Fishing Capital of the World". The very deep hole here between Cayo Costa and Gasparilla Islands has arguably the largest concentration of tarpon in North America, especially from June through August.

This area gets crowded, and unlike Homosassa, this is muscle-fishing, drifting with heavy tackle and live bait for the most part, although some lighter tackle anglers do well by jigging. Tarpon are elsewhere here, of course, cruising the beaches and inlets and presenting other opportunities. Boca Grande also has some good snook fishing, and nearby at Captiva Pass, redfish are abundant in the fall.

The tarpon fishing in some areas of western Florida along the Gulf is world renowned, with big fish the quarry.

GULF OF MEXICO

From Florida to Texas, the entire inshore area of the Gulf of Mexico has attractive fishing. But the big word in the Gulf these days is the fishing to be had away from the shore, out in the blue water, on the canyon edge, where the marlin roam.

From Port Arthur, Texas; South Pass, Louisiana; Destin, Florida; and points in between, the big boats with the ability to run offshore and tackle the sometimes rough weather, are getting into blue marlin that are hefty enough for serious bragging.

"Offshore" means different things throughout the northern Gulf, not only from individual ports, but from day to day at the same port. For the Yucatan Current coming into the Gulf mixes with the strong flow of the Mississippi River at South Pass. It generally moves northeast and then southeast, following the direction of the land mass, but it also shoots off to the northwest and then southwest. It is not only possible,

but likely, to be in billfish country from any of the Gulf ports; it's a matter of how far you go to find blue water.

One-hundred fathom water lies 12 miles off South Pass, for example, and depending on the action of tides and currents, blue water will be from 8 to 20 miles out. Currents change fast, however. Off Galveston, blue water can be 10 miles offshore or 90. This is true throughout the Gulf, and swirls and eddies of current (blue water) that hold billfish are common as well.

But the search for, and forays to, blue water, have been very productive, More and more anglers are doing it now, as the billfish catch increases, and the ability of boats to stand the offshore expeditions improves.

The reward is mainly blue marlin, but also whites and sailfish, and the billfishing community has had its eyes open wide for blues since 1977, when the Gulf produced its first rod and reel grander, a 1,018-pounder caught off of

South Pass. Blues here average under 300 pounds, but 600- to 800-pounders are caught, and grand-class fish are reported seen or hooked and lost virtually every season.

Each billfish port has its own hot-spots offshore; most of these, how-ever, are around the 100 fathom curve. June and July are usually prime, but August and September can be hot in given years. Other species encoun-tered include yellowfin tuna, blackfin tuna, wahoo, and king mackerel.

For the majority of fishermen, however, it is the many other species that are most notable in the northern Gulf. Fishing the offshore oil rigs, for example, of which there are many, is extremely popular. The rigs are vertic-al reef-like structures that attract bait and a host of predators. Deep-water rigs may be a place to locate marlin, sailfish, dolphin, wahoo, and other pelagic species, but the closer-to-shore rigs are magnets for many types of snappers, sharks, jack crevalle, cobia (ling), king mackerel, dolphin, jewfish, various groupers, and sailfish.

Inshore, fishing opportunities are extremely diverse and equally popu-lar. Redfish (red drum) and seatrout (called trout, speckled trout, or specks) are most popular, especially along the Texas coast and in Florida Bay. Tarpon are an attraction in some areas, most notably in the western side of Southwest Pass, Louisiana, where good fishing is had from August through October and 150- to 200-pound fish are possible. Cobia are a popular target, with the beach at Destin producing large fish in the spring. Pompano, bluefish, groupers, and other species attract attention as well. The northern Gulf of Mexico has quite a mixed bag of opportunities.

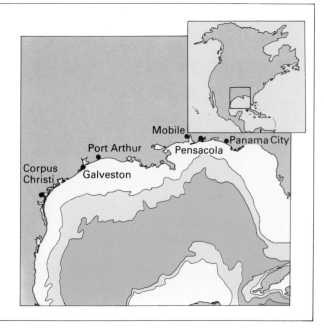

The major ports for billfishing include Port Arthur, Corpus Christi, Galveston, and Port Aransas, in Texas; South Pass, Port Eads, and Grand Isle in Louisiana; Gulf Shores, Dauphin Island, and Mobile in Alabama; and Destin, Fort Walton Beach, Pensacola, and Panama City in Florida. For big game the drill is to run offshore to blue water, which varies in locale but is often found on either side of the 100 fathom curve.

Forays into blue water from various ports along the Gulf of Mexico have produced blue marlin, with some of large proportions.

Hooking Bait

Live shrimp are a highly popular bait for a wide variety of coastal fish, and can be hooked through the top of the head for live-lining, or threaded on a bait hook or jig hook. Live blue crabs are also used for many species of fish; smaller versions take tarpon and permit while larger ones are fished deep for snapper, grouper, redfish, and others. They are hooked through the tip of the shell, often with claws removed. Fiddler crabs are used for snappers, groupers, sheepshead, and other fish. Depending on locale and availability, such species as pinfish, anchovy, menhaden, grunt, sardine, pilchard, mackerel, and herring are used for live bait. These fish are hooked through the lip or back, sometimes with a double hook setup or through the eyes (soft-fleshed fish).

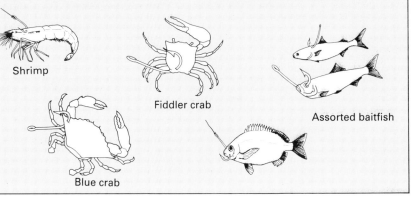

Shrimp

Fiddler crab

Assorted baitfish

Blue crab

CHANDELEUR ISLANDS

LOUISIANA

Chandeleur. The word rolls very pleasingly off the tongue. Sounds very appealing. Could be a street in New Orleans, the name of a nightspot perhaps, or maybe a steamboat. But it is the name of a chain of barrier islands off the northeast coast of Louisiana that provides some exceptional fishing, and which has become renowned throughout the Gulf Coast and Deep South.

Once known only to a few, the Chandeleurs became widely recognized nearly two decades ago when a national television show flew several celebrities, including a sportscaster, professional quarterback, and tackle manufacturer, into the island and broadcast the nonstop action for millions to see. Isolated and uninhabited, and infested with redfish and seatrout, the Chandeleurs were exposed as a coastal warm-water paradise.

Today the scene is a bit changed, but not so much that the Chandeleurs don't warrant consideration as a great place to fish. The passes between islands have silted over, but the Chandeleurs are still uninhabited. Like many places along the coast and inland in the southern U.S., the Chandeleurs have received a lot of pressure, but it yields fine angling – some say as good as ever – for those who

The Chandeleur Islands are east of New Orleans and south of Biloxi, Mississippi, in the Gulf of Mexico, and extend for about 25 miles at the eastern end of Chandeleur Sound. Charterboats and houseboats operate in the islands, using smaller skiffs for fishing and transportation over the flats to and from fishing locales.

are diligent, attentive, and persistent.

In fact, for day-in day-out productivity, there is no place in the entire Gulf that matches the curving string of the Chandeleurs. Red drum (redfish) in the 2- to 4-pound class, and seatrout (called speckled trout or specks) in the 2- to 5-pound range are the quarry. Good redfishing is possible all year long, while the best seatrout angling is from summer through early fall, although many larger fish are caught in April when they appear chasing big

mullet. Fishing is from skiffs or by wading, mostly the latter, and the water is clear enough to provide good sight fishing.

Because of the opportunity to hook so many fish, the Chandeleurs are a great training ground for new speck or trout anglers. But the nearness to the Gulf and presence of deep passes also mean a lot of sharks, so wading fisherman stay in fairly shallow water and keep their fish stringer on a long lead well away from them.

LAGUNA MADRE

TEXAS

Barring a brutal cold spell in between the time this was written and the time you read it, the Laguna Madre area of the south Texas Gulf will be such a great place to fish for redfish – species of culinary fame and the reason for the meteoric rise in popularity of Cajun-style blackened seafood – and seatrout that every sporting magazine will be talking it up.

Gulf of Mexico weather is unpredictable and sometimes brutal but a horrible cold snap is what fishermen in this area fear most. With good reason, of course. On Christmas Day, 1983, this entire region was devastated by a massive cold front that killed nearly all – estimates go from 90 to over 95 percent – of the fish in these shallows and sent a scant few others scurrying for deep water.

It was a colossal loss, but the good news is that the redfish and seatrout are back to the levels of the early 80s, they are getting bigger each season, and the fishing is great and getting greater.

Laguna Madre stretches from Corpus Christi, Texas, almost to the Mexican border, encompassing miles and miles of truly remote water. Some areas are relatively accessible from various ports and beaches, while others can only be reached by boat.

Unlike the territory further up the coast and elsewhere along the Gulf shores, the water is clear here and the bottom possesses lush greenery and white sand holes, with those holes often producing large fish that lie there in wait to ambush bait. Much of the fishing is done by stalking, using boat and foot to look for individual fish or schools that are pushing bait, which is primarily mullet. The fact that virtually all of this fishing is done in

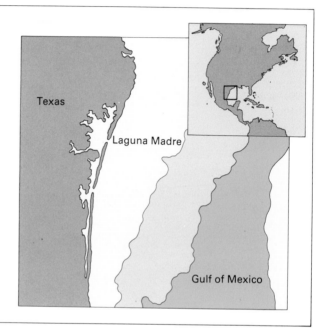

The Laguna Madre area extends for 150 miles, separated into upper and lower sections. Port Mansfield, at the end of the road, is a fishing village whereas Port Isabel/San Padre Island to the north has a wider tourist following and Corpus Christi is a major city. The Padre Island National Seashore protects the remote Laguna Madre shallow flats, which is up to several miles wide.

Observation

One of the tricks for spotting shallow-water fish is to look not at the surface but below the surface and at the bottom. When you focus on the bottom, try to look for something that stands out as being different, and whose movement contrasts with some bottom locales enough for you to detect it. When you see the wake of a moving fish, realize that the forward edge of the wake is behind the fish. Then take that into account when you make a cast that is intended to intercept that fish. It is often important to be able to see fish before you cast to them because you have to be able to approach them without alarming them. Other times it is important to see certain objects that might be harboring fish. Polarized sunglasses are a big help here; glasses that offer wrap-around side protection are best. And a cap with a wide bill and dark underside is also a good aid.

very thin water, and mostly by wading (even if a boat is used to get to locales), makes for great light tackle excitement.

In some places here, however, there is some exciting fishing for schools (locally called herds) of large redfish in much the same manner as is done for schooling inland stripers, looking for activity and then running up to the school, casting quickly and trying to land the fish in time to stay with the school for more action.

Redfish (technically red drum and also known as channel bass) now run up to 10 pounds here. Speckled trout (the local name for seatrout) are mainly caught in the 3- to 6-pound range, but fish up to 10 pounds are here and bigger ones will be showing up in time. Mullet and pinfish are the bait to watch for, and a variety of lures, including topwater plugs, do the trick.

The best trout fishing is in the upper area of Laguna Madre, at the Land Cut, and in Baffin Bay; March through June is best for big fish. The better redfish spot is around Port Mansfield.

Not all the fishing in this section of the Gulf is inshore, incidentally. The many oil rigs out in the Gulf are the only other structure here besides barrier islands, and they produce such species as snapper, king mackerel, wahoo, amberjack, and more.

Left: Redfish are the foremost quarry of anglers along the south Texas Gulf of Mexico, and are sometimes found here in schools.

Right: Anglers troll across the stern of a long-range fishing boat that has ventured from San Diego to the various islands in the Pacific west of the Baja Peninsula.

CENTRAL BAJA ISLANDS

MEXICO

Some places in the world pride themselves on the fact that there is great fishing right at their doorstep. You don't have to go far, they say, to sample what they have to offer. Just visit the lodge, walk out of the door, and you're in great fishing country.

This is a matter of semantics, however. Usually such places are out in the middle of an ocean. Some of them are halfway around the world for many traveling anglers; so it's more like, once you get here, you don't have to go much farther. Never mind that it takes between 24 and 48 hours to get there in the first place.

That's how long it also takes many people to get to the fishing grounds that are far offshore from the western

Situated at great distances from the central and southern Baja Peninsula, the Mexican islands offshore are accessed by long- range sportfishing vessels from San Diego. Short-duration trips focus on the most northerly islands and inshore region, while the longest duration trips run some 1,200 miles to the Revillagigedos.

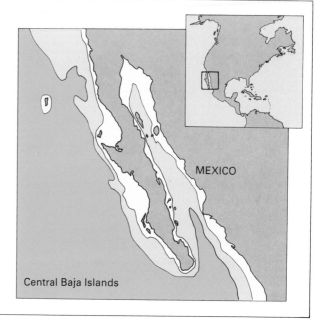

MEXICO

Central Baja Islands

Baja Peninsula, hundreds of miles from the nearest land. Except they're on the water all that time. The reason it takes that long is that they are traveling by boat from San Diego, California, a distance of between 200 and 1,200 miles, depending on the islands. That's more than many cruise ships travel. What some anglers won't do to get to hot fishing, right?

The fishermen who make this trip, however, stay there – up to two weeks in some cases – once they arrive. They have the opportunity to sample some extraordinary angling out in the Pacific, way beyond the reach of day boats, in great surroundings that very few but long-range sportfishing vessels can visit. There, the water is blue, the fish are eager, and the action can be wearying.

This actually takes place at varying distances from Southern California, starting at Guadalupe Island but reaching to the Alijos Rocks and then to the Revillagigedo Islands, all of which are well offshore, and can include numerous island and rock outcroppings closer to the western Baja coast. These volcanic spires rise from the ocean depths, providing great structure to influence currents, attract bait, and draw game fish.

The major interest at most of these locales is now yellowfin tuna, although long-range exploratory fishing got started with the quest for monster wahoo a little more than two decades ago. The prospect of catching scores of big, blazing-fast wahoo, including fish from 60 to 80 pounds, lead to boats ranging in size from 65 to 115 feet, capable of holding 15 to 30 anglers, and geared with plenty of everything a group of diehard anglers would need. Shorter rods, better reels and line, and the prospect of giant tuna, lead to an increasing interest in yellowfins.

The locales closer to San Diego include Guadalupe Island, San Benitos Islands, and the nearby bays, which range from 150 to 350 miles away from San Diego. These locations

are the site of shorter duration trips in the spring and summer, usually between four and seven days. The target species include the ever-popular yellowtail, calico (kelp) bass, grouper, and occasionally bluefin tuna, with albacore possible in early summer. A 54½-pound yellowtail that holds the 30-pound line-class world record was caught at San Benitos a few years ago.

The mid-range trips, lasting from 9 to 11 days, get into wahoo, sea bass, yellowfin tuna, grouper, and dolphin

(dorado). They range a greater distance, fishing more southerly islands off the Baja coast, particularly Thetis Banks and Alijos Rocks.

The Alijos (pronounced ah-lay-hose) are 200 miles west of the village of Cabo San Lazaro in central Baja, and some 600 miles out of San Diego. They are a premier yellowfin attraction, with banks that consistently attract fish in the 50- to 150-pound range. Yellowfin are always in the neighborhood here, and getting into a

Left: With Guadelupe Island in the background, anglers pose with a pair of 40-pound-class yellowtails; these fish are among the most popularly sought species by long-range anglers.

Right: Alijos Rocks, a popular Baja fishing spot, is framed by the arch of a rod of a stand-up fisherman; stand-up fishing tackle and tactics derived from such expeditions.

school of such fish, with all rods on board engaged in battle, is the kind of fantasy fishing that can be possible.

October through January and April through June are the times that the Alijos are fished. The fall and early winter period produces wahoo as well and sometimes striped marlin.

This area is a known big yellowtail hangout, incidentally. Four current California yellowtail world records were set here (as well as one on Thetis Banks), including a 78-pounder, which is the all-tackle and 50-pound line-class holder. That big fish was caught in June 1987. Yellowtail are primarily caught here on live mackerel fished with a weight on the bottom.

Yellowfin tuna at Alijos are not trolled up, as they are in many other locales in Baja area waters. Off Alijos they are chummed, using unweighted free-swimming live mackerel (and jacks and anchovies). Trolling is done, however, en route to various locales, and some tuna, as well as

Stand-Up Technique

Stand-up fishing involves playing large, strong fish while standing instead of sitting in a chair or using the boat to help fight the fish. It evolved from long-range fishing expeditions where anglers have no seats and can only play large fish with their bodies and tackle from a standing position. Although there are several variations in technique, in part depending on what type of harness is employed, the central point is to use a short (less than 6-foot) fishing rod, quick pumping action, and pivoting body movement. In the accompanying illustration (a), the angler is using a rod gimbal but no kidney or seat harness. He has to keep his left arm and back straight, and pivot at the bent knees. The angler with a set harness (b), however, can move the rod upward by sitting back and use his own weight to actually fight the fish.

A

B

WHITE SEA BASS

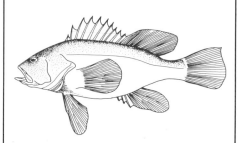

White sea bass are actually members of the weakfish family and have the tender mouths usually associated with those species. Found along the California and Mexican coasts, these fish are usually found in kelp beds that are in fairly shallow water near shore. They feed on small fish, crustaceans, and squid, but they grow quite large, so fairly heavy tackle is used. A lot of fishing for white sea bass is done on or near the bottom using live or cut bait while drifting or anchored. However, these fish will roam the water column, and are caught at other levels as well, sometimes by casters tossing plugs, spoons, or other lures, and sometimes by trollers.

dolphin, wahoo, and marlin, are caught that way.

The longest duration trips are made further south, up to 1,200 miles from San Diego to the Revillagigedo Islands. These islands – Clarion, Roca Partida, San Benedicto, and Socorro – are from 225 to 400 miles from the Mexican mainland at Cabo San Lucas, and obviously well removed from Cabo's day-trip fishery.

They are volcanic formations that still bear the scars of their formation; San Benedicto erupted as recently as 1954 and looks rather like a burnt cone. All alone in the Pacific, and jutting up from extreme depths, the Revillagigedos are like a magnet for many species, including wahoo, marlin, amberjack, skipjack tuna, and rainbow runner.

They are particularly known, however, for yielding monster yellowfin tuna, especially fish of 200 pounds and up. All four of the islands are credited with current line-class world-record yellowfins. The 80-pound line-class and all-

tackle world record is an astounding 388-pound 12-ounce fish that was caught near San Benedicto in 1977 at a legendary place called Lunker Hole. The angler who took that fish also caught a 357-pound 130-class record at Clarion in 1987, proving, at the very least, that lightning can strike twice in these fish-rich waters.

Most of the time fishing conditions are good at the time that these long-duration expeditions are made, so that pleasant cruising and fishing conditions are experienced. Revillagigedos is usually fished in the winter, and the period from late July to October, which is the hurricane season, is avoided.

SAN DIEGO
CALIFORNIA

In the United States, it is often said that California is a state of mind. Customs and vocabulary are often just a little different from those in other places in this large land. So it should come as no surprise that in the San Diego area, "sleepers", "tailers", and "feeders" are part of the lexicon.

Perhaps this could be talk in the financial community, but it is the jargon of fishermen. Big-game anglers, to be more precise, since there are an awful lot of people who fish in this, the most populous state in America.

The aforementioned terms are used to refer to the attitude in which sport-fishermen find striped marlin. These fish are abundant offshore in Southern California, virtually overlooked in the popular angling literature in this coun-

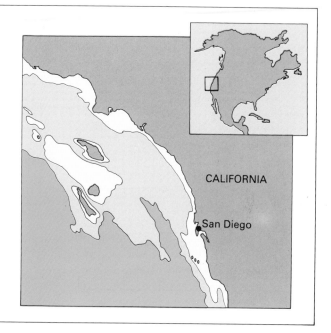

Striped marlin are caught as far away as Point Concepcion, but the bulk of activity takes places off San Diego, from the Mexican border (and in Mexican waters, too) northward to Catalina and San Clemente Islands and vicinity. Good marlin fishing can be had within 40 miles of San Diego at times. Albacore and yellowtail are caught in some of the same areas, although albacore tend to be further offshore. Warm inshore water gives way to cooler breaks out in the deeper locations, where there are islands, banks, and seamounts that influence current and affect baitfish presence.

CALIFORNIA

San Diego

Left: Yellowfin tuna are high on the priority list of long-range anglers; this large yellowfin was caught at Socorro Island.

Right: Southern California marlin fishing rates good to excellent these days; here, a triped marlin is landed.

try, and the staple of the big-game crowd north of the Mexican border to Catalina Island.

It was in this region that the first striped marlin ever caught on rod and reel was taken. This occurred in 1903 in the Catalina Channel, and the catch was second only to tuna in the annals of big-game fishing history.

The offshore waters of southern California today provide marlin fishing that rates as good to excellent, as well as being exciting. The excitement comes not only from the well-known aerial fireworks of striped marlin, but also from the standard method of pursuing them here, which is primarily sight fishing. That is why the term "sleeper" means a striped marlin that is, or appears to be, sleeping on the surface; why a "tailer" means a marlin that is cruising, usually with tail out of the water; and why a "feeder" is one that is below the surface chasing a school of bait.

Bait, in fact, has long been the most popular offering for marlin, although lures have continued to grow in usage. In bait fishing here, anglers stock their livewells with from 50 to a 100 mackerel. These are hooked in the nose and cast ahead of surface-cruising marlin, or dropped back and drifted to deeper-roaming fish. Obviously, this occurs when marlin have been spotted. While looking for marlin, trolling plugs, which are referred to as "jigs" here, are employed, and they do account for many fish.

Researchers think that there may be two origins for the marlin in these waters, the skinnier ones coming from the Sea of Cortez to the south, and the plumper ones from elsewhere in the Pacific. Regardless, the marlin here are not large, like their South Pacific cousins, nor quite the size of the Ecuadorian fish either. A typical catch might be in the 120- to 150-pound range, with some over 200. The large striped marlin are often caught in these waters early in the season, which extends from July through October, but the best fishing overall is in August and September.

The attraction, of course, is schools of bait, which the marlin follow northward, but the many banks and seamounts offshore seem to concentrate the fish. Here, there are upwellings that move bait schools upward, and the marlin take advantage of this. They are predominantly found here where the water clarity is good and where the temperature breaks to 68 and 70 degrees occur. Local skippers focus on such points.

Although these banks are well offshore or long distances northwesterly, ranging from 20 to 100 miles depending on locale, the Southern California offshore waters are frequently pleasant enough for one-day ventures to many distant points. Fair days and rolling swells make for good marlin sighting (tailing fish are often spotted surfing down a swell).

Ironically, it is not the incomparable striped marlin that gets the interest of

Locating Deep Fish

It used to be the case that fishermen looked only for above-water visual clues to help them find fish or to find the places that might be attractive to certain species of fish. But that changed several decades ago with sportfishing sonar. Electronic sonar has become very refined indeed, and is used for bottom depth determination, for pinpointing such objects as dropoffs and reefs, and for locating schools of fish or large individual fish. Although it is still not possible to ascertain which species are seen on sportfishing sonar at any given time, experienced anglers who know their quarry are frequently able to determine what specie(s) are present at the depth and in the location found. They can then drift live bait or jig for those fish, or attract them to the surface, or troll at the appropriate deep levels.

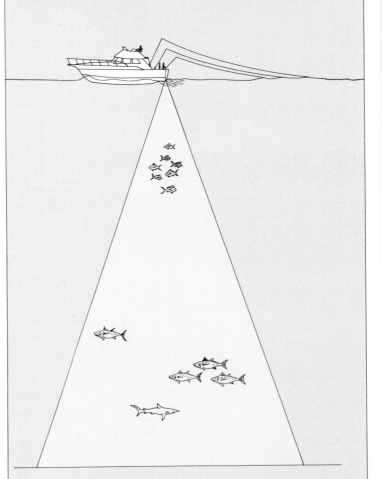

Albacore are the first choice for most of the San Diego fleet, and when these fish are abundant, the action is brisk.

the majority of anglers in these waters, but albacore. Albacore are to Southern California saltwater anglers what walleye are to Minnesota's legions of freshwater anglers(except for a great difference in game qualities). The word goes out fast when the first albacore start to hit the docks each year. This is usually in late June or early July, and a literal mad rush ensues for party and private boat fleets from all ports in the area, not just San Diego. This lasts until October or November.

The California Yellowtail (*Seriola lalandei dorsalis*) is differentiated from its southern cousin by more than range (the latter being in the South Pacific). The California fish doesn't grow as large, or at least it hasn't been caught as large, and it doesn't interact with the other yellowtail. Nevertheless, it, too, is a member of the worldwide family of jacks, and is a fast-swimming, stubborn fighting fish, with a distinctive yellow tail and a yellow stripe that runs from eye to tail along the flank.

Known also as "longfins", albacore are revered for both their fight – bulldog runs – and for their edibility. These strong fish take some muscle to subdue, so fishermen get to play tug-of war with albacore, which really gets exciting when a school is encountered (as it often is). These, incidentally, are the "white meat tuna" that are so popular in small cans in food stores in the United States.

In the early part of the season, albacore weigh in the 10- to 18-pound class, but later they are heftier, in the 25-pound range with some hitting the 40-pound plateau. To catch them, many anglers, especially the party boat fleet, use live anchovies, but trolling with feathers and jigging also gets results.

This, too, is an offshore fishery. Although occasionally there are schools of albacore that come to within 20 miles of the coast, most action takes place in the 50- to 100-mile range, in cooler 60- to 65-degree water. Day trips are made at the shorter distances, but not when the

Yellowtails range in size from 10 pounds on up to 40, but are not routinely caught in the largest sizes. The main grounds are the Catalina, Channel, and San Clemente Islands; the Coronado Islands 18 miles south of San Diego (in Mexican water); and from Oceanside to Point Dume along the coast. Live bait is principally used here for these fish, with anchovies the number one fare, and squid or mackerel distant choices.

The California record yellowtail is a 62-pounder that was caught in the La Jolla area over 35 years ago; however, a 59-pounder was caught off La Jolla in 1988. Three current line-class world records, including that 59-pounder, were established in Southern California waters.

A lot of fishing here is done on party boats; estimates have it that some 850,000 anglers fish out of party boats here in a given season. Albacore and yellowtail are their prime quarries, but such other species as calico (kelp) bass, bonito, barracuda, etc., are on the itinerary.

fish are at the upper end of this limit and beyond.

Another very popular fish in Southern California waters is yellowtail. Also hard-fighting and good eating, yellowtail are a tenacious-fighting member of the jack family that are caught by fishermen in California as well as in Baja waters.

April through October is the fishing season for yellowtail off Southern California, although this is basically a full-year fishery in southerly waters where the large boats venture.

CAMPBELL RIVER

BRITISH COLUMBIA

British Columbia is not a place one associates with crowds, with the possible exception of the cities of Vancouver and Victoria. You especially don't think of crowds on the water midway along an island in the ocean, even if that place is the formidable and historically significant Vancouver Island.

So how is it that on any summer night there will be hundreds of fishing boats scattered throughout the Campbell River area? How is it that when the action is hot, several thousand boats, each with two to four anglers, will be within a few miles of that river, most of them tightly packed into two or three

locations? How is it that a village like Campbell River can be home to 500 guides, and that a resort like April Point Lodge on a small nearby island, could harbor the world's largest privately owned fleet of Boston Whalers?

Tyee. An Indian word for large salmon, tyee has come to be recognized as meaning a chinook salmon over 30 pounds. Tyee, and many salmon of all sizes, filter past Campbell River in prodigious numbers today as they have in ages past. For the waters in the Discovery Passage between Vancouver Island and the mainland are like a funnel for Pacific salmon stocks. A high percentage of

all migrating salmon go through the Passage, some headed to Vancouver Island Rivers, others further to the south or the north.

The Passage is to salmon as Times Square is to New Yorkers. En route this-away and that-away, any fish coming inside Vancouver Island passes by. No wonder that Campbell River has for years billed itself as "the Salmon Capital of the World".

Unlike most other prominent sportfishing destinations, which are of relatively recent discovery, the Campbell River area is bearing down on 100 years of sportfishing tradition. In October 1896, British angler Sir Richard

A guide displays a 35-pound chinook, or tyee, salmon that was caught in the Discovery Passage off the Lighthouse, a locale that draws many other anglers in the height of the season.

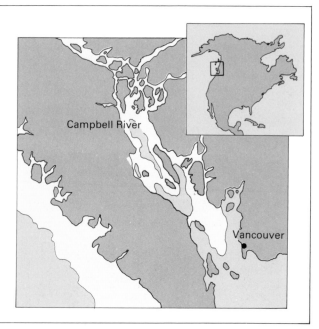

Campbell River is one hour from Vancouver and is accessed by float plane (with water taxi service) or wheeled aircraft from the mainland. Anglers with boat in tow can ferry to Victoria and drive north.

August is the prime tyee time. This is when the big fish, preparing to spawn, are around. The best time for bigger cohos is September and October. For pure numbers, June is tops, with May also a good bet because there are fewer grilse (2-year-old salmon) around. When the grilse are abundant you can catch 50 in a morning. Other coho average 5 to 6 pounds, with bigger northern coho in the 6- to 12-pound range in the fall.

Musgrave wrote in *The Field* of his experiences fishing for tyee with an Indian guide out of a dugout canoe off the mouth of the Campbell River. His largest fish was a 70-pounder, and a model of it, which was once proclaimed as the largest salmon ever taken on hook and line, is still on display in the Natural History Museum, in South Kensington, London.

Musgrave attracted others, who attracted others, and in 1924 the now-famous Tyee Club was started, analagous to the Catalina Tuna Club and for the purpose of standardizing the sport of salmon fishing in British Columbia. The club formulated many sport-fishing guidelines, most of which are still in force for members to this day. One of these includes the use of rowboats.

Nowadays, in the inky blackness of a pre-dawn morning, Tyee Club members tow their rowboats to the fishing grounds, anchor the towing vessel, and row off in fiberglass skiffs, hoping to tempt an early-morning salmon in either Tyee Pool or Frenchman's Pool.

The rowers, of course, are vastly outnumbered in the area by power-boaters, who are more mobile and more efficient, but sometimes sport-fishing isn't about efficiency or success ratios.

Not that there isn't plenty of success for both chinook and coho salmon anglers in these rich waters. There is so much success, in fact, that people come from all over the world to try to pluck some bounty out of the intricate tidal currents of the Passage.

The premier salmon fishing spot, not only here but probably in the whole world, is the gigantic back eddy in front of the Lighthouse where the Strait of Georgia and Discovery Passage meet. This is where there are often 600 to 700 boats fishing, and where thousands and thousands of salmon, waiting to ambush bait, annually fall to the hook. When the run is on, boats routinely have doubles and triples, and all over the water nets are waving and rods are bending.

Another extraordinary spot, though not one that is conducive to heavy traffic or to boaters with a weak heart, is Seymour Narrows. Here, when the tide is high and really moving the current can flow as great as 16 knots, and there may be 50- to 60-foot-wide whirlpools. At 10 knots it is estimated that 1 million gallons of water moves by per second; nonetheless, this dangerous water draws salmon.

And those salmon may be quite large. Several 60-plus pounders are accounted for every season, though it isn't every day that fish of 40 pounds or more are garnered. There is a lot of emphasis on sportsmanship here-

abouts, especially with the larger lodges and their guides, so there is a good deal of fishing done with relatively light tackle, swift waters notwithstanding.

This is especially true for coho salmon, which are abundant in this locale. When there is a good run of cohos on, 30 or 40 can be caught in a day. The sizes run smaller than they do farther to the north, but it is popular to use light line, long rods, and fly reels to fish for the coho, so a scrappy bout is virtually ensured. An

excellent spot for coho is Whilby Shoal on the extreme southern tip of Quadra Island. There is a major kelp bed shoal from green to red buoy and from point to point there, and it supports thousands of fish, especially coho, which feed on massive pods of tiny shrimp.

Although salmon are the main attraction there is some river fishing for sea-run cutthroat trout and for steelhead. The latter enter the area in the fall and winter and provide river fishing that is good but which doesn't

get the attention that is directed toward king salmon.

Because of its protected location, this region is fishable all year long, no matter what direction the wind may be from, which is another good reason for its popularity. That also makes it a good place to hold tournaments, of which there are quite a few, and to book a trip in advance with an assurance of meeting fishable conditions.

Guides are numerous not only because of the number of lodges in the area, but also because these waters

Right: This coho salmon was caught off Quadra Island on a fly skipped across the surface; trolling with fly rods equipped with nylon monofilament is popular and effective here.

Left: Fishermen drift with the swift flow through Seymour Narrows, north of Campbell River, a scenic spot that is renowned for big fish but which has treacherous currents.

COHO SALMON

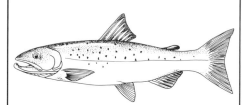

These sleek and silvery fish may not grow as large as their chinook brethren, but they lack nothing in the way of excitement at the end of a fishing line. Known for repeated acrobatics, swift runs, and jolting strikes, coho are the darling of light tackle enthusiasts all along the Pacific. They mingle with chinooks and can be caught at the same time. But the angler who targets coho would do well to scale down his offerings, using, for example, a smaller cut-herring for mooching, as well as lighter tackle.

are tricky, both from a boat handling as well as what-to-do standpoint. Tide, for example, is important here. When the tide is low, fish don't move and are scattered all over. Some places produce better than others at that time. The new and full moon phases produce higher tides and are better times to fish. The depth to work varies as well, although for tyee your lure or bait must generally be just off the bottom.

Mooching with herring is very popular here for salmon, as it is all along the British Columbia coastline, with lighter tackle, smaller hooks, and smaller bait being used for coho. There is, however, a fair amount of fishing done here with artificials and light outfits, and when there last we witnessed an angler subdue a 38-pound tyee at the Lighthouse on 6-pound line. Besides mooching, trolling and jigging are practiced.

With all the activity, the nearby towns, the boat traffic, and so forth, this is clearly not wilderness fishing, which one tends to associate with British Columbia. The salmon do not mind, and neither do the legions of anglers.

Trolling Flies for Coho

Tackle needs consist of an 8½- or 9-foot fly rod for 6 or 8 weight line, with a long extension handle and a salmon fly reel that will hold 600 yards of 8-pound-test monofilament. You can use 8- to 12-pound-test line. Tie a streamer fly directly to the line without a weight, and pull out between 23 and 27 arm-long lengths of line. The fly will troll on or just below the surface. Occasionally it might skip on the surface with a little wake. Jiggle the rod tip sometimes, have a straight pull at others. Watch for a big wake from a large charging fish.

Troll fairly fast over bull kelp beds so that the fly skips over the surface almost like a small big-game bait. This can be done all season as long as the water is not too murky. Early morning calm conditions are best. Hold the rod tightly in case a big salmon happens to take the fly, which they do occasionally.

Above: Boats at April Point return at the end of another day of mooching for tyee, a tradition of long standing in this area.

Right: Big salmon and beautiful surroundings are the hallmark of Rivers Inlet; this king, or chinook, salmon weighed 45 pounds and was caught at the mouth of the inlet.

RIVERS INLET
BRITISH COLUMBIA

Spectacular by nature is what some say of British Columbia. Beauty is her birthright, say others. Indeed, this Pacific Northwest province can justifiably flaunt her inland and coastal attractions.

For an angler, there can be no prettier place to wet a hook than the tranquil coves along the northern British Columbia coast, where there are enough inlets and straits and river mouths to explore that an entire summer could be spent delightfully cruising and fishing. Some folks do just that each season, enjoying not only the fishing and the scenery but also the sight of bald eagles, humpback and killer whales, sea lions, and even the occasional grizzly bear.

The highlight of such fishing exploration, however, is Rivers Inlet. Forty miles long and 7 miles wide at its entrance, Rivers Inlet is situated at the southeast corner of Queen Charlotte Sound, just north of Cape Caution, which is a funneling spot for large numbers of chinook and coho salmon. Fish migrating northward, having come from the Strait of Georgia between Vancouver Island and the mainland, land right at the doorstep of Rivers Inlet. Salmon migrating southward along the coast, having come from the Hecate Strait and Queen Charlotte Sound, swim right by as well. Some of these fish are not only passing through, but are returning to spawn in one of the four major rivers that empty into the inlet. The result is that from mid-June through September, the action is continuous, and Rivers Inlet is one of the world's premier sportfishing locales.

King, or chinook, salmon are the main attraction here, not only because they are plentiful, but because they are

Rivers Inlet is situated to the east of Fitz Hugh Sound along the rugged and roadless coast of British Columbia. Protected from the northwest by Calvert Island, it often offers protected fishing even at the mouth. Access is by twin otter float plane to the Rivers Inlet Sportsmans Lodge, or by private craft, which are usually trailered to Port Hardy on Vancouver Island and launched from there, with a two to three hour boat ride from that point. It is also part of the Inside Passage, a 1,600-kilometer waterway extending along the Pacific Northwest from Seattle to Skagway.

Rivers Inlet

large, bright, and powerful. In fact, it is not unusual to hear of anglers fighting a giant king for hours, although the biggest fish don't necessarily take the longest to subdue. Some just fight harder than others. While one can argue whether tackle (primarily long limber rods and single-action reels), or angler inexperience contributes to this phenomenon, it is a certainty that the nature of these fish is variable. A

40-pounder will usually take 40 minutes to land, however. But I watched a Montana big game guide fight a 45-pounder for two hours last summer, landing the fish about 1½ miles from the point of hook-up. The evening before, another angler hooked a 46-pounder at dusk and didn't have the fish back to camp until 10:30.

And the salmon grow bigger still. An 82½-pound chinook caught in 1951 at

Rivers Inlet stood as the all-tackle world record for three decades until surpassed by an Alaskan fish, and that was eclipsed locally by an 84-pound fish caught at Rivers Inlet in 1986. Two more 80-pounders were reportedly taken here in 1987. At some point a chinook of 126 pounds was caught in a commercial net in the Hakai Pass, which is north of Rivers Inlet.

While the monsters aren't always predictable, 50- and 60-pounders are sure to be caught every year. These are impressive looking fish, deep-bodied and with thick girth, looking not unlike a tuna, although, of course these species are totally unrelated. The salmon feed well during their meanderings, their major prey being herring, anchovies, and needlefish.

King salmon aren't the only catch, either. Silver, or coho salmon, some weighing up to 25 pounds, come into the Inlet in two different runs, and the other species of Pacific salmon, chum, sockeye, and pink, are seasonally available as well.

Salmon fishing at Rivers Inlet has actually been improving in general. This is in part due to a hatchery at the head of Rivers Inlet that was started in 1985 and is operated by the lodges in

the area (40-pounders have already been produced from hatchery stock), and in part due to less pressure. Thirty years ago there were many canneries in Rivers Inlet and lots of traffic. Virtually all of the canneries are now gone, although the spectre of commercial drift-net fishing along the coast clouds the future.

The salmon fishery starts in mid-June at Rivers Inlet, when there is an early run of big kings. July is the month for unadulterated action, as small coho show up as they follow-baitfish schools. Coho get larger as the season progresses, with the biggest fish, locally called "northern coho" being available in late August and September. September is generally the best time to catch a large coho. These fish, pound for pound, are more exciting to catch than big chinooks even though they don't grow as large. The big cohos are active, leaping, tenacious fighters, streaking rather than bulldogging, and some anglers prefer them to kings.

Pink and chum salmon show up in mid to late July. The run builds in late July and peaks in early August. King salmon fishing is good from the beginning of the season through the end of August, with the biggest fish usually being caught in late July and the first three weeks of August. As noted previously, some of these fish are headed up the inlet to spawn, while others are migrating by as they head up or down the coast, accounting for varied sizes and strains of fish.

One of the best locations for all salmon species at Rivers Inlet, especially for large chinook, is a spot known locally as "The Wall", west of Goose Bay along the southern shore. Here, the water drops sharply by a cliff into 90 feet, and is 180 feet deep a short distance offshore, then drops to 400 feet 100 yards offshore. Fish congregate in this spot, allowing for specialized motor-mooching techniques using herring for bait.

Early morning and late in the afternoon are preferred times for catching

Above: Clustered near The Wall in early morning, Rivers Inlet anglers use a controlled drifting and trolling presentation called mooching to fish for coho and chinook salmon and steelhead.

Left: Anglers catch salmon that are migrating up and down the Pacific Northwest coast, either passing through Rivers Inlet or moving in to ascend its tributaries.

Boat Control

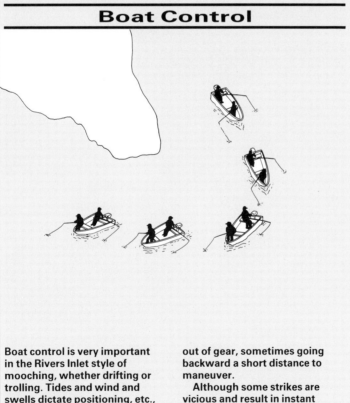

Boat control is very important in the Rivers Inlet style of mooching, whether drifting or trolling. Tides and wind and swells dictate positioning, etc., but you want to achieve a proper roll of the bait as well as keep it in the most advantageous locations. When trolling, or motor mooching, the boat operator frequently (in some cases constantly) puts the tiller-steered motor in and

out of gear, sometimes going backward a short distance to maneuver.

Although some strikes are vicious and result in instant hookups, many are soft, in which fish bump the bait; one has to pay out line quickly to give the fish time to get the bait well into its mouth without feeling resistance. Most fish are hooked just inside the mouth to enable release without harm.

KING SALMON

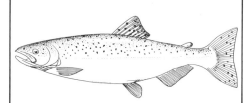

King, or chinook, salmon is the largest salmonid in North America. The all-tackle world record for these fish is 97 pounds 4 ounces, but they can grow bigger, with the largest known individual being the 126-pounder mentioned in the text. It is distinguished from other salmon by its black mouth and gums, and from coho by virtue of the fact that it has spots on both the top and bottom of the tail fin (the coho sports these on the top only). Silvery when at sea, chinook become darker as they approach spawning, ultimately becoming olive or reddish brown.

fish here, with some importance being attached to having lines in the water at first light. Many a large salmon is hooked before the sun pokes over the mountains and filters through the fog that wafts up the valleys. It is cold then, without the sun, and considering that even in summer the water temperature is in the upper 40s. But salmon that have come into the inlet during the night are more agreeable before there is a lot of boat traffic and before the brighter light sends them deeper.

There is plenty of deep water in Rivers Inlet, and a lot of places worth fishing. The inlets of minor tributaries, back in secluded bays hemmed in by spruce and hemlock, are particularly appealing, and at times you can easily forget this is saltwater fishing, not in a pristine mountain lake or deep in a fjord. Then you come upon a sight like Drainey Narrows; there on a good tide, water rushing out of Drainey Inlet produces a 6- to 8-foot waterfall. Out in open water the sight of a breaching whale reminds you where you really are, which is in one of the finest saltwater fishing spots in the world.

QUEEN CHARLOTTE ISLANDS

BRITISH COLUMBIA

The way that folks from northern California through Washington and up the Pacific coastline revere salmon, you'd think that just about any place in the Northwest with great fishing would have been discovered long ago and hit hard for years and years. But a few locations in North America, despite the advancements of the modern era, still haven't been easy to get to economically enough to attract many people.

So it is that the Queen Charlotte Islands, sitting alone off the northwestern coast of British Columbia and 25 miles southwest of Alaska, languished in relative obscurity. The Haida Indians, who maintain control of most of the northern Charlottes and whose ancient village ruins on Graham Island are close to the hot northern fishing area, have not permitted development, making it difficult for fixed-base lodging operations to get started. Couple this with the fact that most of British Columbia's coast is wild and sparsely populated, having excellent salmon fishing of its own, and you can see why few people ventured away from the mainland.

Taking a cue from the popularity of mainland floating resorts that moved from hotspot to hotspot, entrepreneurs recently devised a mothership approach for exploring the Queen Charlottes, using large boats that could be moved to accommodate changes in fish distribution and that could be secured in a protected moorage, complete with a fleet of small sportfishing craft.

The offshore discovery process began, and good news about the Queen Charlotte fishing started to spread. That was just a few years ago and now the Queen Charlottes, especially the northern tip in the Langara area, have become the most coveted place in Canada for big salmon.

And big is no understatement. Here, you need the strongest fishing net

Left: In a setting that is more reminiscent of a freshwater lake than an ocean inlet, anglers frequently catch the chinook salmon of their lifetime.

Right: Early morning is one of the preferred times for British Columbia salmon fishing, as is late in the day.

made to land the larger salmon, and usually it takes four arms to swing a netted fish out of the water and over the gunwale. This is truly 60-pound salmon country. It takes a 50-pounder to raise eyebrows and 40-pounders are routine. In fact, these fish are so fat and chunky that newcomers routinely underestimate the size of their catch, later learning that the fish they thought was 35 pounds in actuality was nearly 50. Reports indicate that nearly a dozen fish 70 pounds or better have been caught in the Queen Charlottes in the past five years, so there are obviously some real leviathans to be had from these waters.

These big salmon got to be so fat from spending several years at large in the Pacific, gorging themselves on herring and anchovies. Their wanderings bring them toward the British Columbia coast, *en route* to natal tributaries to spawn, and that migration path brings many from the Pacific depths past the Queen Charlottes.

As with other British Columbia salmon grounds, there are generally two times when the biggest salmon are more prevalent. One is early in the fishing season, which in the Queen Charlottes is from mid-May through June, and the other is through the month of August. It is uncertain whether that phenomenon is due to two different runs of fish, and, in fact, big fish do appear throughout the summer, being more prevalent in some years than in others (though which ones usually isn't predictable).

The fishing here is none-too intricate, which will come as a surprise to salmon anglers in the heavily fished waters of the interior section of North America, where downriggers and sonar are prerequisites and all manner of lures and trolling presentations are employed. You won't see a downrigger in the Queen Charlottes, and hardware usage is minimal.

Traditional coastal salmon gear involves the use of limber 10-foot rods and single-action or level-wind reels holding several hundred yards of 20-

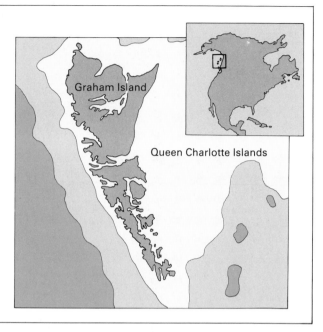

There are about 150 islands that make up the Queen Charlottes. Located between the 52nd and 54th latitudes, they form the western boundary of Hecate Strait north of Queen Charlotte Sound. The most noted fishing occurs at Langara Island, which is the northern-most point of the Queen Charlottes and is actually closer to the Alaskan Panhandle than to mainland British Columbia, and near Rennell Sound on the western end of Graham Island. Mothership operations are accessed by amphibious plane.

Graham Island

Queen Charlotte Islands

or 25-pound line, trolling and drifting with weighted cut herring. The only thing that is intricate is getting just the right roll, or spin, from the herring.

An opportunity seems to exist here for the development of light-tackle salmon fishing; playing these strong, giant chinooks in open water with 4- to 10-pound line is quite a challenge. A few fishermen do use light gear now, but they are in the minority. Some anglers have attempted fly fishing for giant chinook in the Queen Charlottes but so far their efforts have not borne much fruit. This is in part because much remains to be known about suitable locales here (the same places tend to get fished over and over), and also because weather frequently hampers exploration.

Although mooching with herring is the preferred salmon fishing tactic, an opportunity exists for light tackle usage and employment of flies and hardware.

The Queen Charlottes have become known for their large king salmon; this one was caught at sunset.

Using Cut Herring

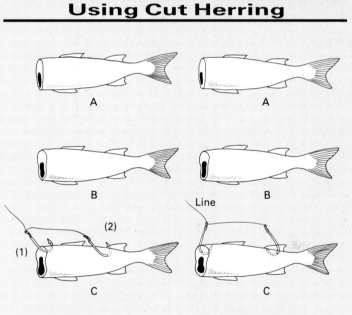

The angle of cut that is made when separating the head from the body of a herring is quite important. This dictates the speed of the roll as the bait is drifted or trolled. An angled cut is made behind the gills by the pectoral fin and the innards are pulled or routed out of the cavity. Snelled salmon hooks in two- or three-hook rigs are used; the manner of placing them is important, but varies with the number of hooks, size of bait, and speed of roll desired. The lead hook is impaled through the head, however, with point inserted inside the cavity behind several ribs and hooked out through the top of the bait.

Fairly heavy sinkers are used – from 2 to 6 ounces – being keel shaped and fished several feet above the bait. A barrel swivel is used a few feet ahead of the sinker and the length of the leader from swivel to bait is roughly equal to the length of the rod.

The Queen Charlottes experience some truly nasty weather, with rain and mist almost a surety in the course of a short visit. Westerly and north-westerly winds frequently pound the archipelago, and some days fishing is only possible in sheltered locales, if at all. Good foul-weather gear is a must here, to protect against both wind and rain.

When the weather is more hospitable, however, anglers are able to get in long days of fishing, with first light coming as early as 4:30 in the month of June and lasting until well past 9 in the evening. It is common for many anglers to fish the morning and evening periods and rest during midday.

King salmon aren't the only fish here, although they certainly are the most coveted. Plenty of coho, or silver, salmon swim among the Queen Charlotte Islands. Cohos become increasingly abundant as the season advances. Small fish are around early, with 10- to 15-pounders becoming available through the summer, and big fish, including the "northern coho" of 20 pounds and over, present from late August into October.

There are also some nice halibut to be caught in Queen Charlotte waters. Halibut are found all along the upper

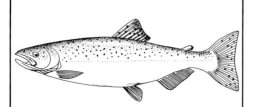

PACIFIC SALMON

The Pacific Northwest sees five species of Pacific salmon during the year: sockeye, chum, pink, coho, and chinook. Chinook are widely known as "king" salmon and coho as "silver" salmon. The big coho of the fall are locally called northern coho, and the early-run chinooks are called spring salmon. All are anadromous fish, spending their lives in the ocean and returning to their rivers of birth to spawn, after which they die. In the ocean for several years, they wander great distances and feed prodigiously. They are highly sought for their food value and extensive commercial fisheries exist.

British Columbia coast, of course, but are usually taken while fishing with bait or jigs fished on the bottom. The halibut are so abundant in sections of the Queen Charlottes that they frequently rise to take the trolled herring presentations of salmon fishermen, which is an unusual thing for these bottom dwellers to do. Taking a 60-pound halibut and a 60-pound king salmon in the same day, let alone the same trip, is a possibility. So far, halibut up to 125 pounds have been recorded by sport fishermen, the larger ones usually coming to people deliberately fishing for this species rather than catching them accidentally. Lingcod and snapper, incidentally, are also caught here.

Because of the difficulties in establishing a fishing operation, it isn't likely that the Queen Charlottes will get over-run with anglers in the near future. If commercial fishing operations don't decimate Pacific salmon stocks and if anglers moderate their take of trophy kings, there will be outstanding big-salmon fishing in the Queen Charlottes for years to come.

SOUTHEAST ALASKA

They call it the "Other Alaska", the part that everyone overlooks. The part that doesn't have all the charter boats and the lodges and the people and the traffic. Six hundred miles long and removed from the rest of the state of Alaska, despite the fact that it harbors the capital city of Juneau, the Panhandle bordering British Columbia is home to some of the finest Pacific Northwest fishing that can be imagined. It has, too, some of the grandest scenery in a section of the world loaded with beautiful vistas, and some of the most outstanding wildlife in North America. That is a lot of superlatives to lay on any place.

But this is Southeast Alaska. With more than 1,000 islands and over 13,000 miles of shoreline, this area has the blessing of always being protected in some fashion from winds whipping off the cold north Pacific. That makes it ideal for the Inside Passage, which was an historical settlement route. Indeed, for several years in the late 1890s, thousands of people passed through the straits here en route to Skagway and then to the Klondike during the rush for gold, many in vessels that were barely seaworthy. Protected waters notwithstanding, there were many shipwrecks.

The passage is great for anglers, of course, who seek a different kind of treasure today, and from craft that would have brought many a nugget a century earlier. Today, that angler arrives by float plane and headquarters at lodges on such islands as Admiralty and Chichagof.

The finned treasures being sought are none of the glamorous billfishes or tunas which are usually associated with the Pacific Ocean, but coldwater salmon and bottom fish. Big, powerful, and plentiful, the fish here attract anglers from all over the world, in a setting that reminds one more of inland, glacial freshwater locales than a salty, tidal environment.

And while some good fishing can be had in the tributary streams and rivers for various salmon, plus steelhead, Dolly Varden, rainbow trout, and grayling, this is usually a side-venture for anglers. It is out in the salt where the main events – fishing for big chinook and coho salmon and monster halibut – takes place.

Left: Although they are overshadowed by their larger cousins, coho, or silver, salmon are abundant later in the season.

Right: The waters of Southeast Alaska are well protected from winds, and provide some of the most scenic angling to be found anywhere.

Improved Clinch Knot

One of the most popular knots for tying line directly to a lure, the Improved Clinch Knot can give 100 percent strength, but only if tied properly every time. To tie it, (1) pass the line through the hook eye, then make six turns around the standing line; (2) thread end through the loop ahead of the eye; (3) back end through the newly created large loop; (4) moisten the knot and line and tighten. Use six turns for line up to 12-pound- test, five for 14- to 17-pound line, and four spirals for 20- pound and over.

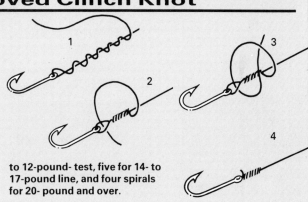

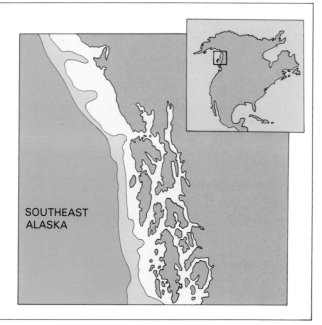

The Alaskan Panhandle is separated from the rest of the state to the north by the Elias Mountains, which are among the tallest coastal mountains anywhere. Admiralty and Chichagof Islands, which are two of the larger islands in the Alexander Archipelago, are the focus of much sportfishing attention, especially around Elfin Cove and Funter. Halibut inhabit the deep waters and salmon migrate through the passage and between islands, en route to mainland rivers to spawn, or to rivers further down the Pacific Northwest coast.

SOUTHEAST ALASKA

The halibut here are big beyond the imagination. They throw back 50-pounders. And that's no chamber of commerce brochure palaver. In fact, this is prime world-record country.

Numerous line-class Pacific halibut world records have occurred in these waters, the most notable being a 356½-pounder on 30-pound line taken in the Castineau Channel in 1986.

The Alaska state record halibut, which is not in the I.G.F.A. records (for various reasons some fish do not qualify for record recognition even though taken on rod and reel), came from Icy Strait, which is in between Chichagof Island and Glacier Bay National Monument; that leviathan weighed 440 pounds.

Although a visitor cannot be assured of catching monsters of record dimensions, one or more 300-pounders is caught every year here, and it is common to tangle with 100-pounders. Twenty- to 30-pound halibut are run-of-the-mill.

These fish put up a tremendous resistance, and it is no wonder that the larger specimens are likened to barn doors. Eighty-pound gear is standard fare here (and supplied by the outfitters) to deal with the biggest fish. But many anglers, shooting for records as

well as big fish on lighter tackle, are using from 12- to 40-pound gear.

Standup-tackle with 20- to 40-pound gear has become popular, and allows anglers to whip large fish in a reasonable amount of time. This is important for saving one's back but also because the hot action often doesn't last long, as it can be tide or hole oriented, and having one person struggling with a big fish for a long time makes it tough for the other anglers on board (usually several anglers are on a boat) to get in on the action.

Usually, two hours before and after a tide change is the prime time. Tides are strong here, which accounts for using very heavy weights; most fishing takes place in 100 to 150 feet of water, but sometimes in over 200 feet.

Most of this fishing is jigging, using plain or baited jigs and fishing on or close to the bottom by drifting. Here, it is fairly standard to use jigs up to 16 ounces adorned with a large (up to a pound) cod fillet. Although halibut are caught throughout this region, Elfin Cove off the northern tip of Chichagof Island and Funter Bay off the northern tip of Admiralty Island, are particularly notable spots. Peak season is from mid-June through September.

There is a smorgasbord of bottom-

dwelling fish to be caught while jigging, incidentally, including yelloweye rockfish, black rockfish, and lingcod. These provide great sport on light tackle, and the lingcod can range up to 50 pounds. Elfin Cove has produced four current world record lingcod, including the all-tackle and 50-pound line-class holder, a 64-pound fish that was caught in 1988.

So good is the bottom fishing that one might overlook the fish that the entire Pacific Northwest coast is most noted for: salmon. Although this area is not known for giant salmon, 40- and 50-pound chinook migrate through this area, ultimately en route to tributaries that wind their way well into the British Columbia mountains.

Known as king or spring salmon in this region, chinook are caught in the salt by drifting and trolling with cut herring. Ditto for coho (silvers). May through July is the prime king salmon period, although these fish are also available into September. Silvers are

PACIFIC HALIBUT

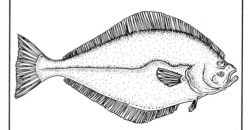

The Pacific halibut is distinguished from its California cousin by being more northerly in range and larger growing. It looks, in fact, like its Atlantic halibut cousin, however, all three are distinct species. Pacific halibut are migratory, and are dark brown on the top and white on the bottom. In the northern portions of their range they are found quite shallow, but may be located at depths of up to several hundred fathoms in warmer, southern waters. Their diet consists of small fish, crustaceans, squid, and mollusks. They feed at different levels, although they are mainly caught while fishing on the bottom, drifting or jigging. Heavy tackle and large baits are generally used for the larger specimens.

Monster halibut are possible from the waters of Southeast Alsaka, especially off the northern part of Chichagof Island, where this fish was taken.

available from July on. As is typical in this area, the bigger silvers seem to show up later in the season, and 20-pounders are possible. Earlier in the season the size ranges from 7 to 12 pounds. Pink (known as humpbacked), chum (dog), and sockeye salmon round out the summer possibilities.

Although protected from wind, this area is noted for wet, cool weather and fog. Ketchikan, to the south, gets 13 feet of rainfall a year. The state government used to proclaim "sun holidays" in the winter for the sake of southeast Alaska residents.

But for fishermen who come prepared for it, this is a minor matter. Because, in addition to really outstanding angling action, they are treated to the sight of brown bears, bald eagles (many are seen each day and thousands descend on the Chilkat River above Haines each fall), sea lions, whales (including occasionally a breaching humpback), the majestic spectacle of snow-capped mountains and fjord-like vistas, and much more. Some well-traveled people have called Southeast Alaska a paradise, aesthetically and piscatorially.

GULF OF ALASKA

Because of the allure of fly fishing, catching steelhead, and tangling with big fish in flowing water, most of the angling attention paid to the state of Alaska has been focused on the many tributaries that host excellent runs of migrating salmonids. However, a great deal of fishing opportunity exists all along the seacoast for a number of prime game species, most notably halibut, chinook salmon, and coho salmon.

Halibut, which were virtually ignored by sportfishermen, didn't get much attention, other than from the enormous commercial fleet in these waters, until salmon numbers were depressed about a decade ago. Only then was it realized that large halibut were *the* bottom fish, and one to be reckoned with on any tackle.

And heavy is an understatement for some of the Gulf of Alaska specimens, especially in and around Cook Inlet and the tip of the Kenai Peninsula. The Homer-Cook Inlet area lays claim to several line-class world-record halibut, the largest of which is a 350-pounder on 130-pound line. Bigger halibut, including a 466-pounder, have been caught on rod and reel in these waters, and still larger ones have been reported by commercial boats.

In the northern Gulf of Alaska, there are now many charterboats that cater to halibut fishing, and three areas stand out: Prince William Sound; Kodiak Island around Long and Woody Islands; and the Kenai Peninsula waters of Kachemak Bay and Cook Inlet. Fishing is from May through September, with August best.

Salmon. of course, are a strong attraction here. The Kenai Peninsula is world-renowned for the strain of huge chinooks that run its Kenai River, and it has been pressured mightily. The Kenai holds several world records, including the 97-pound all-tackle chinook, and Deep Creek on this peninsula holds several others. Although these are river-caught fish, they had to be in the Gulf and Cook Inlet first, so the coastal boater hereabouts does have an opportunity for a superheavyweight. Good spots near the peninsula are in various areas of Cook Inlet, as well as at the mouths of the larger rivers and in Kachemak Bay, plus off the Copper River in Prince William Sound and the Karluk River at Kodiak Island.

Numerous records have been set in these waters for coho and other salmon, too, including all five categories for coho in the fly rod division (in the Karluk River), so the opportunity is here as well. These salmon are predominantly caught in the same locales as chinooks. June and July are prime for chinooks, from mid-July into September for cohos.

Chinook salmon, such as this fish, as well as coho, pink, chum, and sockeye, are also caught in these waters, especially in the tributaries.

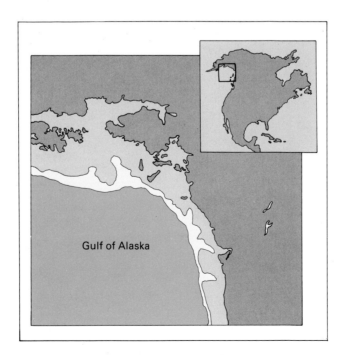

Gulf of Alaska

WALKER'S CAY

BAHAMAS

Christopher Columbus came upon the Bahamas the same year that he discovered America, and was taken with their beauty. He was, it has been reported, searching for gold at the time. It was treasure seeking that drove other visitors here in the early days as well, although those adventurers were pirates, and it was not until 1728, 11 years after Blackbeard (a Nassau visitor) died, that the pirates were driven out. Today, friendly visitors in the form of tourists swarm to these islands, a great many with fishing in mind.

The Bahamas, with some 700 islands or cays, is not without a lot of places to fish, sunbathe, or be otherwise entertained. While this Atlantic archipelago has many places of note, none is more acclaimed than the 100-acre piece of land known as

As the northernmost land in the Bahamas, and the lead island in the Abaco chain, Walker's Cay is 150 miles northeast of Ft. Lauderdale, Florida, 110 miles east of Palm Beach, and 45 miles north of Freeport on Grand Bahama Island. It is frequently visited by anglers boating across the Gulf Stream from South Florida, which is about a four-hour journey in relatively calm seas. Flats anglers fish nearby, jiggers fish the inshore reefs and offshore north and west at Mantanilla Reef (although this is 40 miles away), while blue-water trollers work the edge of the dropoff. An easterly current, and a quick dropoff from the Abaco wall to 100-fathom water and more, means that Walker's Cay is a 15-minute run from harbor to productive big game grounds.

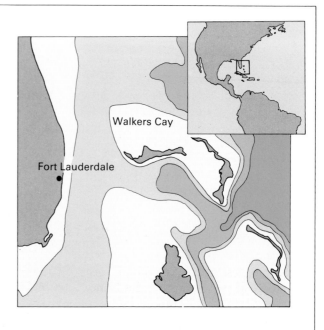

Walkers Cay

Fort Lauderdale

Walker's Cay is the northernmost island in the Bahamas, and is close enough to Florida for boaters to bring even relatively small boats, such as these, to this locale for various types of fishing.

Walker's Cay, which is the north-ernmost spot in the Bahamas, and which itself was named after a pirate.

An anti-submarine base in World War II, the site of a missile tracking station in the early 60s, and a retreat for former U.S. President Richard Nixon, Walker's Cay today is a pure fishing resort, one often labeled as idyllic, peaceful, and secluded, and a frequent inclusion in listings of top ten getaway destinations.

Walker's has as diverse a fishery as one could expect in the Bahamas, and has been the locale for notable catches, with its offshore fishing and reef bottom fishing most acclaimed.

Walker's is least heralded for flats fishing for bonefish, but depending on who you consult, it's either good here or so-so. The latter is the way a bonefish fanatic, looking for miles of flats, lots of opportunities, and big fish, especially for shallow-water tailing fish, would describe it. But since most folks don't fit that category, the bone-fishing is pretty good, and an interest-ing diversion from reef and offshore angling.

Having caught my first bonefish there, and being one of three anglers to each catch a fish out of one school on my first foray, I have a special fondness for Walker's flats, even though they are not extensive. Never-theless, bonefish are found year-round at Walker's, mainly just past the ma-rina by the airstrip, and over at Grand Cays and Double Breasted Cay. The flats also produce barracuda and shark, of course.

When it comes to reef fishing, however, there is no debating the quality of the experience near Walk-er's. There is simply no better place in the Bahamas, perhaps even in this slice of the world, and it takes place at the coral nearby edges and offshore in the deep-water reefs.

On the ocean side of Walker's the coral drops off into 40 feet of water just a short distance away, and this provides action for both red groupers and red hinds (strawberry grouper) in

Left: Although not known as a hotbed of bonefishing, Walker's does offer some flats wading for small bones; each of these anglers is hooked to a bonefish caught from the same school.

Below: Wahoo, barracuda, various tuna, and assorted groupers and other species are found along the reefs, which are fished primarily by deep jigging, but also by trolling; Walker's reef fishing is among the best in the Bahamas.

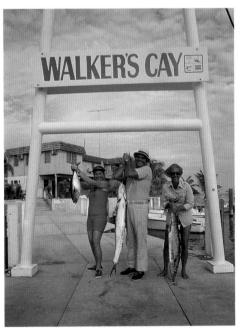

small sizes, as well as Nassau, yellow-fin, and black groupers. Actually these species are present all the way out to 150 feet of water or more, and while light-tackle fun can be had in shallow water, the larger fish are out deeper, and 130 to 200 feet is the range that is usually fished by deep jiggers. The fish they look to tempt in the deeper reef waters include the aforementioned species, plus the occasional African pompano, shark, amberjack, barracu-da, wahoo, and others.

Stout tackle is usually used here because these fish can reach heavyweight sizes, and make vigorous efforts to escape by powering back into the rocky habitat. Twenty-pound groupers, especially Nassau and yel-lowfins, are common, and they may be had up to 40 pounds. Red grouper (called deer grouper by the locals) may hit the 15-pound mark, and black grouper can be in the 40- to 60-pound class or larger (an 84-pounder is the local best).

Reef fishing is productive all year long at Walker's. Jigs tipped with curly soft plastics or with bait are the hot ticket, especially on a moving tide, usually working close to the bottom for the groupers and up the water column to attract the other species.

For many Walker's Cay visitors, reef jigging, though productive, is just a side dish, with the entree being big game. Walker's Cay has the reputation of being a big-game port, hosting several major tournaments annually. The harbor is crowded from late winter through early summer with sportfishing boats, with the main interest being blue marlin.

The water drops to over 1,000 feet deep within two miles of Walker's Cay, and plummets from there to a 3,000-foot canyon. Many humps and other bottom irregularities exist and between this underwater structure and the continuous easterly Antilles Current, the result is an upwelling of bait.

Pursuing the bait and migrating through are such species as blue marlin, white marlin, sailfish, yellowfin tuna, blackfin tuna, bluefin tuna, dolphin, king mackerel, and wahoo. Mako sharks are also on the agenda.

Walker's Cay hasn't produced a lot of record-size fish for these species in recent years, although they had some in the past and they do presently hold a few I.G.F.A. line-class records, including a 75-pound king mackerel on 30-pound line and a 104-pound wahoo on 80-pound line, neither of recent vintage.

There is some expectation that a monster blue, one over 1,000 pounds, might hit the scales at Walker's one day. Only one such fish has been officially recorded anywhere in the Bahamas (that one at Bimini). Gran-

WHITE MARLIN

Found along the Atlantic coast, the Caribbean, and in the Gulf of Mexico, white marlin are more like a sailfish in size and fight than any other marlin. In some waters they are more frequently caught than blue marlin, and are often found in closer-to-shore environs than blues. Many of the same trolling methods are used, although baits and lures should preferably be smaller. White marlin are a good light-tackle billfish; 20- to 30-pound outfits and 2/0 to 6/0 reels are commonly used.

ders have been reportedly hooked and lost by anglers here, although the island record to-date remains at just under 700 pounds. Fish in the 500- and 600-pound class are caught, but the average blue remains under 200.

High-speed trolling with lures is preferred by most regulars here, using this as a way to cover a lot of territory. The best fishing is usually from February through May. March and April are considered prime here for blue marlin but these fish are encountered through the year. Many of the bigger fish are caught in winter, although this is not a heavily fished period due to the possibility of inclement weather.

Other fish that are fairly common through the entire season are wahoo, mackerel, and blackfin tuna. Dolphin action is sporadic off Walker's, but the fish that are caught are fairly large. White marlin make appearances at various times during the year, but they are most likely to be caught during the winter and spring. Sailfish are most abundant in summer and fall. Yellowfin tuna are a summer catch here, for the most part. That's a lot of piscatorial treasure in any angler's book.

Big Fish/Small Boat

Fighting big saltwater fish out of small boats is not only possible but sometimes advantageous, provided that the anglers and crew members are careful and skillful. In addition to being able to maneuver more quickly and also to chase a fish if necessary, a small boat allows an angler to go to the front to fight a hot fish. This allows the skipper to look and move forward as necessary to fight/follow the fish. With stand-up tackle, anglers are now able to stand in the bow of small boats and fight such fish. Some center console anglers actually mount a fighting chair in the front of their boats so the angler can work a fish without standing up. Gaffing or leadering for release may be done from the front if the fish is still green; if tired out, work from the rear gunwale, which is lower.

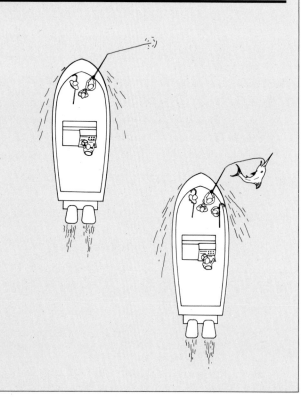

Blue marlin are also caught offshore from Walker's; this blue is about to be tagged and released.

DEEP WATER, GREEN TURTLE, TREASURE CAYS

BAHAMAS

As a group of islands the Bahamas are certainly well known and well visited. Certain islands are heavily trafficked by tourists, and some have received a lot of publicity for their fishing opportunities. Somewhere in the neighborhood of 700 cays, or islands, make up the Bahamas and it stands to reason that a few less-publicized and/or out-of-the-way places exist, including those that offer good, but not heavily pressured,

fishing. Several places like this exist in the northern Bahamas, in the central Abacos and near Grand Bahama.

One such locale is Deep Water Cay. Found on few maps, this 2-mile-long island is reportedly home base for some 200 square miles of flats replete with various typical, finny creatures, but most especially bonefish and permit.

The bonefish here average 5 pounds but are seen up to 10 fairly often. They

have been caught up to 14 pounds, and are present year-round. Permit, too, roam the local waters, in sizes ranging from a few pounds to 25, and some up to 20 pounds heftier. Burroughs Cay, a one-hour run, is a particularly good permit locale. Fly fishing is especially productive here.

Another locale that is situated in excellent bonefish country is Green Turtle Cay, midway along the ocean side of Great Abaco.

Scenic Treasure Cay sports bonefishing on the flats and marlin and tuna action offshore in the blue water.

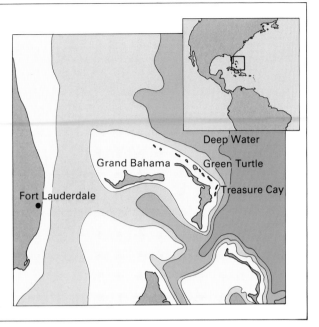

Deep Water Cay is located at the eastern end of Grand Bahama Island, separated from it by Rummer Creek. Two miles long, it is known as a flats fishing haven, with bonefish and tarpon the main draws. Green Turtle and Treasure Cays are in the middle reaches of the Abacos, with unpressured flats and quick access to deep ocean waters.

these three that has significant blue water fishing, however, and this is becoming more of a factor in its angling attraction. The ledge-like drop off here starts less than a mile from the island, dropping from 200 to over 1,400 feet, and continuing from there.

The big-game history here is rather threadbare yet, since it hasn't received much pressure, a lot of fish are being released, and big sportfishing boats have really only started seriously working these waters in the past few years. So far the blue marlin season is similar to that at Walker's Cay, which is 140 miles to the north. The best blue marlin to-date at Treasure weighed 603 pounds. Wahoo, and the other usual Bahamian offshore species are encountered, too.

Fish here are not large, but there are plenty of them year-round, with good-sized schools of bonefish spotted by wading or boating anglers. Poling in search of cruising fish, and stalking tailing feeders is possible along flats devoid of people. A run up north to Little Abaco Island may be worthwhile (also from Deep Water Cay), where larger bonefish are sometimes found in the vicinity of Cooperstown and Fox Town.

Three miles across Abaco Bay from Green Turtle is another locale worthy of note, although not without regular patronage, mainly from the big-game crowd. This is Treasure Cay, where marlin and tuna in the blue offshore water receive main attention. Nevertheless, as with Green Turtle, Treasure Cay has a lot of small bonefish, and the angler looking for a respite from the big water or hoping to get his first bonefish will find that the skinny water near this island is worth investigating.

These locales also have other species of note on the flats, as most Bahamanian waters do, including barracuda, lemon sharks, blacktip sharks, and mutton snapper, and the usual assortment of bottom fish on the reefs adjacent to the flats.

Treasure Cay is the only one of

Outriggers

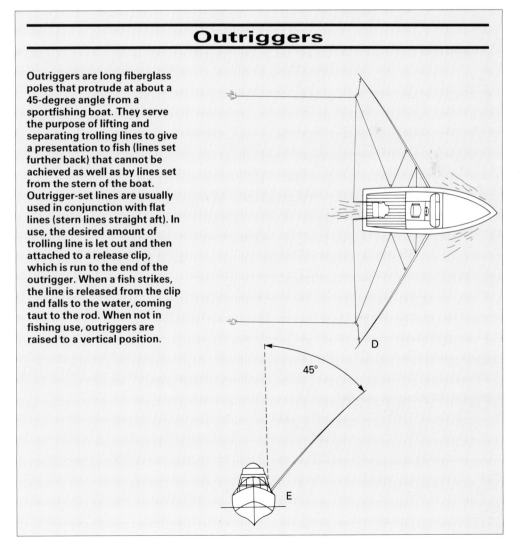

Outriggers are long fiberglass poles that protrude at about a 45-degree angle from a sportfishing boat. They serve the purpose of lifting and separating trolling lines to give a presentation to fish (lines set further back) that cannot be achieved as well as by lines set from the stern of the boat. Outrigger-set lines are usually used in conjunction with flat lines (stern lines straight aft). In use, the desired amount of trolling line is let out and then attached to a release clip, which is run to the end of the outrigger. When a fish strikes, the line is released from the clip and falls to the water, coming taut to the rod. When not in fishing use, outriggers are raised to a vertical position.

BIMINI/CAT CAY

BAHAMAS

If there is a fishing port that anglers are most likely to associate with the Bahamas, the hands-down favorite would have to be Bimini. It is the closest Bahamian island to the mainland U.S., and sits right on the edge of blue water and pelagic fish migration paths. But Bimini, as well as neighboring Cat Cay (a bucolic island that was once refuge for the infamous pirates Blackbeard and Morgan), was also the home of some of the history-making activities that gave big-game sportfishing its start, and which have propelled it along.

Famous angler/author Kip Farrington caught the first Bahamas blue marlin at Bimini in February of 1933. It was Ernest Hemingway who boated the first big tuna taken on rod and reel

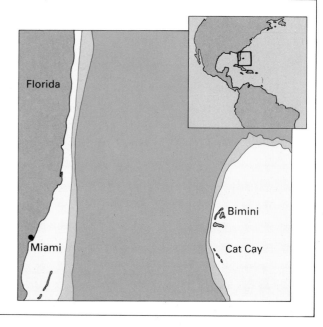

The locale referred to as Bimini is actually two islands, North Bimini and South Bimini, which are 50 miles east of Miami, Florida. Cat Cay is just a short distance to the south, and both are located on the western edge of the Great Bahama Bank, and the eastern edge of the Gulf Stream in the Straits of Florida. Flats exist on the eastern shores, and a steep dropoff, known as the Bimini Wall, on the western edges, continuing to the south. Two thousand feet of water exists within several hundred yards of these islands.

Left: The ports of Bimini and Cat Cay have long been the scene of major big-game fishing activities, and the pioneering grounds for many trolling tactics and tackle.

Right: Giant bluefin tuna, such as this one that was a winner in a major Cat Cay tournament, are pursued in the renowned Tuna Alley blue water in May and June.

in the Bahamas, doing so in 1935 with catches weighing 310 and 381 pounds. His glowing reports about his exploits here through 1941, and the increasing success enjoyed by Farrington, Hemingway, I.G.F.A. founder Michael Lerner, and others put these islands forever on the world piscatorial map.

Many of the world's wealthiest, famous, and best anglers fished Bimini, one of the most renowned of the latter being Captain Tommy Gifford, whose innovations for big-game angling included the outrigger, the fighting chair, and fishing kites. Bimini and Cat Cay have seen other Bahamian "firsts", including the first swordfish, the first blue marlin grander, and the first tuna tournaments (at Cat Cay in May, 1939), etc.

Tuna were a stellar attraction of mega-proportions here, and still are although their numbers have been greatly reduced by world commercial fishing activities and their migratory path apparently occasionally veers away from the Straits. Never a place to vie with the Maritime Provinces up north with half-tonners, the blue waters here have been a place for 300- to 700-pound bluefins, giants in their own right and more than most people care to tussle with anyway. The present women's 50-pound line-class world-record bluefin, a 518-pounder, was caught off Bimini, incidentally.

Tuna Alley, the section of blue water nearest to Bimini and Cat Cay and extending to the north and south a bit, is the fishing grounds, and where there were once many fish caught, an angler is lucky to have a few chances per season, which is roughly six to eight weeks long, through the months of May and June.

The sheer dropoff along the edge of Great Bahama Bank that is prime for tuna is also the locale for billfish, and these, too, have had their ups and downs over the years. Blue marlin were extremely plentiful in the early days here and five to six chances a day were common. That's not the case any longer, but a good number of marlin do migrate by here, some quite large.

As long ago as 1925, renowned author/angler Van Campen Heilner raised big billfish, including an estimated 1,000-pound blue marlin, off Bimini. He reported such in a 1937 book he authored, but never let anyone know previously because he didn't want Bimini, where he'd settled, to be inundated.

It happened anyway in a few years, of course, and although big blues were seen and lost in later years, it wasn't until 1979 that a grander was finally caught. Brought to the Bimini docks by a June tournament angler, the fish weighed 1,060 pounds. It is still the only grander caught anywhere in the Bahamas.

Each season, however, the waters off Bimini and Cat Cay produce 500- to 700-pound blue marlin, usually over 300 to 2,500 feet of water. As in most other big-game areas of the Bahamas, these fish are caught all season long, but the most productive period is from late winter through spring. It is said

Left: Blue marlin are a Bimini mainstay, with some fish being caught throughout the season.

Right: Wrecks and reefs in the Bimini area produce various fish, including large amberjack, such as this specimen.

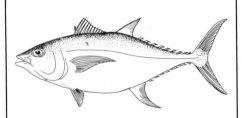

BLUEFIN TUNA

Revered for their fighting qualities, size, and stamina, bluefin tuna are pursued by sport and commercial interests wherever they are found. Actually members of the mackerel family (and called horse mackerel in the Maritimes) bluefin tuna are migratory, pelagic fish that primarily inhabit tropical, subtropical, and temperate waters. Their diet is usually whatever is most abundant in their present location, but includes squid, crustaceans, flying fish, mackerel, small tuna, sardines, herring, whiting, and other fish. Giant bluefins can grow to weights exceeding 1,000 pounds and a length of 10 to 11 feet.

that good fishing could be had in February, but few boats work these waters at that time.

White marlin and sailfish, overlooked by many, have been a regular catch here, although neither will challenge the record books for size. White marlin numbers are down these days, but the better fishing occurs in March. For sailfish, the best chance occurs in summer months. Dolphin are plentiful here, as they are in the Stream in Florida waters. Some big dolphin, in the 50-pound class, show up in winter months, and small school dolphin are abundant in the summer.

Wahoo are a favorite offshore quarry in Bimini and Cat Cay, with large fish possible. The all-tackle world-record wahoo, a 149-pounder, bears a Cat Cay registry, though this was set in 1962. November and December are best for wahoo, but the season extends from October through March. Bimini, incidentally, holds the 20-

pound line-class record for king mackerel with a 77-pounder, although that, too, is an old record. It also has an old record in the 80-pound women's line-class mako shark division, with an 880-pounder. Large makos were much more common in the past than they are now, but these sharks are still caught here.

Although the offshore big-game scene is the strong suit of Bimini and Cat Cay, there is a diversity to fishing here that is on a par with the best elsewhere. Some people consider the bonefishing here to be as good as anywhere in the Bahamas, although among avid bonefishers Bimini does not have that reputation.

Nevertheless, there is no arguing with its production of some big bonefish, as per the record books. Two Bimini bonefish (13 and 15 pounds) are present fly rod world records, and two are line-class world records (15 and 16 pounds). Only two other fish from

Tying the Bimini Twist

Knots to form double-line leaders
Bimini twist
The Bimini twist creates a long length of doubled line that is stronger
than the single strand of the standing line. It is most often used in
offshore trolling, but is applicable in light tackle trolling in both fresh and salt water.

1. Measure a little more than twice the footage you'll want for the double-line leader. Bring end back to standing line and hold together. Rotate end of loop 20 times, putting twists in it.

2. Spread loop to force twists together about 10 inches below tag end. Step both feet through loop and bring it up around knees so pressure can be placed on column of twists by spreading knees apart.

3. With twists forced tightly together, hold standing line in one hand with tension just slightly off the vertical position. With other hand, move tag end to position at right angle to twists. Keeping tension on loop with knees, gradually ease tension of tag end so it will roll over the column of twists, beginning just below the upper twist.

4. Spread legs apart slowly to maintain pressure on loop. Steer tag end into a tight spiral coil as it continues to roll over twisted line.

5. When spiral of tag end has rolled over column of twists, continue keeping knee pressure on loop and move hand which has held standing line down to grasp knot. Place finger in crotch of line where loop joins to prevent slippage of last turn, take half-hitch with tag end around nearest leg of loop and pull up tight.

6. With half-hitch holding knot, release knee pressure but keep loop stretched out tight. Using remaining tag end, take half-hitch around both legs of loop, but do not pull tight.

7. Make two more turns with the tag end around both legs of the loop, winding inside the bend of line formed by the loose half-hitch and toward the main knot. Pull tag end slowly, forcing the three loops to gather in a spiral.

8. When loops are pulled up nearly against main knot, tighten to lock knot in place. Trim end about ½ inch from knot. These directions apply to tying double-line leaders of around 5 feet or less. For longer double-line sections, two people may be required to hold the line and make initial twists.

the Bahamas are in the records at all.

For other diversion, anglers here can fish on the reefs for various groupers, snapper, mackerel, bonito, permit, amberjack, and the like. Bimini claims a present line-class amberjack record, incidentally, with a 92-pounder. Reef angling takes place near Bimini and Cat Cay and also at Great Isaac Reef, the Gingerbread Grounds, and Riding Rocks, in a variety of depths.

There are a number of boat and airplane wrecks, reportedly several dozen, in the shallow waters of Great Bahama Bank, east of Bimini and Cat Cay, and these play host to a vast range of fish.

Permit, amberjack, barracuda, mutton snapper, horse-eye jack, mangrove snapper, yellowtail, and others are part of the smorgasbord, depending on locale (especially distance to deep water, permit being one of the fish found on wrecks that are close to deep water). Tide and depth have some bearing on the fishing, and most are not readily located by wandering and observing, but require the use of loran pinpointing.

CHUB CAY

BAHAMAS

Like Walker's Cay and Bimini, Chub Cay in the Berry Islands is oriented toward billfish, and well it should be. This area is unique in the Bahamas, as can be noticed by looking at a hydrographic or navigational chart. There is a dogleg-like alley of water that comes from the Atlantic Ocean and runs south of Little Bahama Bank, through the Northeast Providence Channel. It turns southeasterly below Chub Cay and parallels Andros Island, running up onto Grand Bahama Bank. This is the spot they call the Tongue of the Ocean. This is the one of the best, and most renowned, locales in the Bahamas for marlin and tuna.

The first time I ran a boat offshore from Chub Cay, it seemed like the chart recorder stopped working a few

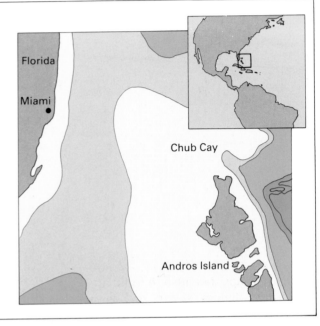

Chub Cay is part of the Berry Islands, a bank of small cays that is 20 miles long and situated at the northern end of the Tongue of the Ocean. A short distance from Andros and Nassau, it is 90 miles east of Bimini. The cays to the north of Chub have good bonefishing and are not fished hard, as the deep waters of the Tongue beckon anglers interested primarily in blue and white marlin.

These trollers are prowling for marlin off Chub Cay in the Tongue of the Ocean, where the blue water drops off into the abyss just a short distance from shore.

yards from the reef. It had not stopped working; it just didn't record water that deep. We went back to shore and suddenly there was the bottom on the chart. Such a precipitous cliff of a dropoff!

And that's where the blue and white marlin are. Blues here average about 200 pounds, with whites going around 50, but blue marlin in the 500- to 700-pound range are taken, and larger ones have been lost. Some large white marlin are occasionally caught here, as attested to by the 148-pounder that is currently a women's 50-pound line-class world record. Better-than-normal fishing has occurred here when a southeast wind pushes over the shallow Grand Bahama Bank, enriching the blue water of the Tongue, and the possibility of catching a grand slam – sailfish, white marlin, and blue marlin – in a single day is present. Sailfish are abundant here at times, but not as well represented in the catch as blue marlin, perhaps because efforts are directed in deeper water and with larger baits or lures than sails prefer.

The billfish season in the Chub Cay vicinity is from March through August, with white marlin usually more abundant in the spring and blues afterward. June has produced blue marlin in the 700-pound range and is considered a prime month, but April through June is when you stand the chance of all three billfish.

Some large dolphin are taken through that period as well, although they are usually caught readily in smaller sizes in the winter months. These smaller dolphin will hit trolled baits well, but they offer great sport on lighter casting tackle. Chub Cay, incidentally, is the only Bahamas locale to currently have a line-class world-record dolphin (it has two, the largest a 76-pounder on 20-pound line). Wahoo, shark, barracuda, and other species round out the lineup, plus assorted reef species.

With most attention here on big game angling, there is some excellent flats fishing that goes relatively undis-

Getting the Belly Out

Big-game fishermen have come to learn that when a large fish turns and puts a belly in the fishing line, they have to quickly make some adjustments in order to keep the fishing line from popping. Backing off on the drag setting and following the line with the boat rather than going forward with the fish, are the keys to preventing a heart-breaking tackle failure. What happens is that when a big fish turns, especially if the boat is moving forward (which it usually is), the drag tension at the fish is far greater than it is at the reel and the stress on the line will be great enough to break it. The solution is to back off on the drag as soon as that belly occurs, then head the boat (backward or forward) in the direction of the line, with the angler cranking quickly to keep pace and re-spool the reel. When the belly is eliminated, increase drag tension and continue fighting the fish, keeping in a straight line with it if possible.

A

200 yards of line

PULL AT FISH IS 4 TIMES GREATER THAN AT REEL

B

BOAT MOVES IN DIRECTION OF LINE, NOT TOWARD FISH, TO REMOVE BELLY

turbed. Bonefish are the mainstay, but permit are here as well. Although the majority of bonefish are small, there are 8- to 10-pounders that are caught here, and some even larger. Ambergris Cay, and the flats north of Chub, are the prime locales, but it is often worth the trip over to Joulter Cays, north of Andros, where large bonefish are a possibility.

ANDROS

BAHAMAS

In the late 18th century, seeking to wrest final control from the Spaniards, an enterprising British captain anchored his boat near Providence Island. He made figures of straw, dressed them like sailors, and included them among a few real sailors who were rowed to and from Nassau. The real sailors laid down in the bottom of the boat on the return trip and this was repeated often to give the appearance of a large invasion force. After one well-directed shot at the Spanish Governor's house, the Governor capitulated and was mortified to find that he surrendered over 700 soldiers and his fort and islands to a small and ill-equipped group with no resistance.

Today, across miles of deep channel from Providence Island, the government equipment and manpower is much more substantial. There, on the east coast of Andros Island, the United States government operates the Atlantic Underseas Test and Evaluation Center – AUTEC – which is a testing ground for submarines. They can do this because the water here – known as the Tongue of the Ocean – plummets to 1,000 fathoms deep right off the shore.

Oddly enough, the place where submarines play experimental tag is not the focal point for visiting fishermen at Andros, who have lots of flats to explore for various species, many of them on the western middle portion of the island.

Bonefish are the main quarry here, and there are good-sized fish to be had, plus many of them, sometimes in vast schools. The best area for these fish is in the bights, the mangrove-studded cays and shores in the midsection of the island, but good oppor-

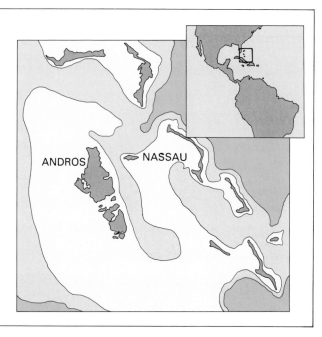

Andros is the largest island (2,300 square miles) in the Bahamas, yet one that is lightly populated and with few fish camps. The eastern edge fronts extremely deep water while the western edge fronts the shallows of the Great Bahama Bank. Andros is bisected, with good angling had in the middle reaches around the North and Middle Bights, along extensive flats and mangrove-lined swamps. Tidal passes or creeks, plus flats, exist on east and west shores, and offer various species. Joulter Cays, north of Andros, are another good locale for bonefish.

There are many flats for bonefishing along the western shore and midsection of Andros.

Releasing Small Fish

Many, if not most, of the fish caught on the flats by fishermen are released without harm. This is not difficult to do and the fish will recover and survive provided care is taken in landing and handling it. Gaffing obviously is not conducive to release unless a large-mouthed fish is lip-gaffed in the lower jaw and quickly returned to the water. The best thing for the survival of many fish, especially if they are exhausted, is that they never leave the water. Wading fishermen can accomplish this more easily than boat or bank anglers, but it is possible to unhook some fish in the water by grasping the hook with needle-nosed pliers and pulling the barb out. A minimum amount of handling is desirable in all cases. If you must handle small fish, do not squeeze them tightly, let them flop around in the boat or onshore, and don't keep them out of the water for a long period of time. For deeply hooked fish, cut the line and leave the hook in the fish, which will corrode in a short time in saltwater.

tunities exist on the east and west sides as well. One of the nice things about Andros is that you can be fishing in a good locale no matter what kind of wind might develop.

Some sections of this island, espe-

cially those inside large mangrove swamps, have never been fished, and are inaccessible to all but the fish. Many flats are near virgin. Sections of the western shore probably don't see more than a few anglers all year.

Bonefish at Andros average from 3 to 5 pounds, with larger fish to 10 pounds a common catch. Fourteen- and 15-pounders have reportedly been caught, and still bigger fish seen, so record-class bonefishing is possible here. One of the known spots for big fish is Cabbage Creek, which is on the western edge and above the North Bight. An average day should yield five or six bonefish, and a good day quite a few more.

There are a lot of other fish to catch at Andros, including small tarpon, ladyfish, barracuda, permit, various snappers and groupers, and blacktip sharks. The east shore flats are more likely to harbor permit, probably be- cause they edge deep water, although this species is found elsewhere.

The tidal passes on the east shore are best for tarpon, and the catch can be a fish in the 60- to 70-pound range. These locales, referred to as creeks, possess diverse opportunities on both shores, and light spinning tackle or fly rod gear produces equally well.

SOUTHERN OUT ISLANDS

BAHAMAS

The so-called Out Islands at one time were considered to be anything that wasn't Providence Island, where the capital city of Nassau is now located. That was a long time ago, however, and for definitive purposes here, we'll talk about the most notable fishing opportunities that exist in the southerly cays and islands of this archipelago on the Atlantic side of the Great Bahama Bank, including Exuma, Long Island, Crooked Island, and Eleuthera. This is predominantly flats country fishing, although in some places there is good reef and/or offshore fishing.

Eleuthera is furthest north and closest to Providence, and one of the southerly Out Islands known for big game. The northern end of this 100-mile-long island abuts the deep water of Northeast Providence Channel, and is on the pathway of migrating billfish and tuna, so it merits attention from the trolling enthusiast. At the southern tip of Eleuthera, a ridge between that island and Cat Island to the south also provides trolling action.

Bottom fishing is particularly good for grouper here, and bonefishing is fair to good depending on where one looks. Perhaps most notable fishing areas are the flats around Harbour Island, at the northeastern tip, where 5- to 7-pounders are possible and fair-sized schools may also be encountered, and St. George's Cay at the northwestern tip.

Moving south, Great Exuma has miles of small cays and flats both west and north that provide exciting sport with small bonefish. Some large bones are periodically encountered, but for the most part, 3- to 5-pounders are the catch, although large schools of fish can be found.

In the same vicinity but slightly east, Long Island is one of the prettiest of the Bahamian Out Islands and a locale that has abundant bonefish and an opportunity for varied adventures. Narrow and 60 miles in length, Long Island can provide lee fishing somewhere on days when this is necessary. Bonefish, mostly small, are found along the entire coast, and in large schools on extensive, wadable flats. Some bones up to 10 pounds cruise the flats, and permit are a possibility. Long Island also offers good reef jigging for assorted species.

Still further to the southeast, Crooked Island has seldom-explored bonefish flats, with the bonus of small tarpon. The latter are found up to 50 pounds, and the bonefish are on the small side but abundant. The flats in all of these areas also sport snapper, sharks, barracuda, the occasional permit, and the ever-present chance of spotting a huge school of silver streakers.

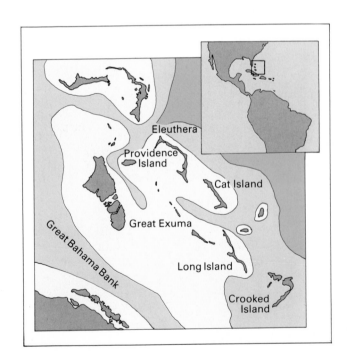

CUBA

It has been said that you can virtually cast from Cuba's northern shore and be wetting your hook in the Gulf Stream. Not quite, but the Great Blue River, as Ernest Hemingway called it, does pass surprisingly close to the walls of the now run-down Malecon in Havana.

Today, that once beautiful seaside boulevard sports fishermen casting for bottom fish. Since there is very little sporting tackle in Cuba, they cast by tossing handlines from a circular *carrete*, using old sparkplugs for weights and a chunk of meat for bait. They fare pretty well, too. But then, so did the Old Man.

Not much in this Caribbean country is as it was 30 years ago, in 1960, not long before Papa rode the *Pilar* out to

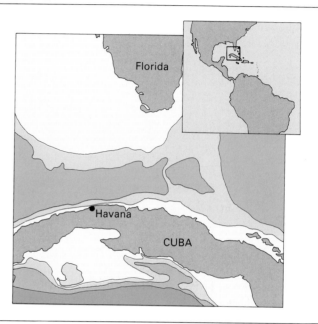

The early part of the season off the Havana coast is known for white marlin, with an occasional blue marlin thrown in. Late summer and fall is reputedly the time for big blue marlin, and dolphin and sailfish occur throughout. In the southern flats the best bonefishing period for shallow-water stalking is said to be from November through February. Considering that deep water exists close to Cuba's southern cays, there is a possibility that good bluewater fishing exists along this coast. Without boats and facilities here, and without the possibility of private boats doing exploratory fishing, there is no confirmation of this.

With the Havana skyline in the background, a young mate sets lines for big-game trolling in the Gulf Stream.

the edges of the blue for the last time. The Stream is still there, of course. It still flows easterly as it has for thousands of years, coursing through the Yucatan Channel into the Florida Straits, curving around Cabo San Antonio and hugging the shoreline past Havana, past the sands of the world-famous Veradero Beach, past the fishing village of Cojimar, which provided the setting for what is arguably the greatest story of the sea ever written.

Each hour the Stream brings with it some 10 cubic miles of tropical water. Hemingway, who considered this the greatest fishing stream in the world, made Havana a port with big-game status through his pioneering exploits here, and he is one American (Ted Williams being another) who is revered in this country.

There is a museum dedicated to Hemingway at San Francisco de Paula, his old estate, where the Pilar rests. And in tribute to Papa each year, anglers go forth in the spring to ply the edge of the Stream in the Hemingway Tournament, an event that was a national competition for many years, but which has had some measure of international participation over the past decade.

One of the early winners of that contest, incidentally, was a pre-revolutionary Fidel Castro. In 1960

Castro personally boated three marlin, to capture the silver cup by virtue of overall weight.

Indeed, the edge of the Gulf Stream on the north shore does attract billfish, although the tournament seldom produces earth-shaking results. Certainly, these are lightly fished waters, and with travel restrictions on many would-be visitors (primarily Americans), meager local tackle and big-game fishing skills, and the likely adverse effect of localized commercial fishing operations, this fishery remains a question mark. Despite the proliferation in angling communication in recent times, and despite the extensive search for new grounds by many anglers, Cuban blue-water fishing remains an enigma.

Even more enigmatic is the virtually untapped and even less heralded inshore light tackle fishing that exists on the south side of Cuba. Very few tourists have visited these waters in the past 30 years, although in bonefishing circles it is remembered that Ted Williams, whose diamond exploits made him a hero in this baseball-crazy country, and who has been obsessed with bonefish, tarpon, and Atlantic salmon angling, was once a regular visitor to the flats around Isle of Pines. There, accounts had it that bonefish roamed in great schools.

Whether that exists today or not is strictly conjecture, although there is reason to believe that it does. Isle of Pines has received some notoriety for its penal colony, and while a few fishermen have been to south Cuba waters, they have not been in the vicinity of Isle of Pines (which has been renamed by Cubans as Isle of Youth). They have been elsewhere, however, and as one who ventured to

BARRACUDA

Fish of the shallows as well as the reefs, barracuda are able battlers that often strike savagely, and frequently jump out of the water when hooked. The great barracuda is the species found throughout the Caribbean, and some specimens are known to host a toxin that produces ciguatera poisoning when these fish are consumed. They should not be eaten. Fish in the 10 to 15-pound range are quite common and the world record is an astounding 83-pounder caught in Nigeria.

Left: Excellent angling for small bonefish can be had on the south shores of Cuba, where mangrove-studded flats are abundant and fish are schooled in great numbers.

Right: Nearly untapped fishing is possible for various species, including tarpon, jack crevalle, yellowtail snapper, and other fish.

the many cays to the east in the Gulf of Santa Anna, I can attest to the fact that bonefish can sometimes be clustered in schools that are measured in the hundreds.

These are small fish, for the most part ranging between 2 and 5 pounds. The bigger bones, which evidently are less social, do not group like this, and appear to be scarce.

Though bonefish have the reputation of being wary and difficult to stalk, it is possible to take several from a single large school on the Cuban flats, to have several bones rush to your offering, and even to allow a hooked fish to swim back and rejoin the school. These are all unusual occurrences, events that seldom happen in waters that are well trafficked.

Nonetheless, such peculiarities appear in virgin fisheries, and one certainly gets quite a rush when hooking a bonefish amidst such a large group and the whole congregation spooks, sending a mass of silver bullets streaking over the marl.

These waters, especially the string of islands known as the Last Paradise Cays, southwest of Punta Macurijes, are rich in many forms of aquatic life, in fact. Small tarpon, plus barracuda, permit, red snapper, jack crevalle, and yellowtail snapper are some of the inshore species, with the likes of amberjack, groupers, and other fish in deeper water off the edge of the flats. Locals talk of 25-pound permit and 30-pound barracuda, although this hasn't been proven.

The tarpon pose something of a mystery here. Baby tarpon are abundant in the shallows and canals and are present all year long. Bigger tarpon are said to be in deeper water, but it is unknown how big they actually get. One Cuban boat captain reported catching a tarpon so gigantic that it had to be cut in three sections to be weighed, which makes for an amusing tale if nothing else.

However, tarpon up to at least 70 pounds roam the freshwater confines of Treasure Lake, which is a renowned

Accommodation on or near the fishing grounds of the Last Paradise Cays are slim, and a mothership operation has been used to house anglers and act as a base for expeditions along the flats.

largemouth bass environment in the Zapata Swamp, not far from the infamous Bay of Pigs. How the tarpon got there remains a mystery, although some locals allege that an underwater passage exists from lake to salty flat. Whatever the explanation, it is quite likely that large tarpon do exist in Cuban waters.

If travel restrictions to Cuba are lifted in coming years, as some observers feel will happen, there will be a rush to explore these fertile flats, canals, and cays, and much will be written about the opportunities. This is especially likely to happen if private

boats are allowed to come into the area. If not, visitors may find themselves in mothership operations such as the one I stayed in, where a shrimp trawler had been converted to accommodate anglers, and small boats were towed to the saltwater flats for actual fishing.

These Cuban waters may be one of the few remaining frontiers for pioneering anglers, and while there is some suspicion that records for weight will probably not be threatened if and when there is further exploration, there is little doubt that fishermen will get their line stretched often.

Working Color Changes

Water that exhibits color change can be a good place to fish. On still days these locations will be noticeable by sight from a good distance, appearing as a dark line on the surface. Where blue-green water turns to an indigo blue is an edge that should be worked well. Usually fish are found in the clearer water and trollers can run parallel to the color change in the blue water. But when this isn't producing it may be wise to weave in and out at right angles to the color change, especially staying with a uniform bottom depth.

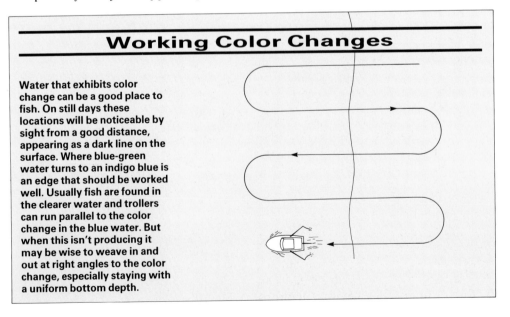

CAYMAN ISLANDS

You would think that for a place that was just a one-hour flight from Miami, Florida, and well out in the western Caribbean, more would be known and publicized about big-game sportfishing in the three-island Caymans. But the history of angling here is just being written.

Perhaps this lack of attention is because of the Caymans' proximity to Cuba; Cayman Brac is less than 100 miles from Cuba's southshore islands and Grand Cayman is about 200 miles away. Private boaters from the U.S. don't just run here for short periods, as they do out in the Bahamas.

The Caymans are not without visitation, however. With at least one beach that has been classified as among the best in the Caribbean, it has attracted its share of sunbathers and water sports enthusiasts. And with outstanding reefs and tropical waters it is explored underwater by thousands of divers annually.

The divers, especially those who use underwater breathing apparatus, know well what some big-game anglers have found from watching the sonar equipment on their boats: the bottom of the ocean drops off a long, long way, just outside these islands. In fact, the word 'dropoff' doesn't begin to explain what happens here, because these islands are mountains rising from the sea, part of the Cayman Ridge and a range of submarine mountains that extend all the way to the Misteriosa Bank.

Described as a "layer cake of life zones", the trench-like dropoff outside Grand Cayman Island is known as The Wall. Here, the inshore reef plummets to 800 feet a few hundred yards from the island, and slopes to 3,000 feet within 3 miles. Beyond that it drops

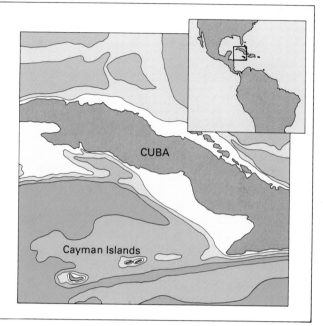

The three islands that make up the Caymans include Grand Cayman, the largest at 22 miles long, Cayman Brac, which is 89 miles east northeast of its larger sister, and Little Cayman, which is between the others and the smallest of the three. The group is roughly 180 miles west of Jamaica. Within a half-mile of Grand Cayman, the ocean floor plummets to extraordinary depths.

Second Chances

It is common to raise billfish and have them look over the baits, with some fish simply swimming off and some taking a swipe and missing. The fish that strike and miss are the ones that hurt the most, because these were active, interested fish. Sometimes such a fish can be hooked by making a quick turn after the strike is received, rather than continuing in a straightforward direction. This is especially so if just baits are used and when lures and baits are trolled together. The quick turn makes the offerings sink, especially those on the inside of the turn. This does little for the hardware, but can make the bait attractive to a hot billfish that just missed its meal.

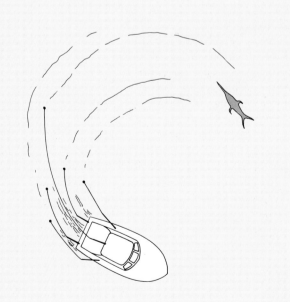

past 20,000 feet into the Cayman Trench, which is the deepest hole in the Caribbean.

If this sounds like the makings of big-game country, especially blue marlin and tuna, it is. With the blue water of the Windward Passage enveloping these islands en route to becoming the Yucatan Current, and year-long tropical water conditions, the stage is set for marlin. Which, it is becoming better known, are here all year long. It was only recently that marlin were taken throughout the year, although the major effort for them is still the months of November through March.

These aren't big blues; the island record to-date is a 584-pounder, which is nothing to sneeze at, but then far short of the possibilities elsewhere in the Caribbean, especially out in the Indies. Blues here are said to average 150 to 180 pounds, which makes this grounds for males (the smaller fish) and juveniles.

Yellowfin tuna and blackfin tuna are also on the Caymans' offshore scorecard, incidentally, as are dolphin and wahoo. The wahoo fishing has been excellent in the past, sometimes very close to shore at Grand Cayman. These fish are all caught close to Grand Cayman, of course, as well as at the Cayman Banks, which is a large shoal area about 10 miles west of Grand Cayman.

Inshore, there is fishing for the various reef species, but also bonefish and tarpon, although, again, for relatively small fish. Loads of baby tarpon exist in the mangroves and inland brackish waters of Grand Cayman and also at Little Cayman. Bonefish are found on all three islands, with the most opportunity existing on Little Cayman and Cayman Brac. They run from 2 to 6 pounds on average, with occasionally larger fish.

PUERTO RICO

In Puerto Rico, it has gotten to the point that during a marlin tournament in the height of the season, a day that produces 25 billfish for all participants is described as a lag in action. Sounds crazy, but that is what is happening, as some phenomenal summer tournament catches have been registered in recent years here, including an outstanding take of 190 blue marlin over 200 pounds in four days by 103 boats in August 1988.

That tally doesn't count the smaller fish caught, the ones that got away unintentionally, the near-misses, and the sightings. With that productivity, it might be understating the season-long catch when local anglers estimate that over 500 blue marlin are caught here each year.

Sandwiched between the Atlantic Ocean on the north and the Caribbean Sea on the south, Puerto Rico is well situated to receive the migration of Atlantic blue marlin. At the eastern end of the Greater Antilles, it is extremely close to deep water, especially on the northern coast. San Juan is the major port for big-game fishing, and the international marlin tournament held there every August is claimed to be the longest-running blue marlin tournament in the world (37 years in 1990). Flats and reefs on the south and east coast are lightly fished.

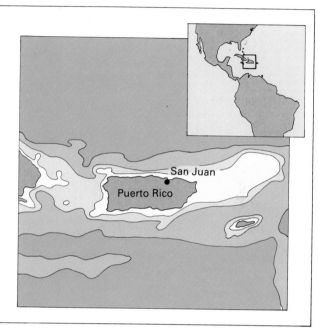

San Juan

Puerto Rico

Left: Many pelagic species, including such fish as this 167-pound yellowfin tuna, are caught along the precipitous dropoff that exists outside Grand Cayman Island.

Right: The sun sets on sportfishing boats in San Juan prior to a marlin tournament. One mile from shore, these boats will be in the magic 100-fathom curve.

BONITO

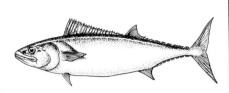

Bonito are actually part of the mackerel family, and are a temperate water fish that are found mostly offshore and in great numbers. They feed on small mackerel, squid, and other schooling fish and don't grow very large. Three- to 6-pounders are common, and these fish are often the quarry for larger predators themselves, especially billfish. They are often taken on heavy tackle while trolling for big game, but when caught on light gear they are a robust battler, diving, surging, running, and generally doing their best to stretch the fishing line.

Obviously, Puerto Rico has a lot of blue marlin in its waters. As well it should. Neighboring St. Thomas is generally viewed as the blue marlin jewel in the Atlantic/Caribbean, especially for big fish, and Puerto Rico is surely a close second. In fact, these two destinations share the pedestal for honors when considering *the* top locales anywhere to fish for big Atlantic blue marlin.

They do, of course, share much the same waters and are in the same migratory path for marlin. They might also be spawning, or at least nursery, areas for young fish as well, as a great many small blues are seen in these waters. Puerto Rico has yet to produce a rod-and-reel grander, however, while St. Thomas lays claim to four, including the all-tackle world record. St. Thomas gets more of a reputation as a result, but the big fish are sure to be in Puerto Rican waters, and there are a lot of visiting anglers each year trying to be the first to set the grand standard.

Local boat skippers see marlin in the monster category every season,

and two fish have been caught that were close to the 1,000-pound mark. One of those is the present Puerto Rican record, a 984-pounder taken in 1985; another giant blue weighed in at 980 pounds. Marlin in the 500- to 800-pound class come to the gaff every season.

Most do so beyond the 100-fathom curve, which is just a mile from the

northern shore of the island, and especially close to San Juan and Arecibo. Some monsters have reportedly been caught a half-mile from shore, but the fishing usually takes place from one to three miles from the northern coast in 100 to 300 fathoms, further when the action is slow. On the west, the run to the 100-fathom curve is about 15 miles from Mayaguez, and

Trolling a Weed Line

Weed lines that exist in offshore waters are frequently a clustering point for small baitfish and attract various predators, most notably dolphin, but also billfish. Virtually any weed line should be fished with one or two trolling passes, working along the edge and sometimes

weaving in an S-pattern through it. If the angle of the sun is low, try to troll into the sun rather than away from it in order to see your trolling lures or baits better and to observe the water better in case the tail of a billfish should appear. If there is a strong current, troll into the current.

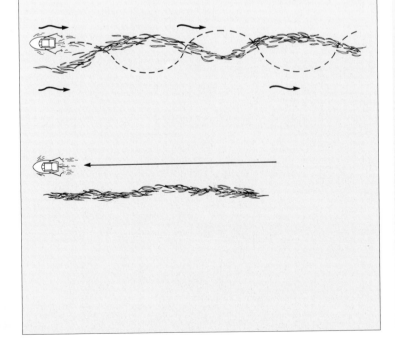

Direction of current

The deepest water in the Atlantic is found not far from Puerto Rico, but trolling on the surface is what attracts the blue marlin.

good fishing can be had there, too, especially in the summer, although charter boat services are much more limited than they are at San Juan.

It is quite likely that marlin exist in good numbers in the blue water around the entire island, but with the exception of the closest grounds to the north and west, these are not as well fished and relatively little is known about them. Reportedly, many marlin exist off the southern coast in the summer, and an eastern seamount is said to have produced a 700-pounder.

The currents, trade winds, deep water, and upwellings offshore all interact to contribute to the marlin presence here. The Puerto Rico Trench runs parallel to the north shore of this 110-mile-long island. Here there are depths well beyond the reach of the most advanced sport-fishing sonar. In fact, the deepest water in the Atlantic, 28,374 feet, is in this abyss.

Puerto Rico is washed by the currents flowing from the Atlantic into the Caribbean and thence becoming the Yucatan Current headed into the Gulf of Mexico. The flow washes around the island to the west in the Mona Passage, which separates Puerto Rico and the Dominican Republic. Blue marlin, it is believed, migrate past here and funnel through into the Venezuelan Basin.

Because the depths plummet off of Puerto Rico and there is a general absence of banks, seamounts, and such structures, a lot of trolling emphasis is placed on watching for bait, feeding fish, and other signs that might indicate the presence of marlin. High-speed trolling with lures has replaced slower trolling with natural baits as the favorite tactic, in part to cover lots of ground while searching.

Puerto Rico is one of the top destinations for big blue marlin, with the summer months being the optimum fishing time.

Blue marlin are here all year-long, but the bigger fish, and the greater numbers, are found from late June through September. The usual emphasis is placed on the two weeks surrounding the full moon. This is the same period that is hot in St. Thomas.

The summer fishery here may be good because that is when blues are the main catch and not one of many species to be caught. At other times of the year, the catch is peppered with all of the typical offshore nomads that one sees elsewhere in blue water around the Caribbean.

White marlin have been on the agenda here in the past, especially in the spring, but are not as plentiful today. Sailfish populate the north coast waters through the winter, as do wahoo, dolphin, and yellowfin tuna. These fish are fairly scarce in the summer months, although a lot of bonito are in the area (and are prime food for blue marlin).

With all the attention placed on marlin in the past, and the absence of major sportfishing centers beyond San Juan, little has been detailed about the inshore fishing opportunities in Puerto Rico. However, snook, tarpon, bonefish, barracuda, snappers, and assorted other species exist here, principally along the southshore where there are flats and bays. Even permit are said to be here.

Media Luna Reef is a tarpon locale and the mangrove flats near La Parguera is a snook spot. Snook and tarpon are found on a number of rivers here as well.

With lots of blue marlin and the chance for big fish, the small-game action inshore is virtually overlooked. However, that would be worth exploring further by anglers who are faced with bad weather days offshore. The trade winds here can produce some rough seas, incidentally, although that seldom stops the big sportfishing boats from venturing forth. Hurricane winds, of course, are another matter, and Puerto Rico was wracked pretty hard in September 1989 by Hugo.

JAMAICA

Proponents of Jamaican big-game angling proudly point out that you can be fishing in suitable water for the highly coveted Atlantic blue marlin just a few minutes from the dock, especially if the dock is at San Antonio or Ocho Rios on the north coast.

And it's true. The water drops to 100 fathoms very close to shore here and there are a lot of marlin in these waters, in part as a result. Local boats, accustomed to raising a good number of fish per outing, rarely travel more than a few miles offshore.

The blue marlin in Jamaica are not very large as a rule, with the normal range being 125 to 350 pounds. An occasional larger fish is caught, but there is speculation that the bigger blues in these waters are to be found well offshore, 30 miles or so, around banks that are hardly touched by present anglers.

Nevertheless, this is a great place to be in the fall for getting action. In a fall tournament a few years ago, 105 marlin were caught in four days, setting a local record. A doubleheader and tripleheader were experienced during the event, which is not your run-of-the-mill experience with blue marlin.

Blue marlin are said to be here all

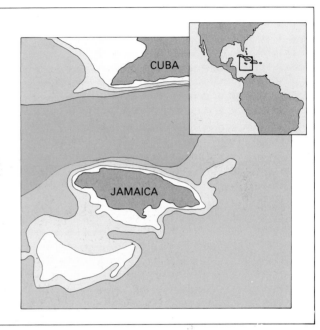

At 144 miles long, Jamaica is the third largest island in the Caribbean. It is 90 miles south of Cuba's eastern shores and situated on the southern boundary of the deep Cayman Trench. A lack of shallow flats limits inshore fishing opportunities but the quick dropoff to deep water provides fertile grounds for marlin, which are influenced by the flow of current through the Windward Passage between Haiti and Cuba and through the Cayman Trench.

year long, although the better fishing is experienced in the fall from September through December. That almost overlaps with the presence of white marlin in winter months, although a few are caught prior to winter. Dolphin, king mackerel, and wahoo round out other possibilities, with an occasional tuna thrown in. The major ports are Port Antonio, Ocho Rios, and Montego Bay on the north shore, and Kingston/Port Royal on the south.

Inshore anglers have some opportunities as well, although these have not been widely explored or developed. Such reef species as barracuda, amberjack, yellowtail snapper, and various groupers are available, and in the coastal rivers, tarpon and snook.

The Rio Grande River, which is west of Port Antonio, has fair-sized snook and tarpon, while the Black River, in the southwest, produces snook up to 20 pounds and tarpon to 100.

U.S. VIRGIN ISLANDS

For many big-game fishermen, say the words St. Thomas, blue marlin, North Drop, summer, and full moon in the same breath, and you have about hit the proverbial nail on the head. Look no further. Well, it's not quite that simple, but the fact is that for many marlin buffs, St. Thomas in the U.S. Virgin Islands is the place to be, bar none. Some call it the blue marlin capital of the world, although what they mean is Atlantic Ocean (with all due respect being given to Hawaii and its Pacific blues).

For one thing, the record books tell a powerful story. There have been only five officially recorded 1,000-pound Atlantic blue marlin caught on rod and reel in the Caribbean; one was off Venezuela, and the remaining four

Christopher Columbus came to the Virgin Islands in 1493, a year after discovering America. The first land he sighted was St. Croix, which he called Santa Cruz. St. Croix is the largest of the U.S. Virgin Islands and the most southerly. Deep water and dropoffs exist off each of the three islands, to the north in the Atlantic at the edge of the Puerto Rican Trench, and to the south in the Caribbean Sea. In the Trade Winds region and subject to easterly winds, the Virgin Islands can see rough water at times, although the prime billfishing time of midsummer is usually fairly calm. St. Croix, however, was virtually destroyed by Hurricane Hugo in September 1989.

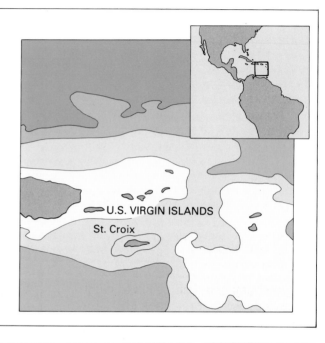

Left: The full moon period in August is the time to be in St. Thomas for the height of the blue marlin fishing and the best chance of catching a grander.

Right: Four blue marlin in the one-thousand pound class have been caught in Virgin Island waters, with the North Drop off St. Thomas being a prime offshore location.

have all been from St. Thomas, (although they were technically caught on the Atlantic side of this island rather than to the south in the Caribbean, but who's quibbling?).

Five current I.G.F.A. world records for Atlantic blue marlin were established in St. Thomas as well. The best of these is the one that every billfisherman has his sights set on, the all-tackle and 130-pound line-class world record catch of 1,282 pounds. Caught in August 1977, that fish was the grandest of many blue marlin records that have been established over the years in nearby waters.

And while the hallowed billfish grounds may indeed be relatively near, they are uniquely situated to provide excellent opportunities and plenty of action. Relatively inexperienced fishermen, being on a boat that sees (or raises) from one to three marlin in a day, think that's pretty good, while the regulars call it slow.

A good day here can be six to eight fish raised, two or three hooked. At the upper end of activity, numbers of fish

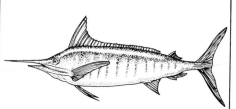

BLUE MARLIN

In terms of size, tackle, and stamina, blue marlin are a tough fish. They may grow in excess of 1,000 pounds. They are, obviously, the premier North American billfish. Blues are highly migratory and are seldom found close to shore. Most of the blue marlin caught by anglers weigh between 150 and 400 pounds. They provide great excitement and are an awesome sight when they spear through the surface in the distance or near the boat and leap high in the air. They may do this repeatedly, then run great distances, sound deep, and resist capture till the angler is weary. Large baits and trolled plugs are the normal offerings, pulled at 4 to 8 knots. Tackle ranges from 30- to 130-pound outfits employed both on flatlines and outriggers, although lighter tackle can be used by the more experienced fisherman.

raised are in the double digits with half as many hookups. This kind of action just doesn't happen elsewhere, and that is why the Virgin Islands, St. Thomas in particular, are drawing fishermen and boats from around the world, particularly in August for major tournaments, but throughout the summer.

What helps make this such a productive fishery is where St. Thomas is situated in the Caribbean and how currents and wind affect the environs. The deepest water in the Atlantic Ocean is directly offshore from the Virgin Islands. It is found in the Puerto Rican Trench, which has depths that plunge over 6 miles. But within 10 to 12 miles of the Virgin Islands, the ocean floor slopes up to a bank that ranges from 140 fathoms up to 40.

This is where the North Drop is located, and this is where there is an upwelling of current and a prodigious amount of bait, due also in part to the prevailing easterly winds. Bonito, tuna, and various predators are routinely feeding here, and the marlin are primarily caught in an area that extends for about 10 miles and is about 2 miles wide, although the entire dropoff from in front of St. Thomas to the island of Anegada is worked. (The so-called Corner, a section here where the dropoff doglegs easterly, is suspected of being a blue marlin spawning location, which, speculation has it, also causes the marlin to congregate in the area.)

The North Drop is between 10 and 12 miles from St. Thomas. In the peak of the season (July, August, and September, especially around the full moon) there are a lot of boats on the dropoff.

High-speed trolling with lures is the main technique in these waters and there is a high percentage of hookups as a result. A bait such as a mackerel might be pulled as an addendum to lures, but mostly it is all lures, smoking and covering a lot of territory. However, some boats prefer baits to get the angler more involved, knowing

that there will not be as many strikes as there would with lures. The strikes, even on baits, are quite violent here and the conventional dropback methods – done because billfish slash at a bait, stun it, and then come in to swallow it – are reportedly not employed for Virgin Island blues.

White marlin and sailfish are also encountered out here, though not as regularly as blue marlin, and such other typical Caribbean offshore creatures as wahoo (St. Thomas holds one long-standing line-class world record for this species), dolphin, yellowfin tuna, blackfin tuna, and various sharks are in the catch.

Sharks pose a problem sometimes here because of their relative abundance, and they have attacked many hooked marlin. Such an occurrence disqualifies a fish from record consideration and is especially hard to avoid where light tackle is employed. With the number of marlin to be raised out here, light tackle fishing has grown in popularity, so sharks are a concern.

Above: Water froths at the stern and pours into the cockpit as a boat backs down on a strong marlin while a fisherman tries to gain line and maintain pressure.

Rigging Mackerel

Follow these procedures to rig a mackerel for offshore trolling. Begin by slitting the belly of the fish, gutting it and removing the anal fin. Taking care to locate the dead center of the nose, use a pick to punch a hole through the nose just forward of the eyes, then cut a small hole dead center under the mouth. Measure the belly length for a double-hook rig, then prepare rig and place it in the fish coming from the cavity. Push the wire leader through the head and lead hook eye, and make a loop that does not bind, then form a Haywire Twist to finish the leader. Using waxed thread or dental floss and a heavy duty needle, sew the bait's mouth closed, then the gill flap and body cavity, ending just beyond the rear hook.

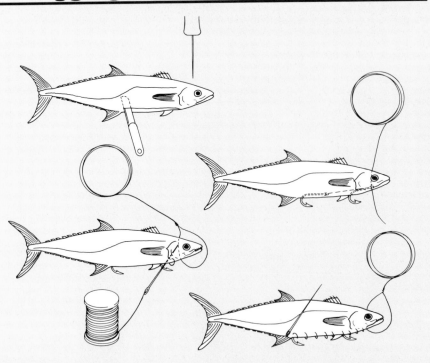

Right: Many small blue marlin are caught in U.S. Virgin Island waters, with these fish being available all season long.

Most of the marlin caught here are released, incidentally, including any fish under 400 pounds in major tournaments, and the feeling is that this is strengthening the current fishery and laying the seed for future granders.

Some of the other fishing in the Virgin Islands takes place inshore, around the reefs and on the flats. King mackerel, barracuda, and various jacks, snappers, and groupers are among the reef catch and provide excitement for those not interested in the muscle fishing of offshore waters.

Tarpon prowl these islands, too, mostly off the northern shore of St. Thomas and along St. Croix. St. Croix provides some bonefishing, incidentally, on flats along the southern shore, but the rest of the islands, with their steeper terrain, do not possess the flats and typical habitat that harbors this species.

Permit, however, are abundant in these islands, especially around St. Croix, and they are an overlooked fishery. Fifteen- to 30-pound fish are caught here by relatively few anglers, as the interest lies predominantly with offshore locations.

However, some visiting tourists, unable or disinterested in fishing offshore, have been privy to sighting from 10 to 30 permit in a day, some actually in schools, on flats that surround St. Croix. The more reliable permit fishing is reportedly on the island's southern coral flats, with the permit coming into these areas from deeper water to feed, and winter being prime season.

Lang Bank, which is east of St. Croix, is a place frequented for dolphin, king mackerel, and wahoo, and is another of the various attractions here of interest to anglers.

Although blue marlin are caught year-round, the prime time, as previously noted, is from July through September for the big fish. White marlin are most abundant in spring. Dolphin and king mackerel are best in spring, tuna in fall and winter, and wahoo through the winter.

BRITISH VIRGIN ISLANDS

Sometimes you wonder why it is that certain places become well known as sportfishing havens before others, or why some take so long to achieve notoriety. Many times the political situation in a country or region is a factor. Certainly the distance from major population centers and the difficulty in getting suitable boats and boat operators is another. Sometimes it is just a matter of people having good fishing in one area and not feeling a need to branch out until forced to by changes in fish distribution, equipment, or the success of others. A lack of suitable boats, and tradition – "that's where we've always fished", or "that's how we've always done it" – are two of the culprits.

In the Caribbean, the big-game limelight has long focused on the United States Virgin Islands and the well-known North Drop locale offshore where the deep water heads toward the Puerto Rican Trench. But this area wasn't known itself as a billfishing hotspot – currently the Atlantic's best – for a long time because it was overshadowed by the fishing offshore from the island of Puerto Rico, which had much accommodation, many boats and darned good billfishing (and still does). Then a few boats went prospecting nearby in the U.S. Virgin Islands and the North Drop off St. Thomas was on the map.

Now the same thing is happening with the British Virgin Islands (BVI) and the deep-water edges closest to its shores known as the South Drop. It's not that people haven't known about the existence of the South Drop or that it had some marlin, but with the great numbers being turned in off St. Thomas, hardly anyone wanted to leave a sure thing and see what was in store

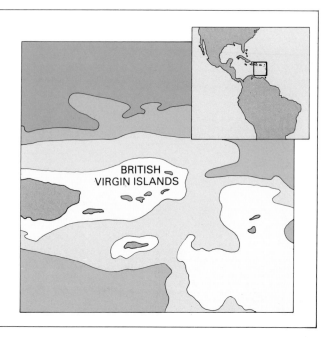

The British Virgin Isles comprise about 50 small islands and cays. The South Drop is east-southeast of Anegada, about a 20-minute run from Virgin Gorda. The Anegada Passage is to the west here and the area can sometimes be buffeted by strong winds and rough seas. Several hundred shipwrecks exist throughout this region.

Hits and Misses

A lot of billfish that strike a trolled bait or lure are missed, which is why there is often a lot of talk in big-game circles about hookups and hookup percentages. With high-speed trolling lures it is not necessary to drop-back line (feed reespooled line to a fish to give it time to swallow the bait before setting the hook), but it is also not necessary to try to set the hook by increasing boat speed. This tactic mainly just peels off more line and makes hook setting harder because of the stretch (presuming the use of nylon monofilament line) involved in long lines. With lures, a billfish is not necessarily hooked when it first takes the lure, and the reel drag has to be pushed forward into full strike position, held there for several seconds, then relaxed to the original setting as the fish runs off. Fish that

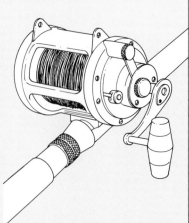

strike from directly behind a lure are easier to hook and less likely to be lost, while those that crash from the side are harder to hook and more likely to be lost.

Deep-water edges exist close to the British Virgin Islands and blue marlin are being caught with increasing frequency here.

nearby: that's a lot of blue marlin, very few boats, and little pressure.

The South Drop turned into a big surprise in September a few years ago when a major big-game fishing tournament was held out of Virgin Gorda and the participating boats spent the first day of the event locally on the South Drop instead of running west toward St. Thomas. The action, which included multiple hookups and the sighting of pods of blue marlin, resulted in hosannas from the anglers and speculation that this could be the hottest blue marlin grounds for the near future.

What is known so far is that there are clearly a lot of fish here, although most seem to be of small size, in the 100- to 200-pound range. Some think this could be a nursery area or spawning grounds, which has also been speculated about the Corner, a section west of Anegada, because groups of smaller (believed to be male) blue marlin have been observed there, too.

While the lack of huge blues, which have occurred off St. Thomas, may serve to keep the trophy seekers out of BVI waters, the abundance of smaller fish and the ability to bring many small blues into trolled baits and teasers should make the South Drop an ideal location for light tackle and even fly rod billfishing.

The South Drop isn't the only location for billfish here, incidentally. The Barracuda Seamount, which is about 12 miles southeast of Virgin Gorda, is another option. This is known for wahoo as well. Obviously the usual offshore species like wahoo, dolphin, and tuna are caught throughout the British Virgin Islands. Inshore, various flats offer relatively untapped opportunities for bonefish and permit, with good sizes reported for each and substantial numbers of bonefish.

Winter and early spring are good fishing times for most of the species in BVI, including white marlin and sailfish. Blues clearly are also available in the summer, particularly the June through September period.

CABO SAN LUCAS
MEXICO

A few decades ago, Cabo San Lucas was an anonymous rickety Mexican fishing village that had a few hundred people and a tuna cannery. Some gringos came down from California to experience phenomenal angling for marlin, and then a few more and a few more. Entertainment celebrities like John Wayne and Bing Crosby were among the visitors to fly private planes to Cabo to go fishing. Ultimately, the word got out, the number of tourists mushroomed, the hotels went up, and today, Cabo San Lucas, and the adjoining East Cape and La Paz regions are internationally known as one of the world's foremost sportfishing centers.

This area is, in fact, internationally known for tourism in general, but the

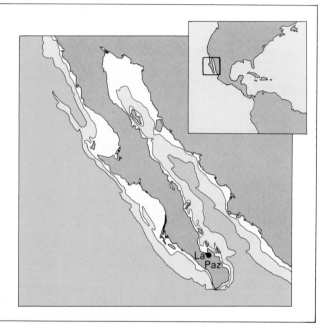

At the tip of Baja, Cabo San Lucas and environs benefit from the fact that the Sea of Cortez meets the Pacific Ocean, with upwelling current and deep water close by. La Paz, which is the capital of the state of Baja California Sur, provides good fishing nearby at two close islands, Isla Partida and Isla Espiritu-Santo, and a little further away at Cerralvo Island. Further south in the East Cape region, Punta Pescadero, Punta Colorado, and Buena Vista are the main fishing sites. East Cape is roughly halfway between La Paz and Cabo San Lucas.

Sportfishermen head offshore at Cabo San Lucas for a tournament; the billfish quest here includes striped, black, and blue marlin, plus Pacific salifish.

foundation for this explosion was, and is, sportfishing. That, because the waters off this southernmost tip of the Baja Peninsula reach far into the Pacific Ocean, where currents moving into the Gulf of California (the Sea of Cortez) contact deep canyons and basins and force an upwelling of water laden with nutrients and attractive to both small and large game fish.

If there was one species that an angler would associate with Cabo it would be striped marlin, although all of the Pacific billfish are found here. Striped marlin, however, are virtually always present off Cabo, with schools of these fish resident at the Cape, migrating into the Sea of Cortez, or migrating from Cortez back into the Pacific.

Striped marlin here range from 100 to 200 pounds, with some larger. It is not uncommon to have double-headers and the possibility of a triple-header exists. Catches of half a dozen or more fish in a day are fairly common, and in the best of times boats have far exceeded that,

although, like anywhere else, there are lean days. Most lean days here are not too bad, and even so, there is the opportunity to pursue abundant and hard-fighting non-billfish species.

Nonetheless, a grand slam of striped marlin, blue marlin, and sailfish is a remote possibility, and on an extraordinary day it is theoretically possible to achieve a super grand slam, with black marlin being the extra species.

Blacks are not as common as blues here, but some very big black marlin have been caught, with June through October good in the East Cape and September through December good off Cabo. Blue marlin in the 1,000-pound class swim these waters, too, although 200 to 300 pounds is the normal size of catch. Their season pretty much overlaps that of the black marlin, perhaps extending a bit longer.

A pair of current line-class world-record blues came from Baja waters as have several line-class striped marlin records, and one swordfish record.

Swordfish are a possible catch off Cabo and vicinity, with July and August offering the best opportunity, especially at the Gorda Banks, which are 27 miles north of Cabo.

The usual size is under 200 pounds, but bigger fish do exist here. Sailfish are most abundant in the summer months as well.

Striped marlin fishing is good to excellent off Cabo San Lucas throughout the year, with summer best; prime time elsewhere here is May through October. Although record-size fish are generally unlikely, action for marlin is not, and it is possible that more marlin (of all species) are caught in the waters off Cabo San Lucas and the East Cape than anywhere else in the world. When the water has remained warm through winter and spring, billfishing has been extraordinary.

Although much of the local food base is fish-dependent, most billfish caught here are being released now. Fishing techniques for marlin involve trolling and live bait angling, using mackerel to catch fish that have been

Striped marlin, such as this one which is about to be released, are the main quarry off Cabo; multiple strikes and hookups sometimes occur.

attracted to a boat and to trolling lures. When chasing striped marlin, local fishermen spend a great deal of time searching for fish and looking for the telltale signs of marlin presence, such as birds, baitfish breaking water, the splash of a breaking marlin, etc.

The foremost billfishing area in this region is at Cabo San Lucas itself, where the Sea of Cortez and the Pacific Ocean meet, and deep water exists. However, the area east and then north from Cabo as far as La Paz is also extremely productive, especially the mid-section of this region, which is known as the East Cape.

This entire region has many other fishing opportunities of note as well. Dolphin, for example, which are called dorado here, are extremely popular, being abundant and caught in good sizes. One shouldn't expect to get a fish to challenge the 73-pound 11-ounce dolphin caught at Cabo San Lucas that is a current line-class world record, of course. Summer is prime, incidentally.

For size, not to mention excellent fight, roosterfish are hard to beat. Numerous current line-class world records for this species have been established from La Paz to Cabo; the all-tackle and 30-pound line-class world record was caught in La Paz and weighed a whopping 114 pounds. As with dorado, one shouldn't expect a roosterfish of this size (which was caught in 1960), but fish up to and exceeding 40 pounds are common. They are caught currently up to 90 pounds.

Late spring through midsummer is the favored period for roosterfish, with La Paz and the East Cape having the most opportunity, These fish are caught fairly close to shore, using both live bait and plugs, with the former being favored.

Some very big yellowfin tuna migrate through here, including fish up to 300 pounds. Migrating schools are fished for the most part, although troughs close to shore from Punta Colorado north beyond Punta Pescadero in the East Cape hold tuna and provide fishing for non-migratory fish.

All of the aforementioned fish are the major targets for most sportfishermen visiting Cabo San Lucas and environs, and there is more than enough to grab people's attention with these species, especially in the prime months. However, there is a lot more available, especially when you consider that scientists claim there are more than 800 species of fish in the confines of the Sea of Cortez. Some of these are bottom- and reef-dwellers that provide entertaining fishing for inshore and small boat enthusiasts.

An exceptionally good area for diverse fishing is at Cerralvo Island near La Paz. Cerralvo is the southernmost island in the Sea of Cortez, and it supports reef fishing for such species as striped pargo, dog snapper, and cabrilla, with the chance of catching a roosterfish or dorado at the same time. These species can be caught inshore along this entire region.

As a closing note, there is good fishing along the western coast of the Baja Peninsula, but with little in the way of villages, boats, and access it goes virtually untapped except for large sportfishing boats that have ventured down the coast from California. One reported billfish hotspot here is off Magdalena Bay, in the middle of Baja California Sur. If road access and facilities are developed in the future, this area will probably be quite a hotspot.

The Uni Knot

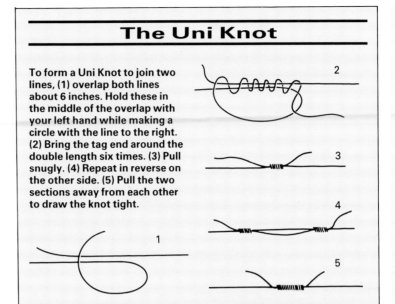

To form a Uni Knot to join two lines, (1) overlap both lines about 6 inches. Hold these in the middle of the overlap with your left hand while making a circle with the line to the right. (2) Bring the tag end around the double length six times. (3) Pull snugly. (4) Repeat in reverse on the other side. (5) Pull the two sections away from each other to draw the knot tight.

Cabo San Lucas and the area around La Paz are known for roosterfish, with many records having been established here.

ROOSTERFISH

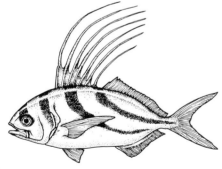

Roosterfish are an exciting and popularly sought Pacific Ocean fish. They are an inshore species that inhabit moderate depths of water and fight particularly well. A member of the jack family, roosterfish look very much like an amberjack in general body shape, although they have an unusual and distinguishing first dorsal fin, which looks like the raised comb of a cock bird. Roosterfish may be found in loose groups, and are often spotted under working birds. Sandy bottomed locales are good to fish, as are bays and sections of mild surf. Smaller fish are usually closer to shore.

SEA OF CORTEZ

MEXICO

"The world's greatest fish trap," and the "world's greatest fish hatchery" are phrases used to describe the richness of the Sea of Cortez, that bountiful gulf between Baja Peninsula and the western Mexico mainland, a richness that is contrasted on the west by the starkness of a barren desert with mountain ranges.

The Sea of Cortez is known for its big-game treasures at the tip of Baja, from La Paz to Cabo San Lucas, and beyond into the deep waters of the Pacific. But the interior section of the Sea of Cortez, which is actually the Gulf of California, has an abundant and diverse fishery for its near 600-mile length.

Many visitors who bring their own boats, especially fishermen from Cali-

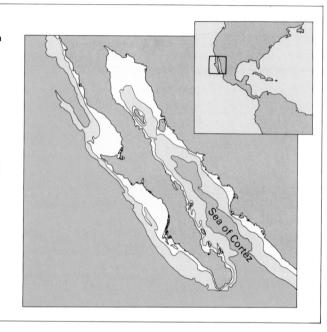

The Sea of Cortez abounds with fish, but also with rocky shores and cliffs, islands, inlets, beaches, and diverse habitats that appeal to those fish. Some of these are located at or near the more accessible locales, such as Loreto, Mulege, and Santa Rosalia in Baja California Sur; Bahia de Los Angeles, Puertocitos, and San Felipe to the north in Baja California; and Puerto Penasco, El Desemboque, Puerto Lobos, and Bahia Kino along the eastern mainland. Migratory species tend to be more concentrated in the southern half of the Sea of Cortez, with its deeper water and greater current influence.

Anglers fish for roosterfish along a deserted beach in the Sea of Cortez; these and other near-shore species are very popular throughout the Sea of Cortez.

Two anglers and a Mexican guide set out in a small skiff, or *panga*, for fishing on the Sea of Cortez.

fornia, New Mexico, and Arizona, come to the area from Kino Bay on the west to Loreto on the east, where the big game (striped marlin and sailfish) are generally less plentiful but the opportunity for other species is just as good, and the light- tackle angling can rate with the best anywhere. Bottom fish, inshore species, and some pelagic nomads are encountered here, virtually all of which are vigorous and hard-pulling.

Roosterfish, for example, which are an extremely aggressive quarry, are one of the somewhat exotic species that exist here and for which the Sea of Cortez has become known. The better fishing for these long dorsal-finned creatures is generally along the coastline of Baja California Sur out to La Paz, but they are picked up in various locales, with April through September the best months.

Jack crevalle are another one of the Cortez fighters that especially appeal to anglers. Related to the roosterfish, jack crevalle are caught in the 5- to 20-pound range in these waters, sometimes in small schools. They are a good fish for the Cortez area as they

are found in a diversity of environments, from rocky shores to beach areas, to offshore. When these fish are ripping through a school of baitfish, they are especially good targets for casters using surface lures and jigs, and are routinely caught by trolling with live bait. These fish, too, are found throughout this gulf, and year-round, though spring through fall is said to be the best time to find them.

Summer, incidentally, is a good time to be fishing the Sea of Cortez for virtually all species, despite the fact that it is very hot then. The warmer waters are especially favored by the migratory fish, including billfish (which are less abundant the further north you go) and dolphin.

Dolphin, known by their Spanish name of dorado here (and mahi mahi further south in the Pacific) are another of the prime species targeted by sportfishermen in the Sea of Cortez. Some large dorado, up to 50 pounds, may be encountered here, although 15- to 30-pounders are more likely. Smaller fish are abundant in the fall. Dorado range well into the gulf, up through the middle islands, but are

more abundant in the southern half of the Cortez. So abundant, in fact, that they have been described as "swarming", a situation which any angler would be glad to encounter unless the too-abundant fish were interfering with attempts to troll up a striped marlin or Pacific sailfish.

Trolling with lures or fishing live bait are the standard tactics for dorado here, and fishermen often look for cruising fish or for some cover (net markers, floating debris, etc.) that would harbor dorado. In calm water early in the day, dorado wakes are spotted – these fish cruise near the surface; boaters intercept them to cast or to put trolled lures in their path.

Billfish, especially striped marlin and sailfish, are a possibility along Baja California Sur from Loreto to La Paz, but the best opportunities for these fish exist from La Paz south.

Sailfish, which are likely to venture closer to shore and in slightly warmer water, are found from Loreto to La Paz, however, with better opportunities occurring from June through October. The area near Loreto, with its chain of uninhabited offshore islands (most

Trolling Strategy

Trolling with lures or bait in a straight line for hours on end is often not the right thing to do, yet it is something that many anglers don't pay enough attention to. Making turns, S-curves, and maneuvering to intercept fish is important in trolling strategy, when individual fish or schools of fish are sighted, or when trolling blindly. Wide S-curves help your trolled lures or baits cover a wider swath of ground, change their action a bit, and put the offerings in front of fish that might have been spooked off by the approach of your boat. The latter point is especially significant when trolling in shallow areas and near shore.

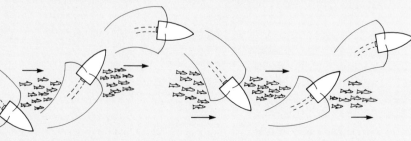

Left: A mate grabs the leader as a billfish shows that it is not quite ready to be subdued.

Right: An angler unhooks a cabrilla, one of many fish that are caught in the rocky, coastal, and inland areas of Mexico along the Sea of Cortez.

Fishing for assorted species in the shallows of bays and inlets is appealing more and more to the winter visitor, to the vacationer without a boat or with a small boat, to the light-tackle angler who doesn't have an interest in bigger quarry, and to the individual who brings a rod for just a little bit of fishing in the mornings or evenings.

Many opportunities exist from Bahia Kino to San Felipe, with notable locales being at the Rio Concepcion estuary at El Desemboque, the estuaries at Puerto Penasco, the rocky shores of Puerto Lobos, and the beaches from San Felipe to Puertecitos. Further down the peninsula, there is good inshore angling from Santa Rosalia to Mulege, along beaches and in inlets.

The coastline throughout the Sea of Cortez is probably 1,000 miles long, with a vast amount of uninhabited area, and sections that seldom get fished. With all the places to explore and all the species to be had, it is no wonder that many visiting anglers use a lot of superlatives to describe it.

notably Carmen and Coronado), is the best bet in the interior gulf for a chance at migratory yellowfin tuna and also a good spot for yellowtail.

Yellowtail migrate northward to the middle of the Cortez, too, almost to the upper third. The islands in the upper Gulf, including Tiburon near Kino Bay, provide good fishing for these hard-fighting jacks from late spring through summer, moving southward in the fall. Bonito, another migrant, are caught here and throughout the Cortez, moving out of the northern reaches with cooler fall weather.

You'd think that all of this would be enough to keep an angler busy, and for many fishermen it is. But the opportunities continue with good to excellent inshore angling, for shallow and bottom fish, throughout the gulf, and especially in the north.

The list of species worth considera-

tion includes several types of corvina, snook, cabrilla, pargo, snapper, amberjack, pompano, ladyfish, vieja, mackerel, sea bass, ocean whitefish, and grouper. A mixed bag. In some areas, casting right up to the rocks is liable to yield one of a number of fish, or to produce a cutoff from something that dives right into the rocks.

For big grouper, the islands from Loreto to La Paz and in the mid reaches have plenty of promise. Tiburon and Angel de la Guarda Islands in the north have reportedly yielded grouper over 200 pounds. The better fishing is when the water is warmer and the fish shallower along cliffs and rocky bottoms.

Corvina, which don't attain massive sizes, but which fight extremely well and make for great inshore light-tackle action, are found along the eastern coastline, primarily in inlets, estuaries, and surf-whipped shores.

JACK CREVALLE

Relatives of roosterfish, pompano, permit, amberjack, and others in the jack family, crevalle jack (or jack crevalle as they are popularly known) are found in Pacific and Atlantic species, although their habits and environs are fairly similar. They tolerate a wide range of environs, including offshore reefs, but are primarily found in harbors and bays, on shallow flats, and around brackish river mouths. They characteristically strike a lure or bait with vigor, and charge hard after a school of baitfish. When found feeding they are readily caught with various tackle.

WEST MEXICO

The western mainland shore of Mexico is most renowned for its beaches, cruise ship landings, and such popular sun and fun spots as Acapulco, Mazatlan, and Puerto Vallarta. But there is much more, including some excellent angling and many miles of lightly fished or unfished waters, from the northern reaches in the Sea of Cortez, south to the open waters of the Pacific.

This area has diverse fishing opportunities, with species including such popular quarry as billfish, dorado, roosterfish, cubera snapper, and corvina among many others, pursued from big charterboat, little skiff, or surf and shore. Moreover, the adventurous can have much of the best angling with little, if any competition.

The northern section of this coast is still within the confines of the Sea of Cortez, and harbors much of the same fishing that can be found on the Baja Peninsula.

Dolphin are perhaps the foremost quarry, being swift, able jumpers, and great table fare. Known as dorado here (which means treasure), they are especially abundant from summer through fall in the northern reaches of the Cortez, though generally moving southward as the season progresses. In the fall, smaller school fish wander into shallower water and provide light tackle opportunities. Fish range from a few pounds to 40 or 50, with the larger ones usually caught in the heat of summer. Live mackerel, if available, are the preferred local bait, although trolling is done as well.

Mazatlan, which is at the southern end of the Cortez, has very good dorado fishing in June, and also yields some large specimens. Two line-class world records were established in this port in the past, one of which weighed a phenomenal 83 pounds 6 ounces.

Another major quarry along this coastline is roosterfish. Many of the line-class world records for this species have been set in the Sea of Cortez, one exception being a fish caught further south along the western coast at Zihuatanejo, which is also a mushrooming billfish locale.

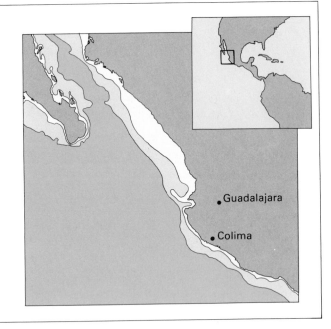

The major accessible locales for sportfishing along the western mainland are, from the north, Kino Bay, Guaymas, Topolobampo (near Los Mochis), Mazatlan, and Zihuatanejo. Kino Bay is close to various islands that offer diverse opportunities; Tiburon is especially notable here. Zihuatanejo, which is furthest south, is accessed from the city of Ixtapa to the south. A close look at a coastal map will reveal a lot of shoreline here without nearby road and without significant access, so there is clearly much to be explored.

Sailfish, blue marlin, and yellowfin tuna are the major targets of offshore anglers who fish out of western Mexico.

Coping With Seasickness

Seasickness, once politely known as *mal de mer*, and now often referred to as motion sickness, afflicts many anglers, whether frequent or occasional visitors to the salt. The result of interaction between the inner ear and central nervous system, affecting the sense of balance, it occurs in varying degrees. The consumption of certain foods and beverages, as well as being hungry or tired are influences; smoke, fumes (especially engine exhaust), and certain smells may trigger motion sickness. To overcome trouble, alleviate known triggering factors. To ease oncoming symptons, lie down, stabilize your body (head especially) by bracing yourself, focus on the horizon, stay outside in fresh air, not in cabins and below-deck areas, eat soda crackers. For prevention, various-over-the-counter tablet remedies are available, though some cause drowsiness; these should be taken an hour before boating. Prescribed medication that works well is an ear patch with time-released Scopolamine. Light dosage Scopolamine is available over the counter in capsule form.

Zihuatanejo is north of Ixtapa, a Cancun-style resort area north of Acapulco that has received a minimum of sportfishing attention due to its small size and out-of-the-way location. Nevertheless, it offers some of the best sailfish, blue marlin, and yellowfin tuna action that can be had on this coastline.

Sails here are caught within a few miles of shore. Blue marlin are caught a few miles further out, and typically weigh in the 150- to 300-pound range, although larger fish, including an existing line-class world record, have been caught. Billfish are present year-round, but the best chance of scoring is in the winter months.

Overshadowed by the more glamorous species, but still with qualities that endear it to anglers in the know, is the corvina. These weakfish-like creatures are perfect for small boat anglers and inshore fishermen who want to work the bays, estuaries, and surfline rips. They are caught in several subspecies and from 3 to 15 pounds, although they get larger.

Another scrappy fish that populates these water is cubera snapper, and bottom fish, including massive grouper and sea bass, are abundant all along the coast in rocky locales.

YUCATAN PENINSULA

MEXICO

The Yucatan Peninsula is one of the foremost archaeological regions of the world, the home of numerous Mayan ruins, some of which are perched high on a cliff overlooking the Caribbean Sea. Such was the thriving ancient culture hundreds of years ago, that it has been estimated that up to 4,000 Mayan canoes navigated regional waters in trading missions at any one time.

Today, the watercraft of this area are more modern, their numbers far less, and their activities most different.

Geographically, the Yucatan Peninsula is to the country of Mexico what the point is to a fish hook. And, even considering the excellent fishing at Mexico's westernmost area in the Baja Peninsula, the Yucatan can arguably be called its leading edge for anglers.

Situated at the northern tip of the Yucatan Peninsula, Isla Mujeres and Cancun are islands. Cancun is connected to the mainland by a bridge; Isla Mujeres is several miles offshore. Billfishing is concentrated to the southeast of these locales early in the season and then further north and northeast as the season progresses and fish migrate through. The entire shoreline north of Cancun is lined with mangroves and virtually uninhabited. Isla Blanca Lagoon is full of flats and mangrove islands, and within a short driving distance of Cancun. The flats and estuary waters of Boca Paila and Ascension Bay along the southern Yucatan are further away, but equally notable.

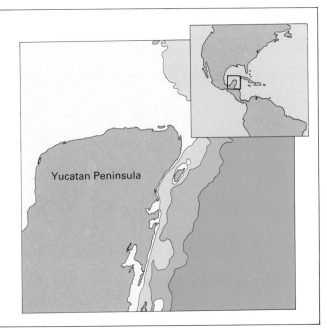

Yucatan Peninsula

Right: With an abundance of sailfish off the Yucatan coast, and many opportunities to tease fish into casting range, this area is particularly well suited to catching sails on a fly rod.

Left: Bounded by the Gulf of Mexico and the Caribbean, the Yucatan Peninsula has excellent fishing both inshore and offshore.

Jutting out into the sea, bounded by the Gulf of Mexico to the north and the Caribbean to the east, this land is situated in such a fortuitous locale as to be blessed with inshore and offshore angling that is truly some of the finest in the world.

The offshore fishing at the tip of the Peninsula – and actually it doesn't take place that far offshore – is focused on the islands of Cancun and Isla Mujeres. These are adjacent to the Yucatan Channel separating Cuba and Mexico and the location of strong northward-flowing currents that channel bait and pelagic fish species along the tip of the Yucatan Coast.

As a result, the sailfish population here is extraordinary, as good as can be found anywhere in the Atlantic. So good, in fact, that the best days have seen multiple hookups, with glorious reports of not just two, but even three and four of these high-dorsal-finned creatures on at a single time. And that is in addition to the white and blue

marlin that are available. Whites are also plentiful at times and they, too, can be the cause of multiple strikes or hookups.

White and blue marlin are caught around the 100-fathom curve off Cancun and Isla Mujeres, which is just a few miles offshore. Whites are often taken a bit shallower, however, and sailfish shallower still. Most of the fishing is done directly offshore or to the northeast or southeast. Arrowsmith Bank to the southeast is less than 20 miles away and is another hotspot, though good fishing close to Isla Mujeres usually dissuades anglers from making that run.

There is no real shelf or quick drop off Isla Mujeres and Cancun, but there is an upwelling of sorts out in the 100 fathom water where current sweeps by. This proves to be productive for dolphin, or dorado, as well as marlin, and attractive to bait.

It is the presence of prodigious schools of bait, especially in the

spring and early summer, that makes the waters off the northern tip of the Yucatan such an attractive area for billfish, especially sailfish. It is routine here to find sailfish balling bait, so trolling methods commonly involve looking for activity and fishing with bait. Dorado, bonito, and other fish find the bait schools, too, and sometimes make it harder to deal just with sailfish. However, the problem of too many eager and hard-fighting creatures is one that most anglers can manage to cope with.

Lots of activity makes this a hot place to try fly fishing, although when the sailfish are ganging up on bait, a fly may not turn their heads. Unquestionably the possibility for light-tackle fishing, using spinning rods and 8- to 20-pound line (these sailfish average 40 to 50 pounds) is great. The best period for billfish and dorado here, incidentally, is in the spring months, and there is still more to be learned and explored about the billfishing.

115

Other species to be caught while trolling for sailfish and white marlin include wahoo, kingfish, and blackfin tuna; grouper, cubera snapper, mutton snapper, and jack crevalle are hard-fighting inhabitants of local reefs and inshore environs.

But the big news inshore the glamor species: bonefish, and plenty of them, plus tarpon, snook, and permit. None of these fish run to giant sizes here, but they are so readily available that experienced anglers say catching one is almost a sure thing.

Some of this action takes place less than an hour's drive from Cancun. This resort city, which was just a small village of a few hundred people in the mid-70s, was carved out of the mangrove coast by the government and made into a Mexican Riviera. An image of what fishing used to be on the Cancun flats is close by, however, especially slightly to the north, 20 miles away at Isla Blanca lagoon.

PERMIT

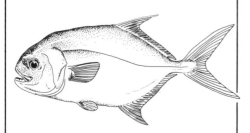

Permit are one of the most elusive, coveted, and heralded of saltwater fish. They are renowned for being difficult to approach, difficult to entice to strike, and difficult to land. They can achieve weights exceeding 40 pounds, although they are commonly caught in the 10- to 20-pound range. They inhabit and are caught on reefs and sandy flats, but are sometimes found at sunken wrecks as well. Small ones travel in schools, which are occasionally large, while bigger permit are usually solitary. These fish are most popularly sought on sandy flats, where they venture on a rising tide to scour the bottom for food, and are often seen cruising or tailing while feeding on the bottom. They feed much like a bonefish does, rooting in the sand for shrimps and crabs.

The Drop Back

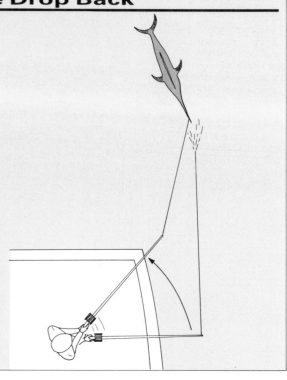

When trolling for billfish with bait or lures, it is a common occurrence to have a fish come after the lure or bait, strike it sharply enough to knock the line out of an outrigger release pin and not actually grab the bait. Or it may swipe at a flatlined lure or bait but not get hooked on the first attempt. Chances are there will be a second attempt by the billfish, but you must be ready for it, grabbing rod, pushing the freespool button, and standing ready. It is good to hold the rod to the side so the lure or bait continues its swimming action. When the billfish comes after it and pounces on it, point the rod directly at the fish and let the line spool off freely. Give the fish time to turn and swallow it, then put the reel in gear and when the line comes tight, drive the hook home hard, more than once if possible.

There are extensive flats here, as well as numerous coves, bays, mangrove islands, and other fishable locales up and down the coast, most of them lightly explored.

What some exploration will discover is that there are plenty of bonefish to be spotted, mostly in small groups, plus permit on the flats. Snook and tarpon (in the 20- to 30-pound class, a few larger) are in good supply around mangrove islands, shores, and inlets. All of these may be caught by waders or boaters, stalking and sighting fish to cast to, which is the most exciting of all inshore angling. A grand slam of all four of these highly coveted species is quite possible on spinning gear, and remotely possible on fly (you'd have to get the permit first, always the most difficult chore).

Even more noteworthy shallow water fishing exists along the Yucatan shore, but well to the south of Cancun. The shoreline drops off sharply just south of Cancun and doesn't offer flats fishing, but south of Tulum, which is the most visited of all Mayan archaeological sites, Boca Paila and Ascension Bay beckon.

Boca Paila is about two hours by auto from Cancun, and was originally fished 20 years ago by anglers taking a long boat ride from Cozumel and camping on the beach. Protected from westerly winds and boasting plenty of easily reached flats, Boca Paila has the motherlode of small bonefish and has long been renowned for its plentiful permit. Tarpon, snook, and barracuda, plus various reef species, are also targeted here.

Much the same can be said for Ascension Bay as well, with its cornucopia of mangrove islands, channels, flats, and creeks. Other fish encountered here include jack crevalle, cubera snapper, and, of course, barracuda. There is year-round fishing on all of the Yucatan flats, but the favored time to visit is from late fall through spring. That coincides with popular tourist travel times, although a cool spell then could diminish flats success. The summer and fall are good times here as well, and less visited.

White marlin are usually taken a little further offshore in the Yucatan than sailfish, although still within fairly close proximity to Isla Mujeres and Cancun.

COZUMEL

MEXICO

Long before the Spanish conquest, Cozumel was a pilgrimage site for Mayan worshippers of Ixchel, the fertility and moon goddess. Perhaps there is some irony in this: today, many sportfisherman make a different sort of pilgrimage to this well-known Caribbean island because its waters are so fertile, and they often do so around the monthly full moon period. Sailfish, which are the premier quarry and perhaps are found more abundantly here than in any other locale worldwide, begin their migration off this island around the full moon in March. Actually the sailfish start to show up in numbers in February (some can be caught all year long) and really get cooking in March, with peak time being from then into June.

The accessibility of Cozumel, which is a prime tourist destination for the usual sun-and-fun resort recreation and which is easily reached from the United States, has brought a lot of private boat anglers as well as tourists who look for a one-day venture to catch their first sailfish. Cozumel is *the* place to do that, and also *the* place to catch sails on fly rod as well as on light tackle. Additionally, this is an excellent place for a realistic chance of getting a multiple hookup, a grand slam (white and blue marlin plus sailfish in a single day), or a super grand slam (the other three billfish plus swordfish).

This may sound a little too rosy to be true, but the offshore fishery has held up for years. It should be pointed out, however that there has been a slight decline in Cozumel catch rates for sailfish in recent years and an increase at Isla Mujeres to the north. But the fishing is newer up north and it is unclear what the reason for, or

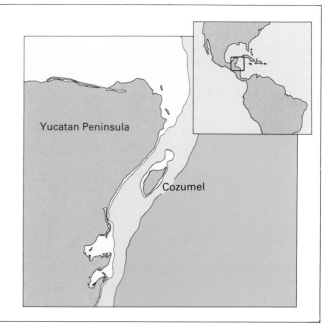

Cozumel is 33 miles long and 9 miles wide and situated off the east-central coast of the Yucatan Peninsula. Twelve miles of deep water separate the mainland from the island, and this is where most of the trolling takes place, often close to the Yucatan near Playa del Carmen in 10 to 60 fathoms of water. Some Cozumel boats run north toward Isla Mujeres later in the season, when the main run of sailfish is more clustered up there. Cozumel is ringed by the renowned Palancar Reef, which supports good bottom fishing, and has a lagoon at either end for flats angling.

significance of, this is. Neverthless, double-digit catches are posted by many boats in the best of times, and a slow day off Cozumel is three or four sailfish (which would be a good day almost anywhere else). Dolphin, king-fish, bonito, and blackfin tuna are also in the offshore mixed bag, sometimes in good numbers and sizes (dolphin especially), although they are usually an incidental catch while billfishing.

Trolling at Cozumel predominantly takes place between the island and the mainland. Sailfish apparently migrate northward with the strong current, coming from the open waters of the Caribbean and working their way up the coast past Cozumel, passing the head of the Peninsula at Isla Mujeres and Cancun, and then moving into the Gulf of Mexico.

The Caribbean is deep here, with well over 100 fathoms of water between mainland and island, and with deep water close to the mainland. There is a sharp drop from 10 to 60 or so fathoms near the mainland, and this is the zone that is heavily worked. Up the coast, the bottom rises to a

Downriggers

Downriggers have been relatively slow to gain wide acceptance in saltwater fishing, although used extensively in freshwater for over 20 years. This may have been due to concern over the effect on life in the marine environment, and also the varied bottom nature of most marine habitat. However, more anglers are using downriggers now in saltwater and for varied applications: getting live bait or chum at a certain depth, and controlled-depth lure presentations. The principle of downrigging is to have fishing line connected to cable and weight via release mechanism to allow lures or bait to get to a pre-selected level, but be free of the weight after a fish strikes.

Line — Cable

Lure

Line

Release

Weight

bank and is not nearly as deep close to shore.

Baitfish are abundant along this area, especially off several coves that exist south of Playa del Carmen, and sailfish migrating through are obviously drawn to this. These billfish come

by in groups, and boats trolling and zig-zagging north-south along the mainland edge frequently encounter pods of sailfish. This is one of the reasons for multiple hookups, as the pod of billfish attacks many of the baits being trolled. After such an

Left: Battling a sailfish on light tackle, as this angler is doing, is the main charm of Cozumel fishing.

Right: A tired sailfish is brought to boatside at Cozumel, and is about to be tagged and released.

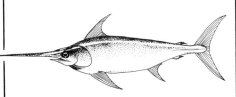

SWORDFISH

Swordfish are the least commonly caught member of the billfish family, although they are among the most widely distributed. Also known as "broadbill", swordfish do have a flattened bill that is wider and longer than other billfish. They are pelagic and usually travel alone, and can be found at varied depths. They are often located in very deep, and cool, water, but will bask on the surface and may be spotted there with the upper tail fin out of the water, a characteristic that has made them susceptible to harpooning.

encounter the savvy skipper may run north a fair distance with the hope of trolling southward and engaging other fish from that pod.

Trolling with bait is still the primary technique here, although some live bait fishing is practiced. Some boats in this region do not favor live bait on the theory that it results in deeply hooked fish and increases the chance of mortality when released; live bait is unquestionably very effective when a pod of sailfish is encountered balling a school of baitfish.

White marlin are also encountered in along the mainland shoals and edges, sometimes caught in the same locales as sailfish. Blue marlin, however, are more likely to be caught further offshore and over deeper water. This occurs in the channel, which has some irregular bottom structure, and usually while fishing larger baits

or lures than would be used for the other billfish. There is still not a great deal of emphasis placed on blue marlin trolling, and seldom does a boat spend much of the day looking for blues unless they are sought to complete a slam. Swordfish, incidentally, are occasionally spotted finning along the surface here, and there is a chance of hooking one by casting a live bait to a sighted broadbill or by fishing at night.

Very little attention has been devoted to reef and flats fishing in Cozumel, and the area has not been publicized for this. Although bonefish are abundant along the Yucatan flats on the mainland (and people make excursions to Boca Paila or Ascension Bay, which are southeast of Cozumel and known for excellent flats fishing), they are not so abundant at Cozumel because the island has little shallow

water. Very few people know that there are some bonefish and permit to be caught on this island, however, and while it may not be world-class fishing, itis good enough to offer a very pleasant day, especially if you don't savvy big water fishing or you experience a heavy blow that keeps big boats off the water, or you just want to take a spinning or fly rod in tow and poke around.

Over a decade ago I found a small lagoon at the south end of the island that harbored bonefish, permit, and loads of snapper. A friend and I located it simply by driving to the end of the island and making every turn we could until spotting passage to the

lagoon after driving over an old Mayan roadbed. In several hours we managed to catch about eight small bonefish on light spinning tackle, mostly by blind-casting with jigs since the tide was high and fish were not tailing. We went offshore the following day but directed four anglers there, who, in a full day of fishing, caught four dozen bonefish.

Another bonefish-harboring lagoon exists at the north end of Cozumel, and is reachable via small skiff. For all I know the southern lagoon may be reachable the same way, but we could find no obvious entrance to the sea from inside it. The fish aren't big in either locale, but the setting is pristine

and peaceful, and the experience is most enjoyable.

The reefs are another matter entirely. Cozumel's other main draw besides angling is also underwater-oriented. The reefs around Cozumel are rated as among the world's finest for diving. Palancar Reef, which surrounds Cozumel, is said to be the world's second largest coral reef. The edges of the reef yield some big groupers, red snapper, and other bottom fish, plus the occasional dolphin and kingfish. I lost several big fish on light tackle while fishing with baited jigs there, and saw nice-sized amberjack and groupers landed. This is an overlooked opportunity.

Right: An angler holds a bonefish about to be released back into the thigh-deep water of a lagoon on the south end of Cozumel.

Left: Other offshore fish to be caught in Cozumel waters include white and blue marlin, and plenty of dolphin; this Cozumel angler is getting his money's worth from a high-flying dolphin.

BELIZE

Does a country that has place-names like Orange Walk, Pull-trouser Swamp, Monkey River, and Double Head Cabbage sound like a renowned fishing locale? Perhaps not, but then that country has a name that no one can positively explain either: Belize, formerly known as British Honduras until independence was granted by the British in 1981.

It is speculated that Belize is a derivation of the Mayan word *belix*, which means muddy river. Belize has some muddy water alright in its plentiful creeks and mangrove backwashes, but also very, very clear water out on the reefs and around its various islands and cays. Muddy or clear, the water of Belize hosts almost as diverse a fish population as its jungle rain forest does birds.

That rain forest was part of the route of the Maya in pre-Columbian days, and it is virtually inconceivable that one hour from the Belize border, at Tikal in Guatemala, there was once a jungle community that was home to 55,000 people in the 9th century. One wonders what fish they encountered.

The impact of the Mayan civilization can be seen even out on the water while fishing. Some of Belize's highly respected flats fishing takes place around a spit of land that should have been part of Mexico. That place, Ambergris Cay, was once connected to the mainland as a small peninsula on the Yucatan, but 1,000 years ago the Maya built a canal there to circumvent the site's coral reef, making Ambergris an island and eventually part of British Honduras.

Mexico's loss was Belize's gain, because that location is one of many in this country that have given Belize a sterling reputation as a place for some

Belize is situated between Guatemala and Mexico's Yucatan Peninsula along the western Caribbean. The shoreline is as yet relatively undeveloped, and flats and inshore fishing predominates along the coast, in and around river mouths, and the creeks, inlets, bays, and other environs. Mangrove-covered cays, islands, and shores are plentiful. An outstanding coral reef, which attracts many divers, extends along the coast, and reefs (Lighthouse and Glover) exist offshore as well. The Turneffe Islands are a short distance from the Belize coast, and they comprise numerous cays within a barrier reef. Sharp dropoffs to extremely deep water exist close to the inshore and offshore reefs.

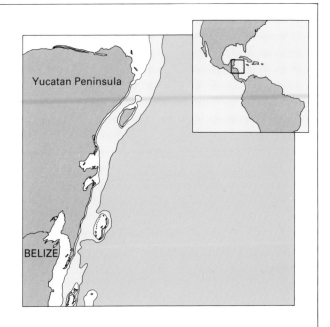

Ambergris Cay, which is a noted bonefish locale, was also the site for the catch of this wahoo; good wahoo fishing can be had off reef in various parts of Belize.

Of Lines and Records

Fishermen who are seeking to break a record, who catch a large fish that might qualify as a record, and who want to know precisely what strength line they are using need to be aware of the peculiarities inherent in fishing line. Space limitations do not permit a lengthy discussion of this point, but suffice it to say that there are "test" and "class" lines. Class line is guaranteed to break under the labeled strength in a wet condition. Test lines generally break at or above (nearly always above) the labeled strength in a wet condition, and there can be great variation in how far above the labeled strength they actually break. The significance of this is especially pertinent where records are concerned.

Records are classified in metric designations. The line used to establish a record in the 4 kg category, for example, can test no greater than 4 kg, or 8.81 pounds. If you hope to establish a record in this category, you should probably fish with a "class" line, as designated on the spool label, in order to be sure that it is the proper strength.

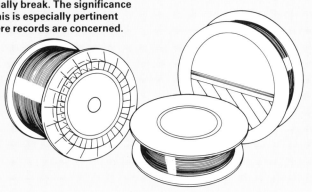

fine light-tackle angling for the fastest and toughest fish of inshore waters and shallow flats. This not only includes such obvious gamesters as bonefish, snook, tarpon, and permit, but also cubera snapper, jack crevalle, and mutton snapper.

The Belize coast is predominantly mangrove-lined. There are many creeks, rivers, canals, and overgrown backwaters that provide great habitat for snook, small tarpon, and other creatures. The Belize and Sibun Rivers, in central Belize and not far from Belize City, and their many tributaries and backwater lagoons and sloughs, are especially notable. Snook here average up to 10 pounds and may be caught to 20, although larger fish have been reported. Small tarpon, up to 20 pounds or so, are also prominent here, and these two fish are the major inshore focus. Other areas along the coast offer the same type of opportunity, although some, such as Ambergris, do produce larger tarpon, including fish over 70 pounds.

Bonefish are plentiful on the various flats along the coast and around the cays here. Bonefish run small as a rule, however, with the average catch being a few pounds and some up to 6 pounds, though few larger, which is typical of this region as a whole. Numerous flats along the coast host these fish, and also permit.

Some of the finest flats fishing in Belize takes place at the Turneffe Islands, which are offshore about 20 miles east of Belize City. This is one spot where the taking of a bonefish, tarpon, and permit on a single day is very possible, and where wading and sight-fishing for schools of bonefish is run-of-the-mill when conditions are right. Here, too, the fish average 3 to 5 or 6 pounds, with occasionally a larger one.

The palm-studded Turneffe Islands lie within a barrier reef that extends for more than 30 miles. There are many mangrove-covered cays or islands here, and the bonefishing, which is what these islands are most noted for,

Left: Bonefish on the flats are the main draw at the Turneffe Islands; they are also found along the coast and various cays.

Right: Offshore fishing in Belize has merit as can be attested to by these anglers struggling to bring a blue marlin aboard.

generally takes place on the eastern shore. Out at Lighthouse Reef, which is some 12 miles to the east, there is also bonefishing, with good angling around Long Cay. This reef is over 20 miles long and offers opportunities for shallow fishing for various other species as well.

There is an abundance of reef opportunity off the Belize coast, in fact. A string of coral reefs, flats, and atolls is just offshore and extends along the entire coast, being part of the world's second longest barrier reef (this extends northward along the Yucatan Peninsula as well). The usual flats fish are found here, too, along with barracuda, grouper, and snapper.

Out at Turneffe, on the southwestern side of these islands, the water spills from a reef to very deep water and this edge is a great place to do some jigging or trolling. The usual reef dwellers are found here, plus king mackerel and wahoo. Wahoo are said to be extremely abundant in these offshore waters and they provide reef trollers with plenty of action, sometimes with several dozen such fish in a day of angling. Wahoo up to 75 pounds have been taken here.

The offshore fishing for billfish is still a relative unknown in Belize waters, at least in terms of the best overall seasons and population density. Although there has only been

limited offshore trolling here, and that only within the past five or six years, it is known that big blue marlin, plus white marlin and sailfish are present. Some observers of the big-game scene think that an untapped potential exists for these creatures.

To date it doesn't seem that sailfish inhabit these waters in the kind of numbers that they do some 100 miles to the north, off Cozumel and the Yucatan Channel. Why that is so remains to be determined, except the flow of current is different here. However, sails begin to show up here in December, remaining through March and into April, the latter being the time that they start to appear in

GROUPER

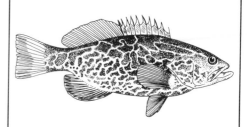

Groupers are actually members of the sea bass family, and bear the broad head and thick body shape of those fish. There are literally hundreds of different types of groupers, however, some more prominent in certain areas than others, Many groupers are found in small sizes, weighing just a few pounds, but others grow to enormous sizes. Groupers are strictly bottom-dwelling fish. Their habitat includes reefs, sunken wrecks, rocky outcrops, bridges, and piers. Many of these fish hide in holes or crevices along the ocean floor, and ambush their prey, which includes squid, crabs, shrimp, and assorted small fish.

number up north. Thus, this area may be on the fringe of the sailfish migration routes.

Marlin arrive a little earlier than sailfish, beginning sometime in October, and they stay through March. Whites and blues run small, with the latter averaging between 200 and 250 pounds. Larger blue marlin have been caught, including fish over 400 pounds, and they have been taken in every month of the year. The fact that there are just a few local boats to fish for big game (and then not too often), and only an occasional passer-by, means that locales, places, and techniques are hard to put together; the more boats fishing an area, the more that is learned.

So far the better spots for marlin are around Glover Reef, Lighthouse Reef, and Turneffe Islands. The water around each of these drops off steeply. Some of these are a pretty fair run from Belize City, and there is a possibility of mothership operations being created.

COSTA RICA, CARIBBEAN

Big fish, lots of fish, arm-wrenching action, more fish jumps in one week than most people see in a lifetime, double hookups . . . these are just some of the reports that religiously filter out of experiences on the Caribbean side of Costa Rica. And this happens routinely.

Costa Rica's lush Caribbean coast is, without doubt, one of the premier places in the world for tarpon and snook fishing. This is *the* place for the caster, the sight fisherman, the stalker, and the angler who wants to use relatively light tackle to have a muscle-match with fish that are tough and big, but not so big as to be overwhelming or to need special tackle and tactics. Something like, say, a 20-pound snook or a 70-pound tarpon.

Though nothing is guaranteed in fishing, even in paradise, on light tackle or fly, the angling in the coastal rivers, lagoons, and open water here is sure to delight all but the most jaded angler. Yes, the tarpon grow bigger elsewhere, but they are nowhere more numerous or less finicky. Tarpon, in fact, are the premier attraction in Costa Rica's Caribbean waters. Here, on good days a party may jump several dozen of these torpedos.

Tarpon all along the Caribbean coast are commonly caught in the 50-to 100-pound range, with some bigger fish possible. Much of the angling is done in rivers and at river mouths, although there are big fish, and schools, outside the river inlets. Most of these are hard (and dangerous) to access unless the sea and surf is calm, but when they are fished, the results are often remarkable.

Both sight and blind casting are practiced here, depending on locale and water clarity, although it is easier and more enjoyable to search out and cast to roving pods of fish, and this is done when and where the water is clear. Tarpon are available all year, but the better fishing is from August through October and January through May. The other months incur the rainy season.

The same seasons apply for snook as tarpon, with August through October being best for big snook. During that period it is possible to encounter a surf run of 20-pounders. Bigger fish are possible as well. There are currently seven world records for this species from Costa Rican waters (including one fly rod tippet record), the biggest of which is a 53-pound 10-

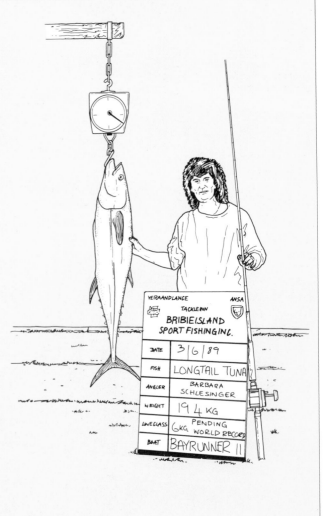

Rules For Records

The International Game Fish Association in Ft. Lauderdale, Florida, is the internationally recognized repository for all-tackle, line-class, and fly rod records for saltwater and freshwater fish. As such, it has strict requirements and regulations for accepting world records. Some of these are overlooked by anglers and may be cause for disqualification. One of the biggest troubles is with scales. Scales used to establish weight for record claims should have been certified for accuracy by an accredited agency or organization; estimated weights and weights made from uncertified scales are not acceptable. There is also a time limit: three months from date of catch for fish taken in international waters, and 60 days for fish taken in continental U.S. waters. Photos of the angler and fish, and the fish plus tackle and scale used must be submitted, as well as a portion of the line used to catch the fish. Anglers who will be fishing in areas where a record catch might be possible, should get a copy of the application form and record requirements.

ounce fish that holds the 20-pound line class and all-tackle world records. That fish was caught in October at Parismina, and shows the size potential possible. A big fish here generally, however, would be in the mid-30-pound range. When small snook are abundant, it is possible to catch dozens in a day.

One of the best aspects of the fishing here is enjoying the jungle treks to and from fishing spots, and soaking up the flora and fauna, which includes rich vegetation and plentiful bird life. You can also catch a few other species for diversion as well. Guapote, machaca, and majarra are small fish that provide fun in the creeks and rivers. And jack crevalle, some up to 25 pounds, are plentiful.

The main rivers that are fished along Costa Rica's Caribbean coast include the Colorado, Parismina, and Tortuguero, each with many tributaries and lots of jungle atmosphere. Regardless of tide the rivers flow well, but during the rainy season they are swollen and muddy, and are not fished. When sea and surf conditions permit, anglers are able to go through the inlets and fish the open water of the Caribbean near shore, but usually angling takes place in the inlets and up the rivers and creeks.

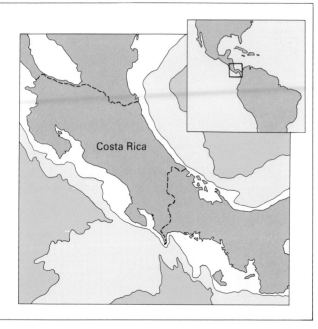

Costa Rica

Tarpon are plentiful along the Caribbean coast of Costa Rica; this is not the locale for monsters, but for plenty of action.

COSTA RICA, PACIFIC

Costa Rica means "rich coast", an appellation that was given it in the 16th century by Spanish conquistadores seeking gold. They didn't find that precious metal, but traveling anglers today find a different sort of treasure along the Pacific coast of this peaceful and scenic country. That treasure has fins, grows large, fights hard, comes in varied denominations, and is plentiful.

The most abundant billfish treasure here is sailfish, but a variety of species can be had along several areas of this coast. While the northwest has been fished for several years, the central and southeastern coastline has only just gotten started.

In the southeast, Golfo Dulce, or Sweet Gulf, is the jumpoff for some

Golfito is the port for fishing Golfo Dulce in the southeast. The Gulf is nearly 30 miles long, and it is about 15 miles to the mouth by Matapalo Point and another 5 to 10 miles beyond that to blue water. From Quepos, on the central coast and a short distance from the capital city of San Jose, it is 20 miles out to the 100 fathom line. There, and further north at Flamingo Bay, the billfishery is still just developing. In the northwest at the Gulf of Papagayo, anglers run offshore to the deep water or fish around the Bat Islands.

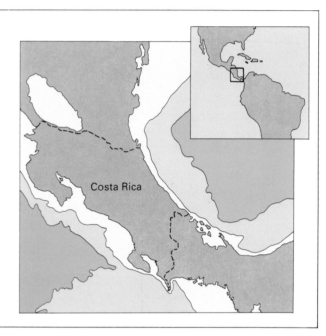

Left: Sailfish are abundant all along the Pacific coast of Costa Rica; this large Golfito sail weighed about 120 pounds, and was released.

Right: Casting and jigging inshore can produce an array of fish, including cubera snapper, roosterfish, amberjack, and grouper.

extraordinarily good sailfishing. This area was only sportfished for the first time in early 1989, and in the first few weeks of operation the Pacific sailfish sightings and hookups were phenomenal. By mid-year, a 170-pounder was boated and two potential record fish were taken.

These are really uncharted billfish waters as of yet, and much remains to be determined. The better times are still not pinpointed, nor is it certain where and when to be looking for the other billfish – blue and black marlin – that migrate through this area. If it is like other billfish grounds on this coast (and it should be), the June through September period, which is also the rainy season, should be best.

Trolling with bait is currently the main billfish technique, but lures have already caught some fish and may be the ticket for big marlin. Sailfish in the 100-pound range have been common,

and the marlin so far are averaging 250 to 300 pounds. Some nice-sized yellowfin tuna are available here as well, plus the expected dolphin.

When the billfishing is slow, or for extra diversity, there is plenty of opportunity for catching varied reef- and bottom species, by trolling, casting to rocky shorelines, or jigging or baitfishing in deep water. Good jigging and baitfishing occurs about 15 miles from Golfito at Matapalo Rock. This is a haven for roosterfish, with individuals from 30 to 70 or more pounds possible. Large cubera snapper, in the same size range, are caught nearby on a shoal. Amberjack, snapper, grouper, and other species are on the menu here as well.

In the central part of the Pacific coast, the fishing is being newly explored and shows potential, too. Again, sailfish are the main quarry and anglers visiting here have reported

raising between 20 and 60 sailfish in a good day of trolling. That is enough activity to keep anyone alert.

This is taking place out of Quepos, and also further north out of Flamingo Bay. Quepos is mostly known for its proximity to the fine beaches of Manuel Antonio National Park, but sailfishing is coming on strong. The sailfish are averaging from 100 to 110 pounds, and are available from December into midsummer. Not many boats have worked this area, so there are many question marks about season, sizes, and so forth. Both blue and black marlin have been caught off Quepos, however, as well as midsized yellowfin tuna, and the prospects do seem pretty bright.

Flamingo Bay has seen more activity, although it, too, is newly being explored. Several tournaments, including one very successful fly fishing event, have been held here in recent

times, and results have been encouraging. A report on one tournament said it was impossible to keep track of the number of sailfish that were raised during the contest, as some boats reported having four or five fish at a time come into the baits. As it was, 102 anglers reportedly caught and released 742 sailfish in four fishing days. That's terrific by any standards.

The summer months are said to be prime here, with sails averaging well over 100 pounds and some being in the 150-pound-plus category. This is the rainy season, but also the time when seas are fairly calm. Evidently sailfish are present all year long, however. Blue, black, and striped marlin are also caught, although in far fewer numbers than sailfish. Other times of the year may offer good fishing as well, but not enough exploration has been done to confirm this. Dolphin and the occasional wahoo round out the fishing report card here.

Along the northwest coast, the fishing out of the long, wide Gulf of Papagayo is a little less exploratory. The Bat Islands here have been productive for billfish and other species, as have the grounds offshore at the 100 fathom mark, and off Catalina Island.

This is a bait-rich area, due in part to the easterly North Equatorial Current, which washes into the Gulf in the summer months, drawing small-game species and larger ones. The black marlin, averaging 300 pounds but caught to over 700, arrive in the Gulf in May and are caught at the Bat Islands by live bait anglers. Blue and striped marlin follow, although they are not as populous.

Sailfish are present through the season, in small quantities till late May or early June, then in heavy numbers into the fall. During the peak of the run, two dozen sailfish (and then some) may be raised in a day's trolling, which, incidentally, is primarily done with natural baits.

Trolling:
Swimmers and Skippers

Lures and baits may be trolled either as below-surface swimmers (just slightly below the surface) or as topwater skippers. Thus, there are swimming and skipping presentations. The swimmers should stay below the surface at all times, except for popping through an occasional wave,

Skippers primarily bounce along the water and wave tops, occasionally darting through a wave or diving under the surface momentarily. A fast boat speed, ranging from 6 to 10 knots, is required, depending on size of bait, type of sea conditions, and direction relative to the wave.

Rigger line

Rigger line

Flat lines   30 yds   60 yds
15 yds

75 yds

Above: These Costa Rican fishermen have boated a nice yellowfin tuna on relatively light tackle, an occurrence that can happen fairly often while trolling for sailfish.

Right: The hard-fighting roosterfish is caught to fairly large sizes in Costa Rica; this one hit a popping plug.

BONEFISH

One of the most coveted of all saltwater fish, bonefish don't grow very large; 2- to 5-pound fish are commonly caught and a 10-pounder is notable. Large bonefish are more likely to be found alone or in small groups, but small fish usually travel in schools. Although bonefish do feed in deeper water, they are primarily located by fishermen when they come onto tidal flats and shoals to scour the bottom for small clams, crabs, worms, and shrimp. Their mouth is under the snout to facilitate feeding, and bonefish are often first detected while feeding in shallow water with their body tilted in a head-down tail-up maneuver, with all or part of the tail fin protruding through the surface. These are referred to as "tailing fish".

Sometimes the chore in offshore trolling here is to keep the dolphin off your offerings and give the billfish a chance. This interference is okay for the first few fish, but gets wearying after a while. However, the dolphin have good size here (up to 50 pounds), and the Gulf was the site of the catch of an 87-pounder that is currently the all-tackle and 50-pound line-class record holder.

These waters also produced several line-class world record dog snappers. They are a hotspot for roosterfish up to 50 or more pounds, and are known for cubera snappers of a similar size, wahoo (in the summer rainy season), amberjack, and an assortment of reef and inshore fish.

It is worth noting that this coastline is tailor-made for pursuing marlin on light tackle spinning or baitcasting outfits or on a fly rod. The number of sailfish, in particular, that are sighted every day make for some very exciting possibilities.

PANAMA

It's a good thing that we're not numerically ranking the locales covered in this book in order of someone's idea of best, second-best, and so forth. What type of fishing, species, and other factors would form the basis for evaluation? Would places that are distant and lightly fished be given equal weight with those that are heavily fished and close to major populations? Would variety of opportunity, size of fish, record potential, ease of fishing, or some similar factor be the major criteria? Such a problem.

If you were to make an attempt at such an evaluation, however, the country of Panama would undoubtedly vie for top honors.

One legend concerning the derivation of the word Panama says that when Cuna Indians were asked where to find gold by Spanish soldiers hundreds of years ago, they responded in their language with the words *panna mai*, which means "far away". Panama as a country is neither far nor near to most of the anglers who are likely to visit it, with the exception of Europeans. Linking Central and South America and hosting the infamous east-west canal passage, however, it is well situated to receive anglers, and well situated to host major game fish, which are found in abundance both near and far from its Pacific shores.

Ironically, the second explanation for the derivation of this country's name is that it came from an Indian word meaning "land of many fish". Among the many fish here are black, striped, and blue marlin; sailfish; swordfish; wahoo; dolphin; yellowfin tuna; mako shark; roosterfish; cubera snapper; dog snapper; bonito; skipjack; jack crevalle; horse-eye jack; and bigeye trevally. You know there have

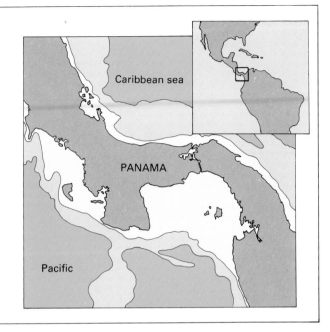

Panama is washed by the Caribbean Sea to the north and the Pacific Ocean to the south, but it is the Pacific that produces the most notable angling, particularly in the vicinity of Coiba Island and Pinas Bay. The waters around Coiba drop off quickly and host many desirable species, though the Hannibal Bank offshore is the prime billfishing grounds in this section of Panama. At the eastern end of Panama, Pinas Bay, near the Columbian border and on the edge of the Gulf of Panama, is the jumpoff for exceptional marlin and sailfish action, much of which takes place 10 miles offshore on the Zane Grey Reef.

Left: Panama is a prime locale for black marlin; this 342-pounder was caught off Coiba Island.

Right: Dolphin, or dorado, are abundant in Panamanian waters, and are sometimes a nuisance because they strike trolling lures meant for bigger game.

to be many fish when you see just how many creatures caught in Panamanian waters currently fill the I.G.F.A. record book, especially in the fly rod categories.

These include dolphin (three), roosterfish, Pacific sailfish, and wahoo fly rod records of long standing. Line class world records include four swordfish, seven Pacific sailfish, five black marlin, and four dolphin, and this is not to mention the records that have been established previously, and broken, here. Most of these and others are light-line/light-tackle catches of considerable accomplishment, further underscoring the point about fish abundance. It usually takes many chances and many lost opportunities before connecting with a record-setting fish on fly or light tackle.

Sportfishing activities here have focused in the western region around Coiba Island, and in the eastern region at Pinas Bay, where prominent fishing camps have operated for many years. The Pinas Bay area has been responsible for most of the aforementioned records, and it is situated close to deep water and the influence of currents that bring clusters of bait nearby.

At Pinas, a great deal of the billfish trolling is done out in the Gulf of Panama, about 10 miles from the mainland at Zane Grey Reef, named after the pioneering author/angler but evidently not because of local exploits. Seamounts there feature drop-offs from 130 to 600 feet deep and it is the main area for marlin. A lot of species are found here, in fact, sometimes so many that it is a problem keeping the non-target fish, such as dolphin, off baits.

Coiba is a 100,000-acre island at the edge of the Gulf of Chiriqui that also has a potpourri of opportunities. Offshore, pelagic species are attracted to the Hannibal Bank, a hump that rises incredibly from 1,000 fathoms to merely 20. When the proper mix of currents washes by here, the marlin fishing is excellent. This bank is also fished for bottom fish and other non-billfish species, but an abundance of all other fish inshore makes it unnecessary to run to Hannibal.

Although billfish are caught off the Panamanian coast at all times of the year, the hot marlin action is from December through April. Blue marlin, which are the least prominent of the three marlin species found here, show up first in December, followed closely by blacks. Blues are more prominent to the east than they are near Coiba, and blacks are the mainstay of the fishery in both locales. Both fish average in the 300-pound range, although fish over 500 pounds are taken here and some blacks in the 700-pound category. The best black marlin taken from Pinas waters was nearly 900 pounds. Blacks are prominent enough in both locales and occasionally a boat lands three to five of them in a day.

Striped marlin become available in March, but they are a less frequent catch than black marlin at any time. That is also the time for the heaviest concentration of sailfish, although sails are present here throughout the year. On the most extraordinary days, boats have reported landing from 15 to 30 sailfish, but ordinarily on a good day about 20 billfish will be raised.

The billfishing slows from late September through early December, which is when the rainy season occurs. That, however, is also when the wahoo fishing is at its peak, and reports have noted days in which several dozen wahoo are caught. Through the rest of the season, they are an occasional catch.

With an abundance of fish, there is plenty of room for the use of light big-game tackle for marlin, spinning tackle for sailfish, and fly rod gear for sails, striped marlin, and small blacks. These waters are one of the foremost locations for light-tackle (and big-game fly) angling precisely because so many fish are raised. The boats used here are predominantly small, in the 23- to 25-foot center console range at Coiba, because the water is often

A Knot For Shock Tippets

This is a fly fishing knot to use when connecting a heavy shock tippet to a lighter line. To tie it, start by making a Bimini Twist in the lighter line (the class tippet) and leaving a 5- to 6-inch loop, then tie a loose overhand knot in the shock tippet and slide the overhand knot over the loop (1). Pull the overhand knot as tight as possible so that it is snug with the Bimini (2). Make three half hitches with the loop and snug each one up tightly (3). Make a four-wrap clinch knot around the shock tippet (4). Snug up and trim off tag ends (5). Make sure the length of shock and class tippets conform to I.G.F.A. regulations for record or contest possibilities.

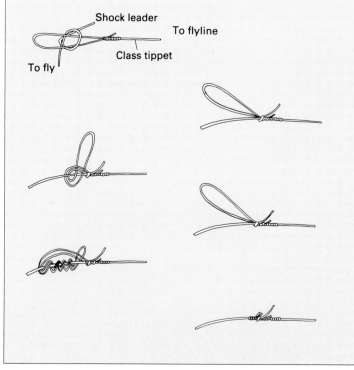

Shock leader

To flyline

Class tippet

To fly

Above: Black marlin are the mainstay of the billfishery in Panama, with peak activity coming from December through April.

Right: There is plenty of opportunity for inshore casting and jigging along the Panama coast, with roosterfish, cubera snapper, and other species on the agenda.

calm, and the ability to fight and land such attractive species from these craft does enhance the fishery. When fishing is at its peak, anglers in Panamanian waters actually switch to lighter tackle to increase the challenge. Surely that speaks reams about the angling.

Not all of the angling here is trolling or billfishing. Many opportunities are present inshore for casting and jigging to hard-hitting, strong-pulling creatures. This is especially true off Coiba Island, where plug trolling and rock jigging can yield cubera snapper, jack crevalle, horse-eye jacks, and roosterfish, plus assorted species. It is not uncommon to ring up a catch of as many as 20 different fish species over several days.

The bottom drops off significantly around Coiba, so you don't have to go far to get into the proper territory. And, with plenty of baitfish schools around, casting to various species that are marauding bait is almost guaranteed during a normal day.

YELLOWFIN TUNA

Found in both the Atlantic and the Pacific, yellowfin tuna don't range as far northward as most other tuna do and don't travel quite as widely as such species as bluefin tuna and albacore. They are, nonetheless, a migratory species, usually found in warm temperate water, usually offshore but sometimes near shore if the warm water is present. Also known as Allison tuna in some locales, yellowfins grow to more intermediate sizes than their brethren, and they are the most colorful tuna, with bright yellow fins. In small sizes they look very similar to blackfin or bigeye tuna. Flying fish, squid, and various small fish make up their diet.

LOS ROQUES, RIO CHICO, RIO ARUCA

VENEZUELA

These three areas of Venezuela aren't even remotely close to one another. But they are all recent saltwater sportfishing discoveries that are distinguished from hot offshore billfishing at La Guaira, and they rate highly for three of the most esteemed fish of the flats and shallow backwaters: bonefish, tarpon, and snook. In addition, they each provide such excellent action that they are magnificent training grounds for anglers who want to: a) get their first licks in on game fish they have read glowing magazine articles about; b) learn to spot, stalk, play, and land these fish knowing that mistakes are easily forgiven because opportunities are abundant; and c) use light tackle and fly rods to maximize their sport and increase their skills.

One couldn't find better grounds to do such things than the flats, lagoons, and mangrove creeks in Venezuela. The best way to achieve these goals is to fish in a place where there is nearly continuous action, where one sees a lot of fish and has plenty of opportunities. That is not only when skills are amplified and/or refined, but when new developments take place by veteran anglers through experimentation. One does not mind deviating from tried-and-true fishing methods (or lures, flies, etc.) when there are a lot of fish to be caught and comparisons between angling efforts are readily made.

Surely one of the best places in the world to become educated on bonefish is Los Roques, Venezuela. Bonefish, known here and throughout most of the Caribbean as *macabi*, are not just plentiful, but bountiful. Rather than being seen in singles or in small

pods, they are seen in vast schools.

These bonefish are located on the flats of some 20 islands that comprise Islas Los Roques (islands of rocks), which is about 80 miles north of Caracas and well beyond the equally notable sailfishing grounds along coastal Venezuela. Los Roques is at the 12th latitude and to its north side is the 2,000-fathom-deep water of the eastern Caribbean Sea; the next land to sight north of Los Roques is Puerto Rico, hundreds of miles distant.

Out on the Los Roques atoll there are all manner of easily waded coral, sand, and grass flats. The tide fluctuation is not great, so shallow water bonefishing is virtually always possible, and nearly every type of feeding situation can be encountered.

Los Roques is a 30-mile-long atoll that is about 80 miles north of Caracas. It is one of Venezuela's national parks, where further development is prohibited and commercial fishing is tightly controlled. The Gulf of Paria adjoins Trinidad, but the fishing is focused on the mainland estuaries along the western and southern sector of the bay. The village of Rio Chico is several hours east of Caracas by auto, and near the Tacariqua Lagoon, which is a national park and wildlife refuge.

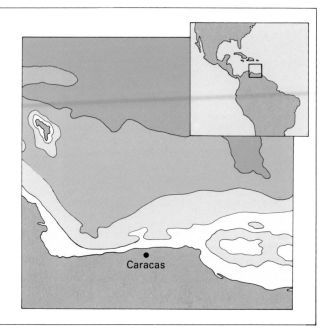

Right: Los Roques has plenty of bonefish, and the shallow flats almost always provide wadeable sight fishing.

Left: With Grand Roque in the distance, a fly fisherman works the Los Roques flats for bonefish.

The majority of bonefish here are caught on falling water, which is a bit unusual (rising water floods the flats and brings fish in to feed in most locations), and are found in classic tailing situations. While singles and small fish are encountered, bonefish are also seen in large schools, sometimes numbering many hundred individuals covering large expanses of the flats.

Since the fishery has not been overly pressured as yet, it is possible to catch several bonefish from a school, in what can be best described as near-virgin conditions. That will probably change as more and more people prowl the Los Roques flats.

The average bonefish here is small, in the 2- to 3-pound range, but there are 5- to 10-pounders. It is conceivable that larger ones exist, but do not show up because they are loners and more wary than eager young fish.

The beautiful flats and reef edges provide opportunities for other quarries as well. Permit so far have not been numerous, but some limited fishing for snook and small tarpon exists in lagoons and near mangroves in the summer. Of course, barracuda are often seen on the flats, and various snappers are taken as well. Very few

Bonefish average a few pounds at Los Roques, but larger fish are possible; easily waded flats and a lot of fish make this a good locale for the angler who has never caught these elusive speedsters.

SNOOK

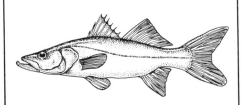

Known also as *robalo*, snook are a coastal fish that are primarily found in warm, tropical waters. They sport a distinctive black lateral line and are one of a few saltwater species that can also do well in freshwater or brackish water. They are often found in the far reaches of freshwater rivers, as well as in lagoons and canals. Cover-laden places are their preferred habitat, and these include mangrove-lined banks as well as around such objects as bridges, docks, pilings, oyster and sand bars, along dropoffs and island edges, and in deep holes.

people bother with the reef edges, where it is likely to have action on a whole host of species. The possibilities here are really unexplored.

Although Los Roques can frequently be windy, enough protected water exists so that it is possible to get out of the brunt of winds. With a water temperature that seldom varies from 80 degrees, the Los Roques flats are quite comfortable otherwise, with generally hard bottoms, while cold fronts and muddy water do not pose a problem here as they do in other bonefishing sites.

Dirty water is another matter along the mainland coast, however, in the back bays, lagoons, and creeks that support hot fishing for snook and tarpon.

A developing eastern hotspot for this is in the Gulf of Paria, which is between Trinidad and the Venezuelan mainland, and several hours from Caracas. There, the Aruca River and assorted tributaries feed a brackish-water, jungle-like estuary that hosts snook up to 20 pounds and tarpon up to 50. Larger tarpon have reportedly

Barbless Hooks

When fish are so abundant that they are caught easily, or when a fishery is fragile, it is a good idea to use barbless hooks on certain lures and flies. Although hooks can be purchased without the barb for fly tying purposes, most of the time it is a simple matter to make barbed hooks barbless by pinching the barb with a pair of pliers. Sharpen the hook point so that it will penetrate readily after de-barbing. When fishing, be sure to maintain a taut line when playing a fish (except for bowing to jumping fish), so that the barbless hook will not slip out. Unhooking fish that are taken on barbless hooks is

relatively simple, and can often be accomplished with the fish still in the water. The hook will back out of the fish's lip or jaw by hand or with a pair of pliers, and no tugging or twisting that might damage the skin will occur.

been seen here, but the average is in the 20-pound class, just right for light-tackle mayhem. Snook are abundant in the mangrove- and deadfall-lined areas, and can average several pounds in size.

There is still much to be learned about this estuary, although visiting fishermen have reported great fun in such exploration, especially in tall mangroves and winding backwaters where monkeys chatter, ibis fly overhead, and the still lagoon surface is rippled by a school of rolling tarpon.

The stained and milk chocolate water that results in these areas in the rainy season doesn't produce nearly as well as the darker, cleaner water, which has to be looked for.

The dry season from November until April produces cleaner water, which some theorize is the time for

best (and bigger) tarpon action. Schools of sardines are said to come into this area beginning in September, followed by mullet in November, and this also greatly enhances the tarpon prospects.

The other developing hotspot for light-tackle snook and tarpon fishing is also a mangrove-lined lagoon situation. This is at the Tacariqua Lagoon near Rio Chico. Perhaps some of the finest small (up to 50 pounds) tarpon angling in the world can be had here amidst small mangrove islands and in backwater bays and creeks.

The tarpon of Tacariqua are mostly under 15 pounds in size and the snook average 2 to 4 pounds. Larger snook in the 6- to 8-pound class are caught as well, and reports say they have been taken to 20 pounds. Casting tight to the edge of the mangroves is the norm

in these dark, tannin-stained waters, with streamer flies and an assortment of surface and shallow-running plugs. However, bigger fish are reported in the channels and in the open lagoon waters. As often happens in such places, early and late in the day is favored for the bigger fish.

Relatively few people have been to this locale yet, and the absence of big fish so far may deter the trophy seekers. On the other hand, much remains to be learned about the Rio Chico and Gulf of Paria regions (as well as the Boca Grande delta by the Orinoco River). Optimists will note that Venezuela's Lake Maracaibo holds the all-tackle world record for tarpon, a 283-pounder caught over 30 years ago, and though that locale is on the far western coast, who knows what lurks in these waters?

Mangrove edges in several areas of inshore Venezuela offer opportunities for snook and small tarpon.

LA GUAIRA
VENEZUELA

Current means a lot. Because of their influence on navigation, the flow of currents was instrumental in determining which areas of the world were first discovered, explored, and colonized. The world climate is affected by strong ocean currents. Baitfish and gamefish abundance is determined in large part by currents – their temperature, their movement, their peculiarities.

The North Equatorial Current sweeps westward from the northwest coast of Africa, coursing over 3,000 miles of the Atlantic and sweeping into the Caribbean Sea below Barbados and Grenada, striking the northern coast of Venezuela. There, just west of Caracas, that country's capital and most densely populated city, an eddy current works counter to the main flow. Added to this is the steady contribution of nutrients from the Orinoco River, one of South America's most prominent watersheds. Together, these natural circumstances create a situation that brings, and also holds, baitfish and large predators in the area in great quantities, quantities that at times produce an awesome amount of action.

Out on the two banks offshore from the village of La Guaira roam four species of billfish, attracted by the abundance of bait along the dropoffs washed by the current. In the peak of their availability, these fish provide some of the finest big-game fishing to be had anywhere in the world.

The tales of marlin and sailfish action off La Guaira, while stupendous to anglers of today, are barely half of what could be experienced 30-odd years ago, when the first sportsmen pioneered offshore fishing here. But in intervening years not a great deal

happened to explore or exploit the fishery with sportfishing craft. So it came as something of a surprise to many people when better boats and equipment ventured to La Guaira in the early to mid-80s and raised 20 to 40 fish per day per boat.

Today the numbers aren't quite that high, but they are exceptionally good. Where most captains in most other ports will be glad to talk of hooking or catching a couple of sailfish and perhaps a single marlin in a day, success at La Guaira is measured in slightly better form. Seeing 20 fish in a day is not uncommon. In the best of times, up to 40 strikes is possible.

As a result, La Guaira may be the best place in the world to have a good shot at registering a grand slam – sailfish, blue marlin, and white marlin – or even a super grand slam (those three plus swordfish). A few years ago, two friends accomplished the super grand slam feat on the same boat two days apart, which must be a first and sounds like a statistic for the *Guinness*

Book of Records. Other super grand slams have been achieved, and sometimes more than one grand slam is recorded in a single day.

Speaking of records, La Guaira is one of only a few places that have

Nearly all of the billfishing in Venezuela is done from boats leaving Macuto, the resort area that is closest to Caracas, or from La Guaira. La Guaira Bank is to the northwest. Here the seafloor rises to a bank that runs east-west for several miles.

Caracas

yielded a 1,000-pound Atlantic blue marlin on rod and reel. This was accomplished in November 1984 and the fish weighed 23 pounds over that magic number. Other granders have been hooked and lost, and other big

Left: The offshore waters of Venezuela that harbor renowned billfishing are a relatively short distance from La Guaira, especially in large sportfishing boats.

Right: A Venezuelan sailfish comes to the boat for unhooking prior to release.

Rigging a Balao

To rig a balao, which is one of the most popular baits for sailfish and white marlin, start with a hook that has been prepared with wire leader using a Haywire Twist (1). Keep about an inch of tag end protruding as shown, making sure it is in the opposite direction of the bend of the hook. Insert the hook by lifting a gill plate and sliding the hook point into the cavity (2). Guide the point of the hook around and out the bait (3), then slide the hook eye under the gill plate and push the protruding tag end of wire through the top jaw (4). The hook should align with the bait; if the bait is curved or hooked it will spin and not troll properly. Using a small rubberband, loop it around the lower jaw and secure it (5), then snap the bill off close to the jaw (6).

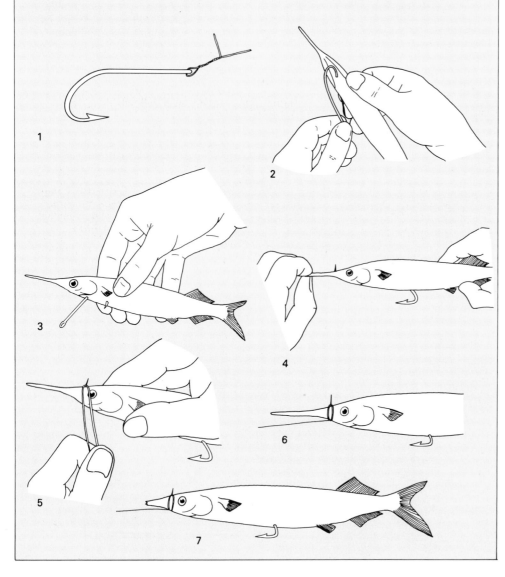

comes to within 150 fathoms from a dropoff that goes to 400.

Bait and lures are trolled in the depths here, with bait more productive for white marlin and sailfish and lures (or large bait) more productive for blue marlin. One needs to have a cooler supplied with rigged baits when the action is hot, because double-headers are fairly common on sailfish and tripleheaders are not unknown.

Anglers have reported being amidst water filled with sails or white marlin, and experiencing flurries when every bait in the water was struck. Such action would seem to indicate an opportunity for light-tackle fishing, if not records, and La Guaira was the locale for a 2-pound line-class white marlin, established a few years ago.

Whites here average about 55 pounds, sails a bit larger. These are great for the light-tackle fisherman, including attempts with spinning and fly gear.

Blue marlin, which are more frequently caught at Playa Grande, average in the neighborhood of 250 to 300 pounds. The grander mentioned earlier indicates the weight possibilities, however. Swordfish range from 100 to 200 pounds and some are taken at night on the banks by anglers using light sticks ahead of bait.

Other species to be encountered in these rich waters include wahoo, large dolphin, and yellowfin tuna. In September yellowfin show up in great numbers, and the action then is described as a blitz by some fishermen. It's described as a nuisance by others, who are specifically targeting billfish.

The search by most visiting anglers for billfish is concentrated on the fall months, especially September and October, although billfish are present in Venezuelan waters all year long. In fact, white marlin are abundant here at the same time as they are usually gathering much farther north in the North Atlantic, which seems to clearly indicate that these are not the same fish, although it is unknown where

blues have missed the half-ton mark by mere pounds. So the big bruisers are here.

The prime billfishing spots are two banks – Playa Grande and La Guaira – that rise off the ocean floor in cliff-like fashion. La Guaira is roughly 10 miles straight offshore (20 from the town of Macuto) and shallower, rising to within 50 fathoms of the surface and extending for several miles. Playa Grande is a few miles further out and

SAILFISH

Although they are the smallest member of the billfish clan, sailfish are among the most popular with anglers because they can be taken on light tackle, including spinning and fly rods, and they put up a strong fight, with repeated aerial displays. They are almost always fought standing up, and 12- to 20-pound tackle is commonly used. Sailfish are distinguished by their high first dorsal fin, and are between 3 and 7 feet long. They are occasionally found inshore, but are mainly caught in offshore environs, and around the edges of reefs, dropoffs, or current eddies.

they go when they move on from the Caribbean.

While sailfish are most earnestly pursued in the fall, they are known to be equally as abundant in the spring, from March into June, but scarce in the winter. Blue marlin, too, are primarily sought in the fall months, although they are less prominent then than they are in the months January through to April.

Part of the reason for an emphasis on fall fishing is that this is when most visitors choose to come here. Locals speak of a year-round season, with peaks in both the fall and the spring.

Speaking of peaks, the scenery in this area is pretty agreeable, too. La Guaira is located along the coast, on the opposite side of the mountain range that separates it from the capital Caracas. Inshore fishing, for a variety of species, especially tarpon, is notable to the east and west, as is the fishing on the offshore flats around islands. In fact, it is notable enough for a separate section, elsewhere in this book, to have been devoted to those areas.

Above: A white marlin clears the surface as they are noted for doing; whites are the most prominent marlin in Venezuelan waters, but large blue marlin are here, too.

Left: Yellowfin tuna can be thick off La Guaira in September, with large fish possible.

SALINAS
ECUADOR

Observing and stalking the quarry sounds like hunting, or like fishing on tidal flats for bonefish. Not like something you would do in the wide-open ocean over deep, indigo water.

But if you were to do such a thing in the offshore salt, it would either be very dull if there was very little to see, or it would be very exciting if there was a lot to see. The latter is the case in one of the world's most renowned big-game fishing spots – the Pacific Ocean off Salinas, Ecuador.

Known for a number of outstanding fishing opportunities, Salinas is a chart-topper where striped marlin are concerned, and stripes are its foremost attraction to the many anglers who come here annually. It isn't the record potential that does it (although Salinas was the sight of two long-standing fly rod records for striped marlin). It is the sheer number of fish to be encountered and the excitement of stalking and baiting them that turns everyone on.

In this section of the eastern Pacific, the striped marlin trolling technique requires having all eyes scanning the ocean swells, looking for a sickle-like tail. When a tail (and sometimes dorsal fin) is sighted, the boat is quickly maneuvered to drag the trailing baits across the path of the marlin. Sometimes the tails are sighted at great distances and the boat captain has to goose the engine to make sure that the fish is headed off and falls behind the line of four or five rigged balao. The boat is slowed to about 5 miles per hour once the marlin comes behind it and then it's a matter of waiting until the fish lights up (turns a neon blue) and attacks.

A minority of striped marlin actually

Salinas itself is not a general tourist attraction, as are many of the world's big game fishing hotspots. Anglers have to fly to Guayaquil, Ecuador, and then traverse through desert flats by auto for two hours to reach it. Not far from the once revered black marlin grounds of northern Peru, and just 2½ degrees south of the equator, Salinas (and nearby Manta) is strategically located to take advantage of the mixing of formidable ocean currents.

ECUADOR

Salinas

Left: Striped marlin are the mainstay of the Ecuadorian billfishery; these fish are plentiful and provide excellent light-tackle action.

Right: Eight hundred and ten pounds is a lot of black marlin, but Ecuador can produce such fish; this one was taken off Manta.

charge one of the baits. Some move off immediately, others look the various baits over and follow for several minutes before drifting off. The watching, waiting, and anticipating make for some anxious but enjoyable moments in themselves, especially since between 20 and 30 fish might be spotted in the course of a day.

The number of opportunities for striped marlin is one of the things that separates this locale from others where these fish are present. Another is the fact that they can be caught on relatively light tackle for some outstanding action. Striped marlin are especially noted for repeated dazzling aerial displays in which they hurtle dozens of yards at a time, and for their stamina.

Still another influence is the interaction of powerful currents. The most prominent current along the western coast of South America is the Humboldt Current, a cold northwesterly flowing stream of water that moves toward the west as it nears the equator. The Equatorial Current at the equator produces eddies that spin off and head back toward the Ecuadorian coast. These eddies, which possess warm tropical water, actually push the colder Humboldt offshore. The eddies contain baitfish and gamefish.

Some 10 to 12 miles offshore there is a sharp drop in the ocean floor, which rises back again before plunging into great depths. An abundance of baitfish in this area causes the striped marlin to skim the surface waters and accounts for the sightings.

Of course, other marlin are present here, too, perhaps not in the same numbers as stripes, but with no less interest from sportfishermen. Black marlin seem to be found more inshore than striped marlin, while blues are likely to be further out over deeper water.

While the billfish, which provided good angling in years past, were thrown a whammy in the early 80s by El Niño, they have rebounded to the point where even monster blue marlin have been taken by sportfishermen

A blue marlin comes over the transom in the waters of Salinas; large blues, including fish over a thousand pounds, have been caught here.

(longliners have reportedly taken numerous granders). In May 1985, the present I.G.F.A. 80-pound line-class world record Pacific blue marlin of 1,014 pounds was caught off Salinas, and anglers have been trying to put another grander on the dock since. An 810-pounder was taken in 1987, followed by a 900-pounder in 1988.

Black marlin aren't usually found in those sizes, although 500- to 700-pounders have been hooked. The average for these is more in the 350-pound class, and the average for blues is about 400 pounds.

That's good, especially since the blue marlin are pretty much available all year here. From May to January is considered the better period, however, with the best period for blacks being April and May and again in the fall. Prime time for striped marlin is just about any time. However, a lot of fishermen like to have an opportunity for variety, and make September through November their preferred period because of all the options that are available.

Another notable fishing opportunity here is with bigeye tuna. These fish average in the heavyweight division, and several records have been set in Ecuadorian waters. Currently, four line-class world records for Pacific bigeye tuna have Salinas addresses, the most recent and largest being a 341-pounder on 80-pound line caught in January 1988. Three other records, though set three decades ago, were taken to the south off Peru. January through March is peak time for these bruisers off Ecuador.

A number of other species are caught here, too. Swordfish are in these waters, but there is little attempt made for them. Sailfish and dolphin are encountered by trollers, too, and inshore anglers (although there are few, what with all the offshore action to be enjoyed) have a chance at various species, including corbina and roosterfish.

There is some concern for the future of the billfishing here, as the commercial fleet, in the form of longliners and gillnetters, has become prodigious in recent years. The sportfishery itself is not noted for its conservation efforts, either, and there is little tagging or ordinary catch-and-release being done. It is understood that the catch belongs to the boat crew.

The lack of release efforts is contrary to the trend in most other places, but in this situation, the sport catch is sold to local Ecuadorians, for whom the fish is an important food source.

Perhaps it is just as well, then, that most of the striped marlin that are seen finning offshore do not attack the baits. But as visiting anglers know, when the marlin are there and they light up to charge, that telltale moment or two of strike anticipation is one of the high points of the visit.

STRIPED MARLIN

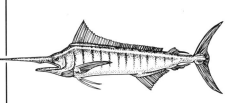

One of few fish that are known to spend almost as much time in the air after being hooked as in the water, striped marlin are a favorite with fishermen for their graceful greyhounding leaps and repeated tailwalking. These pelagic tropical water fish are a denizen of the Indian and Pacific Oceans. They are a highly predatory species, feeding on a wide range of bait. Trolling with various types of bait is especially popular for striped marlin, using either whole rigged baits or strip baits. In some places, fishing with live bait is common. Though more acrobatic than their blue or black marlin cousins, they do not grow as large. The all-tackle world record is a **494-pound** New Zealand fish.

Regaining Line

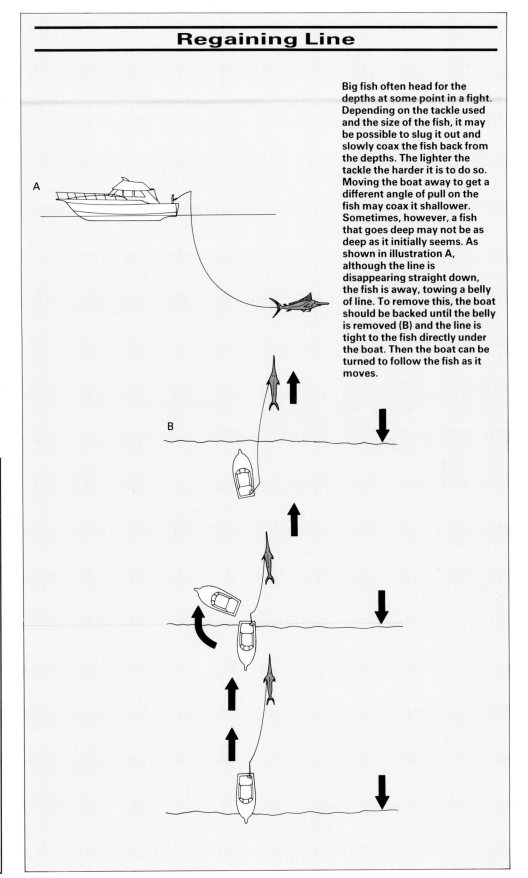

Big fish often head for the depths at some point in a fight. Depending on the tackle used and the size of the fish, it may be possible to slug it out and slowly coax the fish back from the depths. The lighter the tackle the harder it is to do so. Moving the boat away to get a different angle of pull on the fish may coax it shallower. Sometimes, however, a fish that goes deep may not be as deep as it initially seems. As shown in illustration A, although the line is disappearing straight down, the fish is away, towing a belly of line. To remove this, the boat should be backed until the belly is removed (B) and the line is tight to the fish directly under the boat. Then the boat can be turned to follow the fish as it moves.

OCEANIA

Lots of water, relatively few people, great sporting opportunity. In a nutshell that characterizes the angling perception of the Pacific in the Southern Hemisphere.

Distant, promising, pretty. Virgin waters, new discoveries, record-size fish beckon. Indeed, over, along, and near the many atolls, reefs, volcanic islands, and archipelagos of this vast territory swim some of the mightiest fish in the world, some present all year, other passing through on annual migrations. These include pelagic creatures that are strong and grow large enough to dominate entire categories of the record books. And some species that are found nowhere else.

New discoveries may still be made here, perhaps in some idyllic lagoon, or on the dropoff of an uninhabited island. Robinson Crusoes take note.

KONA
HAWAII

There are just a few places in the world where a fisherman can legitimately expect to catch a huge blue marlin. But when you consider the good and bad points of each locale, including the length of the season, weather conditions, size and experience of the local fleet, and so forth, there is one place that has so much in its favor that it cannot be equaled. The Kona coast along the western shore of the island of Hawaii, in the chain of the same name, is that place.

Known as "the big island" because it's 4,000 square miles make up almost two-thirds of the land throughout this Pacific archipelago, Hawaii is no stranger to fishing, sport or otherwise. Rich fishing grounds here attracted early ocean-roaming Polynesians, as attested to at Ka Lae, the south cape where thousands of bone and shell fishhooks have been excavated.

Sportfishing for the giants of the sea started here 70 or more years ago, and led to experimentation, success, and records that have paced the billfishing scene worldwide.

Although all of the Pacific billfishes can be caught here in varying quantity, the blue marlin is king, and the water off the Kona coast is the kingdom. This is the land of 500-pound-plus fish. In fact, to stand a chance of winning any of the major marlin tournaments here, and elsewhere in the islands, you have to put a blue of 600 pounds or better on the scales to be a contender. At that, fish in the high 600-class or into the 700-pound range usually take top honors.

And then there are the granders. While every other blue marlin locale in the world measures its big fish over

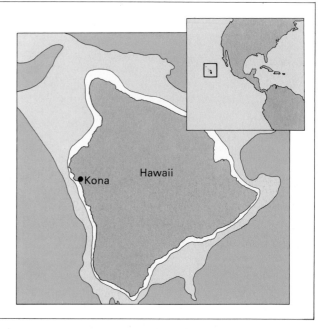

The island of Hawaii is truly a mountain rising out of the sea. Known as Volcanic Island, it has two peaks over 13,000 feet high; one, Mauna Kea, sports a world-famous observatory, and the other, Mauna Loa, has been one of the world's most active volcanoes. Active, red hot marlin are sought by boats leaving Kailua Kona and Keauhou Bay. Azure blue billfish water is found a short distance from shore. The Kona coast is on the leeward side of Hawaii, so nearshore waters are protected and generally calm.

time, Hawaii measures them by which 1,000-pounder is the first of the year (a few seasons ago it happened on New Year's Day), which is biggest, and which fought the longest.

The Pacific blue marlin records have long been dominated by Hawaiian fish, and currently these islands possess eight records. Three of them are fish over 1,000 pounds in the 30-, 50-, and 130-pound line-class divisions, all caught off Kona. The latter is also the all-tackle world record. Weighing 1,376 pounds, and landed in May of 1982, it is not the biggest blue that has been caught on rod and reel in Hawaiian waters. A 1,805-pounder was taken a few years ago off Oahu; it didn't receive record recognition because more than one angler handled the tackle (which is against I.G.F.A. regulations). Neither did the 1,649-pounder that used to be the Kona best. The pros think that one day a two-ton Pacific blue marlin will

come to the hook here. If so, it could just as likely happen to a tourist on his first big game fishing trip as to a seasoned billfish angler.

Big fish are caught each year by occasional anglers on board charterboats. This speaks well of the opportunities available here, and also of the skill of the captain in being able not only to attract such a fish, but tutor an unskilled angler and expertly handle the boat. But that is one thing that is characteristic of billfishing off Hawaii, and the other islands. The skippers and crews are as skillful and experienced as anywhere in the world.

They have, in fact, been responsible for many innovations in billfishing, from Konahead lures and others of this genre, to high speed fishing, to the use of "birds" (wooden flying fish imitations used as teasers). These innovations have increased local productivity and spread to other billfish grounds throughout the world.

Giant blue marlin are more frequently seen in Hawaiian waters than in any other locale; Kona is an especially prominent place for such fish.

The Kona coast may be the most attractive place to fish throughout the islands because of its proximity to deep water and the comfort that is usually experienced in fishing here. Whereas rough seas are frequently found on the windward side of this and other islands, Kona is on the lee from the prevailing northeast trade winds. It also has the protection of two towering volcanoes (one of which, Mauna Loa, is still active) and it usually has calm to mild sea conditions near the shore. This means that more days of fishing are possible and that conditions, especially in prime time, for running baits and fighting fish are among the best.

Billfishing is done very close to shore here, as there is no shelf to speak of. This is a volcanic island that rises out of the sea, and the dropoff to 100 fathoms plus is almost instantaneous from the Kona coast. Five minutes from the Kona harbor puts you in the same territory that has produced many of this island's big

DOLPHIN

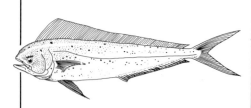

Known in Hawaii and other locales as *mahimahi*, and dorado in still others, the dolphin is also referred to as dolphinfish by some anglers in order to help distinguish it from a porpoise, which is traditionally, but incorrectly, referred to as a dolphin. These blue water creatures feed on squid and flying fish, and small fish clustered around floating sargassum weed and kelp. They are commonly found around objects well at sea. Most are located and caught by trolling at a fairly high speed, usually in search of other species. Dolphin are a prized game fish, not only because they are excellent to eat, but also because they are excellent battlers, running hard and leaping high and often.

Leader Regs for Record Fish

Double lines and leaders are not required for records, but one or the other are almost always used in big-game fishing. In order for a fish to be eligible for a world record, it must meet the criteria established for leaders and double line by the International Game Fish Association. These state, "Double lines are measured from the start of the knot, braid, roll or slice making the double to the farthermost end of the knot, splice, snap, swivel or other device used for securing the trace, leader, lure, or hook to the double line." The double line for saltwater fish is limited to 15 feet for all line classes up to 10 kg, and is limited to 30 feet for line classes over 10 kg. The combined length of double line and leader cannot be more than 20 feet for line classes up to 10 kg, and 40 feet in line classes over 10 kg.

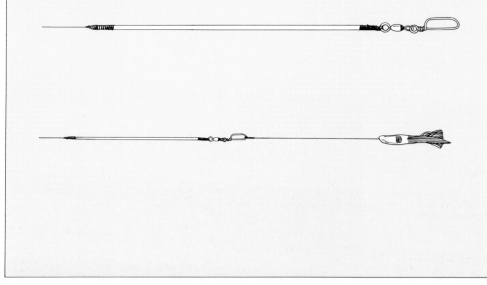

fish. In May of 1987, for example, a major tournament was won with an 813-pound blue marlin landed before noon on the first day of the event, at the area in front of Honokohau Harbor known as Juliet, virtually within sight of Kailua Kona's boat docks. That fish, incidentally, is currently the women's 130-pound line-class world record.

Many fish are taken a short distance away as well, especially off Keahole Point, north of Kailua Kona, and offshore from the Captain Cook Monument (Cook was first to discover these islands and was killed here in 1779), which is south of Keauhou Bay. It is about an hour from harbor to both of these locales.

This is heavy-tackle country. Standard fishing involves 80- to 130-pound tackle because of the opportunities to run into monsters. It is generally understood that visiting anglers who want light gear should bring their own. However, lighter tackle, including 30-pound-test, has become more popular, and so a little more interest in this is being displayed nowadays.

The best time to fish here is from late spring through early fall. Many of the biggest fish have been caught in May, but granders have come in virtually all months, and there are billfish to be had here all year long.

Understandably, the outstanding blue marlin action off the Kona coast tends to dwarf the other angling opportunities here. Among billfish, black marlin are occasionally caught and swordfish make the odd appearance. Spearfish are abundant enough for three smaller specimens to have made it into the record books.

However, big yellowfin tuna (up to 200 pounds), plus bigeye tuna, wahoo, dolphin, albacore and skipjack tuna are also found in these waters. The months June through September is generally good for these species. Bottom fishing here has increased a bit in recent years, with the hard-fighting amberjack and trevally as the quarry.

There is some fishing to be done elsewhere on the island of Hawaii away from the Kona coast, especially off Hilo. However, strong trade winds heavily influence efforts in those locales.

Right: The drop to 100 fathoms occurs very close to the Kona shoreline; this, plus being situated in the lee of prevailing winds, makes the Kona coast especially favored by marlin anglers.

Left: High-speed trolling plugs and other innovations in big-game trolling got their start in Hawaii, and spread to other areas because of their effectiveness.

HAWAII

The big-game fishing overflow in the Hawaiian Islands, if you can call it overflow, may take a second string to the prime fishing off the Kona Coast (see Kona, on p. 150), but Hawaii's second string is as good or better than the first team in many other billfish locales. That may be saying a lot, but Hawaii has a lot. And if it wasn't whipped by the trade winds so often resulting in rough water on the windward side of its islands, the fishing would be so good in so many spots, and for so much of the season, that the question would merely be which way to turn when you left the harbor, rather than which harbor.

Of course, it is the geographic position of the Hawaiian Islands all alone in the Pacific, rising from miles-deep water thanks to volcanic action, that puts it smack in billfish country in the first place. And billfish, plus assorted other species, are found off all of these islands.

Oahu, for example, is famous for Honolulu, Waikiki Beach, and so forth, but it was off this island that a 1,806-pound blue was caught a few years ago, the biggest grander of all time on rod and reel. The Kewalo Basin in Honolulu has the second largest fleet of sportfishing boats in Hawaii, and the fishing centers around the Molokai Channel, up Waianae coast on the lee side of Oahu, and Penguin Bank. Penguin is across the Kaiwi Channel; the bank rises from a point roughly south of Diamond Head on Oahu and continues to Laau Point on southwest Molokai; it often has a great deal of activity from all species of fish.

Big yellowfin tuna, plus dolphin and wahoo, are other attractions off Oahu, especially in the spring. The fishing

along the windward shore and the north shore can be good, and possesses the same species as elsewhere, but it is much harder to fish because of the prevailing winds and resulting rough seas.

Maui is another island with good fishing, despite the fact that its waters don't drop off quite as precipitously as at other locales. For some, the closer-to-shore waters provide excellent wahoo, dolphin, and small tuna fishing for trollers, as well as amberjack, snapper, and giant trevally for inshore bottom bumpers. Hawaii has some large giant trevally, and boasts three world records for this species, including the all-tackle and 80-pound line-class holder, which weighed 137 pounds 9 ounces.

Marlin fishing can be productive here throughout the season, including winter, which is usually slack elsewhere in Hawaii. A good many of the winter billfish here are striped marlin, perhaps because of slightly cooler water temperatures then, and they run up to 150 pounds. Blues in the 600-pound range have been caught off Maui and the total take of billfish exceeds 600 for the season, which isn't too shabby.

Not a great deal of charterboat fishing is done on Kauai, the westernmost island, which is noted for good yellowfin tuna, wahoo, and dolphin. Lanai and Molokai Islands have good dolphin action, and a lot of hard-to-access water. The windward waters of all of the islands don't get fished as much as many people would like for obvious rough-water reasons, but they have produced well when the seas have been calm enough for big boat efforts, and it is known that they have a lot to offer. Which, obviously, is true throughout the islands.

All of the Hawaiian Islands are in billfish country, though some are more comfortable to fish than others due to the impact of the tradewinds and the sea conditions that result.

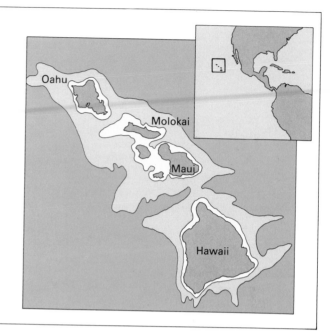

Most of the big-game fishing attention in the Hawaiian Islands is focused on the Kona coast of the big island. But Maui and Oahu have much to offer in this regard, too, with most marlin efforts being directed on the lee side of the islands in or beyond the 100-fathom curve. The Northeast Trade Winds pelt the windward shore and make fishing difficult most days, impossible on many.

Taglines

The use of taglines in trolling lures for big-game fish has become common practice, and originated in Hawaii. Taglines are used to keep the fishing line from rod to lure off the water, which affects action, by raising it high. It also reduces the amount of slack between the time a fish hits and the fishing line goes from outrigger to rod tip. A tagline is very heavy line (up to 300 pounds) that extends down from an outrigger and is attached to a rubberband, which in turn is attached to the fishing line. When a fish strikes the trolled lure, the line breaks the rubberband, there is a split second of slack for the fish to turn on the lure, and then the line comes tight and the hook is set.

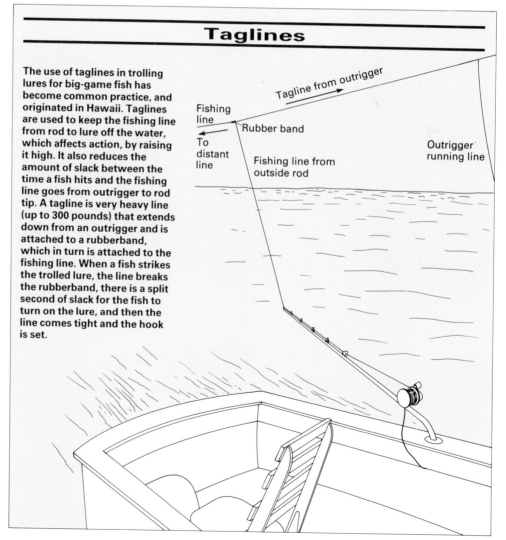

CHRISTMAS ISLAND

It sounds like the title of a fairytale. Few have heard of it or know where it is if they have heard of it. It belongs to a chain of islands that are virtually unknown and it is part of a country that is probably even less well known. Given all this, it is little wonder that the fishing potential in this mystery place was virtually unheard of until early in the 1980s.

But then a sportfishing camp opened, anglers visited, and in just a short time, Kiritimati Island became known internationally as a premier bonefishing spot, perhaps one of the world's best. Its stature continues to grow annually for bonefish, and more is being learned each season about the notable reef and offshore fishing potential as well.

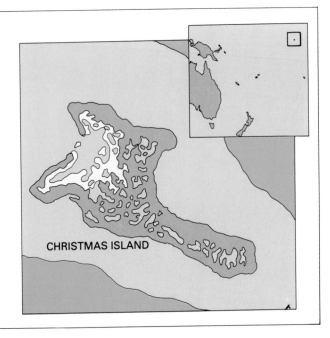

Christmas Island is situated in the mid-Pacific, but thanks to its location relative to Hawaii is fairly accessible. One of the world's largest atolls, it has plenty of lagoon waters and many acres of wade-able knee-deep flats for bonefishing, as well as attractive offshore fishing not far from those shallows. It is situated close to the equator, so fishermen are likely to get fried if they don't take precautions. And it is known for frequent tradewinds through a good part of the year, although sheltered lagoon waters can usually be found.

CHRISTMAS ISLAND

Left: An atoll in the Central Pacific, Christmas Island was recently discovered by sportfishermen and has become known for premier bonefishing.

Right: Though some large bonefish have been reported at Christmas Island, most of the fish run to the smaller sizes, but there are many of them.

Kiritimati Island, better known to the world as Christmas Island, is a 240-square-mile atoll that is part of the Line Islands in the Central Pacific Basin. Northeast of Samoa and Northwest of the Marquesas, it is situated just above the equator, but is still 1,300 miles and nearly three hours traveling time by plane south of Hawaii.

Part of the Republic of Kiribati, Christmas Island has links to actions in the Pacific Theater during World War II and to American military operations in post-war years, but only a serviceman with spare time and fishing rod could have told you much until recently about this place.

What they would have said was

"bonefish galore." They would have told you about big bonefish, little bonefish, bonefish by the hundreds. And that is what the modern-day anglers have found as well.

Christmas Island is indeed as fine a location as there is in the world for anyone who wants to have his first bonefish experience, and to have numerous opportunities to cast to, and hang onto, these flats speedsters, using fly or spinning tackle. Someone who fears the wily bonefish, who thinks his casting skills are inadequate, who needs to learn how to spot fish on rippled coral flats, who needs to learn what it takes in terms of presentation and playing skills, *ought* to come to a place like Christmas Island. For there is nothing like learning the game by having lots of chances to play. If an experienced flats fly caster can take more than a dozen fish in a day here, which, by most standards is exceptional bonefishing, even a neophyte can score.

Christmas Island's bonefish are generally in the smaller sizes, from 2 to 5 pounds, which is typical of places where there are large schools of these fish. However, there are bigger bones here, and there's a reasonable chance of taking fish up to 10 pounds. Some larger specimens have been reported, too, though opportunities for monster bonefish are not great. Nonethless there is a report of a 23-pound bonefish here, which is 4 pounds greater than the long-standing all-tackle world record and a bit hard to believe.

Almost surely there is also good bonefishing on the other islets in the Line Islands, and in the atolls and islands in the relatively close Gilbert and Phoenix chains. Very few people have ever sampled them, and there doesn't seem much likelihood in the near future of doing so unless private boat anglers can make the long voyage from distant ports.

With bonefish the prime discovery, it took a while to find out that there was some excellent potential here for other fish, including offshore angling.

In recent years there has been some exploration of the offshore waters by the lone sportfishing vessel in the area. Reports indicate that a world-class wahoo fishery exists, plus good opportunities for marlin, tuna, and other species. A lot has yet to be learned, however, and it seems this is only the tip of the iceberg.

Nevertheless, that tip reveals a wahoo fishery that sometimes results in double and triple strikes, and offers trolling as well as fly casting potential for very rambunctious fish. Wahoo to over 80 pounds have been recorded off Christmas Island, 100-pounders have been seen, and even larger fish have been snared by commercial fishermen. These streakers are available at any time of the season here.

Also available year-round and quite abundant are yellowfin tuna. Small yellowfins, up to 60 pounds or so, offer action at any time, and bigger fish, in the 100- to 150-pound class, are possible. Other tunas, including skipjack, are locally abundant, and one may come upon a vast school of tuna while trolling offshore.

Billfish are present in these waters seasonally, and a large question mark remains in this realm, only because there simply has been little concerted effort directed at these fish. Pacific blue marlin up to 500 pounds have been caught by sportfishermen in recent years, and larger fish have been taken by the commercial fleet.

At times, plenty of Pacific sailfish have been encountered, producing multiple strikes on occasion, and with fish up to 100 pounds. The major period for billfish action is from late spring through September.

The potpourri of opportunities continues when one takes into consideration the kawakawa, mahi mahi, barracuda (some very large), and assorted other creatures that are seldom disturbed by anglers here. One of these is the giant trevally, a fish that grows to enormous proportions here and which is beginning to get recognition by flats and offshore fishermen alike.

The Albright Special

An important knot for saltwater fishermen, the Albright Special is used for connecting lines of vastly different diameters, as with shock leaders in fly fishing, and also to tie nylon monofilament to wire leaders. To tie it: (1) make a loop in the heavier line and pass 8 inches of lighter line through it; (2) tuck the light line between thumb and forefinger of your left hand; (3) wrap light line back over itself and the loop ten times; (4) pass standing end of light line through the loop; (5) pull gently on the tag ends; (6) pull firmly on the standing lines; (7) clip tag ends.

Left: Plenty of wahoo swim in the waters off Christmas Island, resulting in multiple strikes at times for trollers.

Right: The reef and offshore trolling fishery still is in its infancy at Christmas Island, but yellowfin tuna, such as this fish, plus skipjack are among the species that are found here in fair numbers.

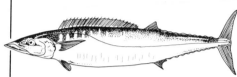

WAHOO

Wahoo are the hardest fighting and most well respected members of the mackerel clan. They grow fairly large and fight like fish even bigger, often being mistaken for other fish when caught while trolling for big game species. These fast-swimming fish are noted for peeling a lot of line off a reel in a hurry after striking, and will make a long run. They are a highly mobile fish, feeding on flying fish, herring, mackerel, and other schooling species. Steel-blue in color, with bright vertical markings, they are found in bluewater environs around the world.

A 73-pound line-class world record was caught offshore a few years ago, making this the fourth of the line-class trevally records set at Christmas Island. Bigger fish, even some exceeding the all-tackle world record of 137 pounds, are thought to swim in these waters.

Inshore fishermen, working the edge of the coral reefs and the shallows in the lagoons have an opportunity to cast to these fish, and fly fishermen could have fun trying to establish new tippet records (one was established here in 1984). Trevally are extremely strong, stubborn fighters, and they present quite a different challenge from that found in bonefishing.

At Christmas Island, it is rather nice to be able to do a little bit of everything and to have good fishing opportunities for all of these species. Couple that with the usual delights of being on a large coral atoll far removed from the rest of the world, and it's easy to see why this is becoming an increasingly popular sportfishing destination.

TAHITI

When the fabled Captain Cook arrived in Tahiti in 1769, he was not a captain but a lieutenant whose mission was to observe the transit of Venus across the sun. Building a fort east of Papeete on Matavai Bay, Cook and his crew were able to use it as a base from which they charted the surrounding islands. Cook called them the Society Islands because "they lay contiguous to one another."

Those islands, now considered a section of French Polynesia, are part of an archipelago that is surrounded by deep, blue South Pacific water. It is water that is without a continental shelf and situated along the migratory route of some of the world's largest and strongest game fish.

No less an authority than Zane Grey himself discovered as much in the late 1920s when he was exploring the South Seas. Grey set up a camp on the beach at Puunui, a village on Tahiti-iti, and landed a 1,040-pound blue marlin in the region of Vairao Bay. The size of that catch, and some of the circumstances that went along with it, are somewhat analagous to what exists in Tahitian fishing opportunities today.

There are still big blues in these waters, for instance. In recent years there have been quite a few marlin caught in the 700-pound class. Fishing pressure, however, remains relatively light, in part attributable to the distant location (Tahiti is halfway between California and Australia) and the fact that there is good, well-established big-game fishing in Hawaii.

Nevertheless, a lot of hours can be put in between strikes in Tahitian waters. Even 70 years ago, Zane Grey reportedly went 83 days here once without a fish. This writer fished for marlin in Tahiti in 1978, and found that there were few people on the water, but that one spent a lot of time waiting for a strike. Although our party caught other species, we raised just one marlin in three days.

That may not sound at first like a world-class fishery, but realize that as recently as 1986 commercial fishermen here caught blue marlin weighing 1,560 pounds and 1,307 pounds. It's a wonder those fish weren't attacked by sharks, which is said to have occurred with Grey's big fish. Sadly, many large blue marlin have been mutilated by sharks while battling the fisherman.

Both trolling lures and bait are used in Tahiti for marlin, the former more so than the latter, but it is bait that has caught some of the biggest billfish.

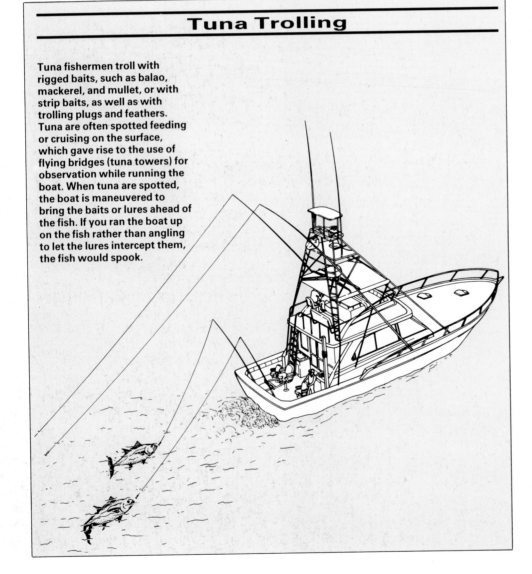

Tuna Trolling

Tuna fishermen troll with rigged baits, such as balao, mackerel, and mullet, or with strip baits, as well as with trolling plugs and feathers. Tuna are often spotted feeding or cruising on the surface, which gave rise to the use of flying bridges (tuna towers) for observation while running the boat. When tuna are spotted, the boat is maneuvered to bring the baits or lures ahead of the fish. If you ran the boat up on the fish rather than angling to let the lures intercept them, the fish would spook.

In the Society Islands, Tahiti (which is the largest island in French Polynesia), Moorea, and Bora Bora are especially known for their marlin and tuna fishing opportunities. While Bora Bora is 165 miles from Tahiti, Moorea is just 11 miles away, and the trough between the two islands is a major fishing spot. Because Tahiti is located at a central spot in the Pacific basin, it experiences low and high tides at about the same time each day. Low tides occur around 6 A.M. and 6 P.M. and high tides occur at noon and midnight. The Tahitian word for midnight, *tuiraa-po*, also means high tide.

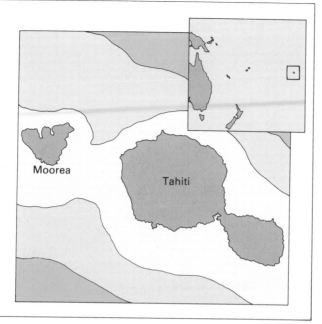

Other prime species to be found here, incidentally, include mahimahi (dolphin), wahoo, bonito, yellowfin tuna, bigeye tuna, and albacore, plus various reef dwellers. Swordfish are known to be caught in the region by deep longliners, but they aren't pursued by sportfishermen. November through March seems to be the best fishing time, but that may only coincide with the peak travel period.

Needless to say, Tahiti and her sister islands are among the prettiest places in the world, with fairytale-like vistas, emerald lagoons, pristine beaches, deep blue skies, and splendid mountain peaks. Combine this with warm, friendly people and it is hard to imagine a more enjoyable place to fish.

An angler watches for signs of marlin while trolling with the island of Moorea in the background; Tahiti offers big blue marlin, tuna, wahoo, dolphin, and other species.

MICRONESIA

Hardly anyone can tell you where Micronesia is let alone what kind of angling it has to offer. In fact, sportfishing is still virtually unknown in that part of the world and the true potential has yet to be determined. This is really an untapped, virgin angling location. Well, almost. A few people have been here and the reports have been coming through, although they are incomplete.

Take billfish, for example. Given the location of the Micronesian atolls in the Pacific, it would seem that these fish might be plentiful. Marlin haven't been targeted by sport fishermen here other than accidentally, in part because there are no proper boats available. However, when a big-game sportfishing boat was brought to the Caroline Islands here a few years ago as part of a touring mothership operation, the anglers on board caught over a dozen billfish in several weeks, including both sailfish and blue marlin, the biggest of the latter nearly hitting 500 pounds. Reportedly, these were the first sport-caught billfish in Micronesia.

First or not is almost irrelevant. What is significant, however, is that these fish are there. They are accompanied, in fact, by virtually all of the

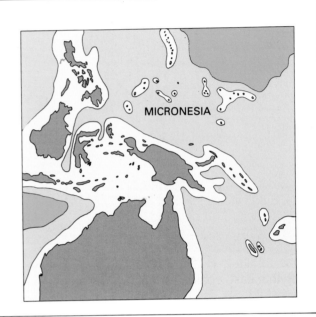

Micronesia is less than 10 degrees above the Equator, and situated between the Marshall Islands and the Philippines. It is made up of hundreds, perhaps more, of small islands and atolls, clustered among several groups of islands. The Caroline Islands have been explored by a few fishermen, especially around Truk and Ponape (Pohnpei). Lagoons, reefs, dropoffs, channels, and varied interesting terrain exist here, much of which has never seen sportfishing activity.

other fish species that are found through the central Pacific, including dolphin, wahoo, and assorted tunas.

The coral reefs, atoll channels, and lagoons abound with sportfish, a full listing of which is still unknown. Angling reports from these virgin waters have been replete with unabated action and clearly a light-tackle paradise exists. Large barracuda, yellowfin tuna, dogtooth tuna, bigeye tuna, bluefin trevally, wahoo, dolphin, and

the usual assortment of groupers and snappers and sharks are caught close to the atolls.

With so few boats and so few fishermen to date, the better locales throughout the vast area of Micronesia have yet to be fully identified. Some speculate that there are flats in this region that could yield both bonefish and permit, making for a Christmas-Island-type discovery, but this is sheer conjecture.

Bathurst Island in the Northern Territory is known for excellent barramundi fishing, which these shore-based anglers are doing, and has underexplored potential for marlin offshore.

DARWIN
AUSTRALIA

Australia may be the smallest continent but it is one big country. From Sydney to Perth and Tasmania to the "Top End", it is virtually large enough to equal the continental United States in size, and it has some of the most diverse fishing imaginable. The largest island in the world, and bounded by the Pacific and Indian Oceans, Australia has angling opportunities galore.

Many of those opportunities are hard to access, however, and still barely explored. While the saltwater fraternity knows full well about the remarkable billfishing that this country has to offer, it really only knows about the east coast, especially the Cairns – Lizard Island locale. New discoveries are still being made here

The Top End of the Northern Territory abuts the Timor Sea on the northwest, the Arafur Sea on the north, and the Gulf of Carpentaria on the east. Nhulunbuy is an aboriginal preserve that sports a bauxite mine, and provides a jumpoff spot for fishing north of the Gove Peninsula, around its barren and desert-like islands. Bathurst Island is accessed by plane from Darwin, with fishing primarily concentrated on barramundi in the creeks and lagoons. Many of the rivers, estuaries, and lagoons to the east and west of Darwin have notable barramundi fishing as well.

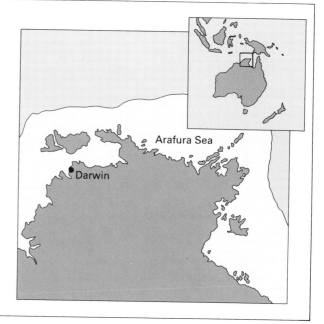

where big game is concerned, and relatively new discoveries have yet to be publicized or marginally exploited.

Western Australia, as an example of the latter category, has a good, but vastly underfished billfishery. Only since the middle of the 80s have a few anglers sampled blue, black, and striped marlin action off Exmount, some 800 miles north of Perth, and off Dampier, still further north.

Totally new billfisheries have recently been heralded in the Northern Territory, and this coupled with the extraordinary inland fishing here, make Darwin the jumpoff for outstanding adventure, and untapped fishing.

The Top End, as the remote northern region of the Northern Territory is called here, has billfishing in two distinctly different locales. Neither of these has received more than an occasional visit by ardent billfishermen, but both have great potential.

The easternmost of these locales is some 50 miles north of Darwin in the waters around Bathurst Island. Bathurst is known for its barramundi fishing (more about that shortly) but until a few years ago, no one had ever fished the blue water here for billfish. The first exploration here in unknown waters and by anglers inexperienced in big-game tactics, produced a remarkable showing of sailfish and black marlin, proving that the opportunity exists, although seasons, sizes, and tactics have yet to be defined. That, of course, is how Cairns, Lizard Island, and many other locales, in Australia and elsewhere, got started.

The other billfish possibility here exists off Gove Peninsula, over 350 miles to the east. There, black marlin have been caught off Truant Islands and The English Company's Islands, reportedly in sizes over 500 pounds, as well as many sailfish. A few charter boats have been working this area from Nhulunbuy, and reports are that light-tackle fishing starts in March, with plenty of sailfish action, and that larger blacks show up in October and November.

Both of these locales sport opportunities for other pelagic fish, including dogtooth tuna, longfin tuna, wahoo, queenfish, tanguigue (a mackerel), barracuda, several species of trevally, and so forth, either around island reefs or while trolling the offshore environs. The islands off the Gove Peninsula are especially a potpourri of opportunities for light-tackle angling for willing, aggressive fish.

Most of the coast of the Northern Territory bordering the Arafura Sea from Gove Peninsula east has seen little, if any, sportfishing ventures. There are many bays, lagoons, reefs, and islands that could provide virgin fishing if there was access and if the fishing wasn't so good elsewhere that there was little motivation to explore this region. Also these are aboriginal lands, and access permits are required.

BARRAMUNDI

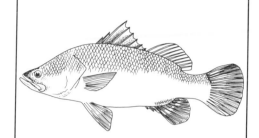

Although barramundi are mostly associated with Australia, they are also found further north as far as the Philippines and southern China. Known also as giant perch and barra, they are a distant relative of the snook and the Nile perch, and thrive in brackish water. Barramundi are not known as open-water feeders, but as structure and object-oriented fish that lie in ambush for mullet, minnows and other small fish. They can be caught in and around thick cover, including mangrove-lined banks, and characteristically head for roots and snags when hooked, in an effort to get free.

Left: The hard-fighting queenfish is among the various species that inshore fishermen can catch in the Northern Territory.

Right: Barramundi are caught in the estuaries and tidal rivers of the islands and coast of the Northern Territory, and are a highly respected game fish.

Despite all of this potential, the Top End is most known for its estuary angling for one of the best sportfish in the world: barramundi. This cover-streaking hard-fighting leaper is caught in the estuaries and in the rivers that abound throughout the Northern Territory and while these fish are found in various parts of Australia, they are nowhere else as abundant as here. Three current line-class barramundi world records have been established in the Northern Territory, the biggest of those being a 59-pound 12-ounce fish, which is the 16-pound record, formerly the all-tackle record, and just 14 ounces shy of the current all-tackle mark (caught relatively nearby in Papua New Guinea).

Unquestionably, barramundi fishing in the Northern Territory is a true angling adventure, the type of fishing that doesn't exist in many places in the world anymore. For one thing, this is the land of Crocodile Dundee fame, sparsely populated, wild, and sometimes dangerous.

The Palomar Knot

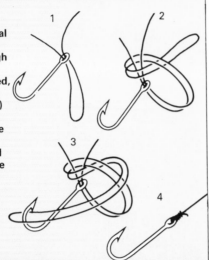

The Palomar Knot is a good fishing knot to use for terminal connections for light tackle angling applications. Although a little difficult to use at first when large lures are employed, it is easily mastered and very strong. To form a Palomar, (1) double about 6 inches of line and pass the loop through the eye of the hook; (2) tie an overhand knot in the doubled line; (3) pass the loop over the entire hook; (4) moisten the knot, pull on both ends, tighten, and clip the tag end. Use a greater length of line when tying this knot to large lures.

Tidal fluctuations play a big role in barramundi fishing, with low tide drawing fish into holes and concentrating them.

Fishing takes place in remote areas, in jungle-like habitat. Mangrove-lined rivers and tropical lagoons and estuaries are the grounds, and casters fish amidst heavy cover, including vegetation and mangrove roots, and have a great struggle keeping larger barramundi from reaching sanctuary once hooked. A lot of tackle gets tested to the maximum by these fish, and many a lure is lost. The fishing, to say the least, is challenging.

Perhaps as challenging, is the fact that good barramundi fishing waters are also frequented by saltwater crocodiles, which are aggressive, known man-eaters, and highly respected by fishermen. Signs warn against swimming, and boaters do not venture close enough to risk an encounter. So serious is this matter in the Northern Territory that a visitor can actually purchase crocodile attack insurance. Now that's adventure.

Barramundi fishing is one of playing the tides, which can fluctuate severely here. The best fishing time is during low tide because it draws barramundi out of the mangroves in creeks, lagoons, and other spots, and concentrates them in holes, channels, and the like, making them more accessible. Trolling and casting are both popular, using diving and rattling plugs on bait-casting tackle. Fishing is primarily done from small skiffs, 12 to 15 feet long, but also by waders.

Bathurst Island has some excellent fishing for relatively large (20-pound) barramundi, but the bulk of the fishing takes place around Darwin in jungle rivers and mangrove-lined lagoons. The Daly River to the southwest of Darwin, and the Mary River to the east, are among the better locations for this activity.

Consituting one-sixth of the land mass of Australia, the Northern Territory is sparsely populated and replete with world-class sportfishing potential. Tourism here is rapidly growing, and it seems that more of that potential will be enjoyed by visiting anglers in the near future.

CAIRNS, LIZARD ISLAND
AUSTRALIA

The odds are 100 to 1 that when you mention Australia to a saltwater fisherman, the first thing that he thinks of is Cairns. The modern-day mecca for black marlin fishing. The Holy Grail for granders. Home of the Great Barrier Reef, which has often been described as the Eighth Wonder of the World.

No less a figure than the pioneering angler and world famous author Zane Grey, in his book, *An American Angler in Australia*, said that Australia has "fish and fishing which will dwarf all the rest known in the world". Grey based this upon his experiences with black marlin and great white sharks, and though written in 1937, it is quite true even today.

Simply put, there is no finer place in the world to catch black marlin, and unequivocably no greater place to have a chance of catching a 1,000-pounder than the northwest coast of Australia, along the Great Barrier Reef from Cairns to Lizard Island. In fact, they record granders here by the score – and then some – each season. Among the more sensational occurrences in the past here has been the capture of two granders in one boat by different anglers in a single day, and two granders by the same angler in one day. Talk about a place where dreams come true . . .

Nine line-class world-record black marlin from this region are currently in the record book, including two fish over 1,300 pounds, the largest of those being the 80-pound line-class record holder, a 1,347-pounder taken in 1979.

Black marlin records have been set and surpassed in nearly all categories off the Great Barrier Reef for over 20 years. Still bigger fish, including a 1,442-pounder, have been caught and

the talk is often about whether a 2,000-pound black might swim in these waters. As with most marlin grounds, there are those who claim to have hooked and lost fish of such gargantuan proportions off northwest Queensland.

Important as it may be to big-game fishermen, the black marlin is just one

of over 1,400 species of fish found in and around the Great Barrier Reef, many of which are coral denizens with amazing appearance and behavior. The reef, which extends for 1,250 miles and encompasses 80,000 square miles, is a coral jungle amidst a cobalt blue sea of striking beauty and remarkable clarity.

Whether one is a beginner or a veteran angler, there is no finer place for seeking big black marlin than the waters off the Great Barrier Reef from Cairns to Lizard Island.

The Coral Sea waters along the northeastern coast provide the world's foremost black marlin fishing. The seaward side of the Great Barrier Reef takes the brunt of ocean swells and currents, and not much farther offshore the bottom slopes quickly into very deep water. Currents and upwelling here serve to push up bait, and marlin have sometimes been seen and caught in quite shallow water, not far from the reef. Cairns is the major port here for black marlin activity, but the waters northward to Lizard Island are as, or more, productive overall.

Cairns

mothership operations came into being to increase fishing time, since runs of 60 miles or more had been made in the past in a day. Most of the fishing now is done for several days, overnighting on the same large boat that is used for fishing, or staying at a mothership and using a sportfishing boat for daily trolling activities.

Exploration gradually took place to the north with the result that Linden Bank, the Ribbon Reefs, Agincourt Bank, and other shoals, reefs, and passages up to Lizard Island produced fish. Lizard Island itself is actually about 150 miles north of Cairns, and some 17 miles off Queensland.

Black marlin fishing here is done in various ways, including lure trolling, dead bait trolling, and live bait fishing. Live bait is likely to be used on calm-sea days. Dead bait trolling, using kawakawa, scad, skipjack, rainbow runner, and other baits, is very popular. Some baits used weigh 15 to 20, or more pounds, which is larger than the fish that many people ordinarily catch on light tackle when fishing inshore in almost any locale.

Virtually indestructible, and constantly growing and regenerating itself, the reef parallels the Continental Shelf dropoff of the Coral Sea for much of its length. Not far from the reef, the bottom of the ocean drops away from 100 to 1,000 fathoms. Shoals rise and drop here, and these are the feeding sites for mackerel, dolphin, and various tunas, which in turn draw both marlin and sailfish.

Cairns has been the jumpoff for most of the fabulous marlin fishing, venturing both to the north and south. Much of the angling is done such a distance from Cairns, however, that

Left: Sportfishermen stand ready for action at the dock in Cairns.

GAME FISHER

Right: Striped marlin are an occasional catch off the Great Barrier Reef; these and most other marlin are released here.

Big-Game Reel Drags

The drag function on a big-game fishing reel is its heart and soul, used to put striking and fighting pressure on the fish. It must be in proper working order. Using a force gauge or good spring scale that is attached to the fishing line, determine the amount of pressure that it takes for line to slip off the drag by pulling line down from the tip with a smooth continuous motion. Adjust the drag tension knob until the proper amount of tension is applied, depending on the strength of tackle being used. The usual standard is 33 percent for fighting drag and 50 percent for strike drag, with the drag lever being reduced from the strike position once the hook has been set and the angler is locked up. To periodically test the drag, pull line off as shown; if the tip bounces, it is an indication that the drag washers are uneven and need to be worked on.

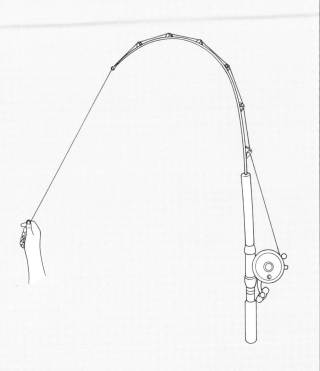

Black marlin are here all year long, but the best action, and biggest fish, are from September through November and sometimes into December, which is the spring and early summer in this part of the hemisphere. Smaller fish are reliably caught from August through January, and in the early and late months there is opportunity to use lighter equipment (80- and 130-pound tackle are used most of the time anyway).

Striped marlin are among the offshore catch, although they do not show up as frequently as blacks. Sailfish are part of the action, too, although not in the same volume as further south off Cape Bowling Green. Blue marlin are primarily found further south along the eastern coast, too, but a few monster fish that have been tagged and released in Queensland waters, though originally believed to be black marlin, were later suspected to have been very large blues. The first blue marlin to be caught in these waters was a 315-pounder taken off No. 10 Ribbon Reef, and that only happened in late 1988.

The catch-and-release ethic in this area, and in all of Australia, is exemplary. Local anglers were tagging and releasing black marlin long before it was fashionable to do so, and granders as well as near granders and smaller fish have been tagged and released for many years.

Some anglers have had the good fortune to recapture fish that were originally tagged on their boats earlier. One fish tagged off Queensland was recaptured almost 4,500 miles away. Obviously, the body of scientific information has benefitted from this, not to mention the fish population, and it has become the situation here (and in New Zealand as well) that keeping a marlin is frowned on by local club members unless the fish is a potential record.

Offshore trollers from Cairns to Lizard Island do catch other species as well, incidentally, though outside this area one seldom hears much

BLACK MARLIN

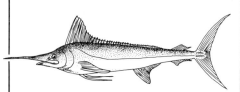

Black marlin are a fish primarily found in tropical waters of the Pacific and Indian Oceans, although they have occasionally appeared elsewhere. They are more likely to be found around islands and shorelines near deep water than their blue marlin counterparts. More large black marlin have been caught than blue marlin, although blues are found in more locales. Fish under 400 pounds are likely to be males and larger ones females. Blacks are the only marlin with rigid pectoral fins that cannot be folded tight against the body. Their size, strength, and leaping abilities make them one of the world's most esteemed gamefish.

about that. Trollers take smaller marlin and sailfish, plus dolphin, bonito, wahoo, yellowfin tuna, dogtooth tuna, cobia, sharks, and mackerel.

For the casting and jigging buff, the reef offers many opportunities for bending a rod, using surface-chugging lures to fish where baitfish schools are being harassed, or fishing deep. Perhaps the best of the reef dwellers is bluefin and giant trevally. These amberjack-like fighters are extremely strong and put up a great fight, with many fish being lost when they manage to bulldog their way to a breakoff on coral. January through July is a good time to be plying inshore waters for these species.

Another popular inshore fish here is the coral trout (which is akin to a grouper). This is highly valued for its table qualities, as well as being a good catch on light gear. Clearly the Cairns to Lizard Island section of Queensland has a wealth of opportunities for fishermen, although interest is overwhelmingly for the mighty black marlin.

CAPE BOWLING GREEN
AUSTRALIA

Left: Giant trevally are a popular inshore and reef-dwelling fish in northern Australia.

Right: Sailfish have been reported in good-sized schools off Cape Bowling Green, and an excellent fishery exists here that complements the marlin angling later in the season further north.

Cape Bowling Green is in northeastern Australia's Queensland district, and south of Cairns. Accessed from Townsville, it lies along the Great Barrier Reef, with Continental Shelf waters being further offshore than to the north. A mixture of currents plus abundant inshore reefs and shoals serve to attract baitfish and small billfish.

GREAT BARRIER REEF

Townsville

It would appear from all the publicity that Australia receives for its monstrous black marlin, that these were the only billfish and that the Cairns – Lizard Island stretch of the Great Barrier Reef was the only place worth visiting. Not so, although there is no place finer for big blacks.

Anglers interested in a little more variety, however, plus lighter tackle fishing for billfish (heavy tackle is the norm at Cairns because of the many opportunities for big fish), are finding that the Cape Bowling Green area near Townsville is among the finest places in the world to fish. Sailfish are more prominent here, and black marlin are plentiful in smaller sizes.

Although not terribly far from Cairns geographically, Cape Bowling Green faces a different offshore situation because the edge of the Great Barrier Reef and the Continental Shelf extend much further offshore. While big marlin no doubt cruise the outer waters, the distance that has to be run to get there, often in heavy seas, makes this usually unfished. But it is possible that mothership operations, as experienced further north, will be used to explore that region more fully.

However, many reefs and shoals exist along this great coral bed in shallower blue-green water (20 to 40 fathoms), and they do possess smaller billfish. An abundance of bait here, due to a mixture of currents and the richness of the bay, attract the billfish, and watching for schools of bait and bird activity is a common element of this fishery.

Sailfishing here has been phenomenal at times, with reports indicating that big schools of these billfish have been sighted. For local anglers and charterboat skippers, the nice thing about this fishery is that really good action can be had from March through September, This means that the winter months (June, July, and August) can be spent here for light action, while the end of the year can be spent further north geared up for granders.

Although marlin of several hundred pounds have been caught out of this area, the fish run much smaller on average (60 pounds or so, lighter early in the season and heavier later), and the tackle is scaled down to 20 pounds and less, with 8- to 12-pound (4 and 6 kg) being very popular. Two fly rod tippet records for black marlin have been established off Cape Bowling Green, incidentally, the largest of those being a 94-pounder on a 16-pound tippet, and also both the men's and women's 2-pound line-class records. It stands to reason that you have to get a lot of opportunities to make those kinds of catches happen. With the exception of possible records, virtually all of the billfish caught here are tagged and released.

However, there is potential for truly giant fish from this port but very far offshore. Some 78 miles east-northeast of Townsville is Myrmidon Reef, a small reef on the edge of an enormous dropoff. It is seldom fished at what is believed to be peak time, in November and December, because of all the big-fish action at Cairns. But blacks over 1,000 pounds have been lost here on some of the few forays that have been made, and reportedly a 989-pounder has been weighed. This with so little fishing attention. Some Australian observers expect this to be a hotspot in the future if appropriate boats and accommodation can be arranged to bring about a concerted fishing effort.

Other species that are caught in the environs of Cape Bowling Green, incidentally, include the various reef species, plus kawakawa, tanguigue, trevally, and assorted tunas.

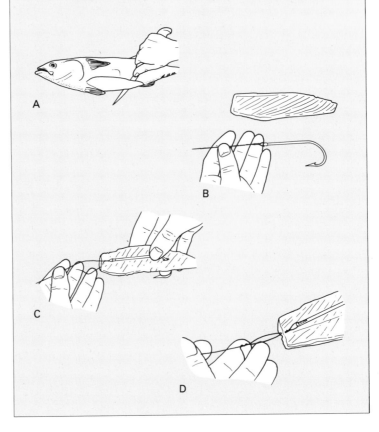

Rigging a Strip Bait

Strip baits are about the easiest trolling bait to rig, and they are very effective. Strip baits are made from various fish, with such species as bonito, small tuna, and dolphin preferred for their durability. To fashion a strip bait, cut an appropriate length from a fish's belly (a) and trim it as illustrated (b). With wire leader partially rigged to hook, leave a long tag end that faces the barb (b) and insert that leader end into the bait close to the forward section, then insert the hook in the middle of the tail section (c). The strip should be flat, not pinched or curled, to skip properly without destructing in short order. Wrap the end of the wire around the leader several times (d). Cut off excess but leave enough tag end available to re-rig when it comes to time to change baits.

A
B
C
D

A virtually untapped fishery exists off Lord Howe Island, shown here, with potential for billfish, tuna, and other species.

BRISBANE, CAPE MORETON

AUSTRALIA

Back in the days of the Tangalooma (Moreton Bay) Whaling Station, Brisbane was the shark fishing capital of the universe. Even today, the eastern coast of Australia, including the waters off Brisbane as well as to the south in New South Wales, rank with the best in shark fishing. Great whites, blues, makos, hammerheads, and tiger sharks of proportions that would make even Crocodile Dundee blanch have been captured in these waters, and the record books are replete with line-class and all-tackle entries from this vast region.

Cape Moreton, in particular, has achieved fame with its great white sharks, but the angling interest these days from worldwide fishermen leans more toward the billfish, and the waters off Brisbane and Cape Moreton hold all the species.

And while the Australian billfishery is generally synonymous with black marlin, Cape Moreton offers perhaps the best chance on this continent of catching blues, and big ones at that. In fact, it may be one of the hottest blue marlin grounds anywhere.

In February 1989, the Australian blue marlin record was shattered by an 815-pounder caught, according to reports, in 150 fathoms of water about 16 miles from Cape Moreton. Local anglers had thought such big fish were present, and speculation has been inevitably fueled now about the possibility of a grander being caught in these waters.

Whether it is or not remains to be seen, but a lot of effort is going to be made to find out. In the meantime, anglers will be catching many smaller blues, and at times here the catching of these can be extremely good. Reports of double and triple strikes, and even a remarkable tagged-and-released tripleheader, have filtered out

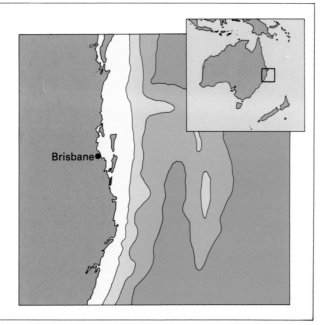

The good fishing of the Cape Moreton/Brisbane area is not far from the popular tourist locale of the Gold Coast, so this is one locale that is not so out-of-the-way in the vast continent of Australia, although it may be a two-hour run to get to the big marlin grounds. South of the infamous Great Barrier Reef, this area has reefs and rocky humps offshore from shallow Moreton Bay, and much of the marlin action is to the northeast. In New South Wales down the coast, incidentally, there is excellent fishing for inshore and mid-depth species, including some of the world's best yellowtail angling.

Brisbane

and reef fishing, with action available for a good number of species.

A potentially hot fishery is developing off Lord Howe Island, which is southeast of Brisbane and some 435 miles from Sydney. The waters in the vicinity of Lord Howe feature rocky pinnacles, immensely deep water, and sheer dropoffs. There has been almost no fishing pressure here until a few years ago, but impressive catches of blue marlin, sailfish, wahoo, yellowfin tuna, and yellowtail have been registered, and some monstrous blues have been sighted. Many more species are available, and some huge bonefish have been taken as well on coral reefs, there being no real flats to speak of here. This could be a sleeping giant in years to come.

from Down Under. Many fish seem to be in the 300- to 400-pound class. Stay tuned.

Blues notwithstanding, there are also black marlin, stripers, and sailfish here, sometimes within relatively short range of shore when the east Australian current moves inward. The striped marlin and blacks are small, but good targets for light tackle fishing efforts. These marlin average 65 to 90 pounds.

The season commences in summer, from October or November through to March, with the striped marlin and blacks early and the blues available from January through June. Seasons could be a little different as this fishery is still a developing one. Sailfish, meanwhile, are extremely popular from February on, and other species to be had include various tunas and dolphin.

Inshore there is much to be had as well, with cobia, trevally, kawakawa, and the like. Between here and the neighboring waters in New South Wales (a territory with some excellent angling in its own right), almost all of the I.G.F.A. kawakawa records have been set. Fraser Island, north of Brisbane along the southern Queensland coast, is a locale for interesting surf

Releasing Billfish

Careful handling of a billfish about to be released takes care and skill, and is sometimes beyond the means of relatively inexperienced anglers. It is also something that may require the work of two or more crew members, especially in the case of large fish. Billfish to be released, however, need to be steered next to the boat, with a pair of wire cutters or knife handy. Smaller billfish can be grabbed by the beak and the hook removed if it is readily accessible. If the fish is hooked

deep, damage should be avoided by cutting the wire or mono leader as close as possible to the fish; where trolling lures are used, be sure that the lure is up the leader and in hand so an expensive bait is not lost. It can be re-rigged later. Keep the boat in slow forward motion. In some cases it may be necessary to hold the unhooked fish for a few moments till it gets re-oriented. Usually, it is well enough to swim off on its own after being set free.

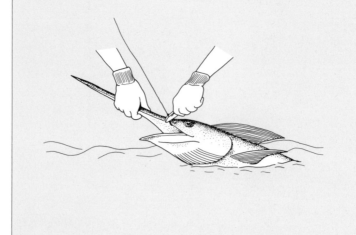

New Zealand's Bay of Islands has diverse fishing opportunities, although it has been principally known for its marlin.

BAY OF ISLANDS, NORTH CAPE

NEW ZEALAND

Turn back the clock. It is 1926 and the world's most famous and successful author of western novels, Zane Grey, is invited by the New Zealand government to visit and fish in its waters. Grey, then also a big-game angler and pioneer of great renown, holder of several world records, and well traveled international sportsman, accepts and ventures to the Bay of Islands on the northern coast of North Island. Here, in 1913, is where the first marlin ever caught anywhere was taken on rod and reel.

When he returns, Grey calls this locale an "Angler's Eldorado". And well he should. While there he caught the first broadbill swordfish ever taken on rod and reel in New Zealand waters. Within weeks of setting up

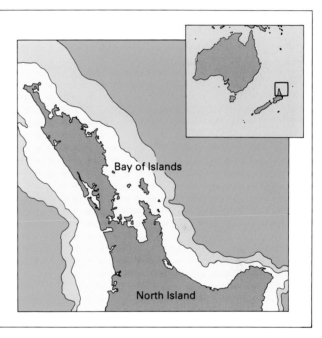

Fishing in the North Cape-Bay of Plenty region is done from Russell and Paihia in the Bay of Islands, Whangaroa to the north, and Tutukaka at Whangarei to the south. The Poor Knight Islands south of the Bay of Islands, and the Three Kings Islands northwest of Cape Reinga (a tumultuous spot where the Tasman Sea meets the Pacific Ocean), are among the popular locales, with marlin trolling done in 55 to 150 fathom depths, lesser for striped marlin and greater for blues and blacks. Even greater depths and ranges can be explored through multi-day trips. These are known as cruising here, where parties book a charter boat for up to a week and travel great distances from home port in search of the currently hot fishing grounds.

camp at Urupukapuka Island he also caught a black marlin, six yellowtails, 17 mako sharks, and 41 striped marlin (including a 450-pound world record). He also introduced that area to trolling with teasers and to using big-game tackle that had the reel seated atop the rod, not below it as was commonplace then in the British Empire.

Now fast forward to September 1989. An article appears in a national angling publication in the United States, written by a New Zealand boat captain, reporting on fishing at Three Kings Islands, north of North Cape and the area Grey fished. In six days spread over two trips, the author and friends hooked 80 striped marlin, landing and tagging 15 over 200 pounds, not to mention an incidental

yellowfin tuna of 110 pounds and yellowtail of 66 pounds. The report includes several accounts of multiple strikes, and the too-good-to-be-true account of strikes on all five lines at the end of one day. *Blitzkrieg* is what it sounds like; breathless is what the author says.

Couple this report with the knowledge that a 902-pound blue marlin was caught in March 1989 east of the Poor Knight Islands and your eyebrows have to be raised. Does something sound wrong here? Is there some place in the world where the fishing is as good or better now than it was 60 years ago? Even allowing for the discrepancies between amount of time fished and the sophistication of equipment and techniques, the present day angling sounds awfully good.

Well, in the Bay of Islands and Far North environs of New Zealand it really is good. No, it's not undiscovered still, and no, the fishing hasn't been as good as in days of yore. In

fact, foreign long-liners dealt a crushing blow to billfisheries here, especially swordfish, and only recent prohibition of these vessels in New Zealand waters may halt the slide. Nonetheless, the Bay of Islands region is one of the world's premier places for big striped marlin, not to mention for also having a chance at blues and blacks, mako sharks and yellowfin tuna, and an assortment of other species if the back-testing fish aren't enough.

For striped marlin, the record books tell it all. No less than twelve I.G.F.A. records are New Zealand fish, including the all-tackle and 50-pound line-class holder, a 494-pound stripe taken in January 1986 out of Tutukaka southeast of the Bay of Islands. It is true that here a 250-pound striped marlin, which would be a trophy anywhere else that the species is found, is just a good fish, since 300- to 400-pounders are caught every year.

Scientific reports indicate that the

striped marlin here belong to a South Pacific stock that grows larger than their northern cousins. Their migration pattern brings them to the North Cape in late December, and they continue onward to the Bay of Islands and then further southeasterly. They are available in this region of the North Island from January through May, with the peak in March and April.

Although there is evidence of these fish being in other areas of New Zealand, such as along the west coast (some striped marlin have been caught off New Plymouth), little fishing has been done for them beyond the northeast coast of the North Island, and there may be new grounds opening up in the future.

Migration pattern and fishing seasons are the same for the other marlin species, although their abundance isn't the same. With blues, the opportunity is always present for a big fish, however, and the search continues for current-day granders. New Zealand's

Left: Very large striped marlin, as well as blue and black marlin, are on the agenda at the Bay of Islands, which Zane Grey declared an Angler's Eldorado early in this century.

Right: Mako sharks have long been a frequent catch in New Zealand waters; this one is small by local standards.

MAKO SHARK

Of all the sharks, mako are the most coveted and estimable fighters. These blue-gray, streamlined, solitary, and pelagic sharks leap very high, fight doggedly, make strong runs, dive deep, and even charge the boat. Close relatives of the great white shark, makos swim with short, powerful strokes, and appear to be more sleek than other sharks. They are also excellent eating, being akin to swordfish in texture, Makos are usually found offshore and taken while trolling for billfish, although some are caught on dead or drifted baits.

Using A Pole Gaff

A pole gaff is a stick or pole of varying length with a gaff hook attached to it. Smaller lengths are used for smaller fish and when fish will be gaffed in the lower jaw to be released alive. Longer pole gaffs are used for larger fish and big boats.

As with any type of gaff, a pole gaff is not supposed to be swung like a club or bat, and it should not be used for fish that are still vigorous. Wait until a captured fish is still and within easy range (not extended reach) of the gaff hook, usually fatigued and on its side. Reach across its back so the base of the pole is against its body and then firmly pull the hook up toward you to sink it into the upper back muscles of the fish. Lift it aboard if the fish is light enough to do so. Don't gaff the fish underneath, in the belly area, which produces a bloody mess. And realize that a shark, once gaffed, will writhe violently, sometimes twisting the gaff handle out of your grip. Attaching a small rope to either end of the gaff and to a boat cleat will help save gaff and fish should this happen.

largest blue marlin is a 22-year-old fish that weighed 1,026 pounds and was caught in the Bay of Islands.

Besides the marlin, the offshore fishery includes trolling for such species as dolphin, yellowfin tuna, yellowtail (called kingfish by Kiwis), and the occasional swordfish, as well as pursuing hammerhead, thresher, and mako sharks.

Makos continue to be a fish of renown here, as when Zane Grey fished New Zealand. Three makos from this area of New Zealand are in the line-class world record books, the largest of those being a gargantuan 1,060-pounder.

As if this isn't all diverse enough, there is a formidable light tackle fishery here, offshore as well as inshore, just begging for more attention. Yellowtails can sometimes be found in schools and taken on jigs and plugs, and this provides some arm wrenching light-tackle action in deeper water. They can also be caught in small sizes inshore, in bays around wharves and reefs.

Kawahai, trevally, skipjack tuna and tope provide other opportunities, and these fish are virtually ignored by local anglers, except as it pertains to acquiring them for marlin bait. Kawahai are a particularly notable fish, good on light spinning or fly gear, and known for leaping, hard-fighting activity, and little known outside of New Zealand and Australia. These fish are often found in schooling situations, providing some very fast fishing.

Tope, which are a little-known shark found in shallow inshore areas, provide good light-tackle action, and Parengarenga Harbor has been the site of numerous tope line class world record catches. White trevally, which are a powerful but small fish, are also fairly abundant, as are snappers, which are the most pursued small game in New Zealand and highly desired for table fare.

The northeast coast is particularly conducive to inshore small-boat light-tackle fishing, since it is in the lee of prevailing winds and has a great concentration of sheltered water. There are numerous harbors with notable angling opportunities for those who prefer the calmer salty environs.

With all of these opportunities, and those yet to be fully developed, no wonder that some call this a modern day Eldorado.

Left: An angler admires a small kawahai; these fish are virtually unknown outside of New Zealand and Australia, and are a great light-tackle quarry.

Right: Whakatane, shown in this aerial view, is the gateway to excellent offshore fishing in the Bay of Plenty.

WHAKATANE, BAY OF PLENTY

NEW ZEALAND

New Zealand sits like a castle with the Pacific Ocean as her moat. Surrounded by water, it is almost equidistant from the equator and the South Pole. The closest neighbor, New Caledonia, is 900 miles to the north. Australia is 1,000 miles away across the Tasman Sea; 4,500 miles of South Pacific water separate New Zealand and South America.

Isolated and formed from nature's fiery volcanic past, New Zealand is known for its rugged beauty, its landscape of cones and craters, its fertile soil and verdant greenery. Some know of its exceptional freshwater fishing (trout), fewer still of its saltwater treasures.

Those saltwater treasures are many, and varied, and they are particularly

Bay of Plenty fishing centers out of Whakatane in the east, where it is a 30-mile run to White Island, and out of Tauranga and Mount Maunganui to the west, where it is 22 miles to Mayor Island. Deep water exists throughout the bay, but underwater humps that rise from the depths provide some outstanding bottom fishing, while cruising species like marlin and tuna are found scattered throughout. Although the area to the north, near Mercury Bay, is a known fishing location, the are to the east of the Bay of Plenty is seldom fished, and because of the closeness of extremely deep water to shore, seems to represent good marlin opportunity.

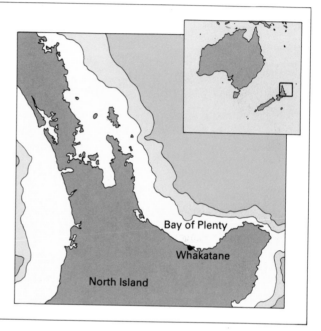

notable for visiting sportfishermen in the middle of the northeast coast of the North Island, in a locale appropriately named by Captain Cook as the Bay of Plenty.

The Bay of Plenty, especially the eastern region, has been overlooked for its sportfishing potential for years, in part because more was known about the Bay of Islands region to the northwest, but also due to limited large boat access as the result of a long-standing sand bar problem at the entrance to Whakatane, which necessitated arrivals and departures based strictly on high tides.

Whakatane is a quaint timber and farming village that tourists used to know more for jet boat trips up the Rangitaiki River. But in the past 15 years it has gained recognition as a gateway to the world's greatest yellowtail fishing, exceptional light tackle inshore fishing for kawahai, and for good grouper, tuna, and billfishing. Much the same can be said of the port of Tauranga, in the west of the bay.

New Zealand is a corker (great one), as Kiwis say, where yellowtail

SOUTHERN YELLOWTAIL

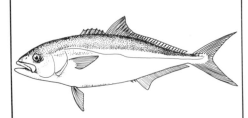

Southern yellowtail (*Seriola lalandei lalandei*) occur in the Pacific from the equator south, with a series of complex groupings in scattered areas. They are distinguished by a yellow tail and a brass colored stripe along the flanks from snout to tail. In New Zealand they are called kingfish, but are also known as yellowtail kingfish, king yellowtail, amberfish, and Cape yellowtail. They are closely related to the greater amberjack.

Left: Big yellowtails, including some weighing over 100 pounds, have made this area of New Zealand the prime place in the world to find this species.

Right: Giant groupers are also abundant in the Bay of Plenty, being taken off rocky pinnacles that jut up from deep water.

are concerned, holding 17 out of 21 world records for southern yellowtail. These include the 50-pound and all-tackle record of 114 pounds 10 ounces, which came from Tauranga, and the 130-pound line-class record of 95 pounds, which was caught out of Whakatane at White Island. Whaka-tane has also produced several fish in the 100-pound class, and it is thought that 125- to 130-pound yellowtails are also to be found here.

Yellowtail, which are in the jack family, are primarily a bottom-dwelling fish that are much like amberjack in shape and fight, being one of the toughest, most stubborn bulldogging fish to catch. New Zealanders call them kingfish. Although

they are sometimes found near the surface in a school, and inshore in small sizes, the monsters for which the Bay of Plenty is noted are primarily caught by anglers fishing volcanic pinnacles well offshore.

White Island, located about 30 miles offshore, is still an active volcano, smoldering and occasionally having mild eruptions. In its vicinity are pinnacles that jut from the deep ocean floor to within 50 to 70 fathoms of the surface. The monster yellowtail reside in the crags of these underwater peaks, and they present a challenge to anglers who use stout tackle, strips of bait and heavy weights, and plenty of muscle to capture the big fish. Enticing them is not actually much of a

chore; hauling them out of the depths and keeping them out of the rocks is, and a fisherman has to really stick it to the fish, or, as Kiwis say, give the Mickey to them, to land the giants. Many of the big fish are not landed, and it is not uncommon to catch yellowtails with several hooks and leaders in their mouths, the result of making it to the rocks and breaking off in earlier encounters with anglers.

Forty- to 60-pound yellowtails are common, and 60- to 90-pounders are likely to be encountered. Although these fish are here year-round, most visiting angler fishing is done from December through April, which is summertime in the southern hemisphere and also the period when

Good fishing is had around and near White Island, an active volcano in the Bay of Plenty.

Locating Structures

Saltwater anglers use Loran to help bring them in the vicinity of structures worth fishing, as well as sonar devices to pinpoint when the boat is over the precise location. Such structures might include old wrecks, natural or artifical reefs, or underwater humps/ banks/ledges. In shallow enough water, these locales are fished by drifting or anchoring and either jigging or bottom fishing with cut bait for bottom dwelling species. In some cases, especially with wide-ranging fish like shark or tuna, chumming is most productive.

pelagic fish are most available. February and March have proven best.

Other species are caught by deep fishing in these areas, too, with perhaps the most notable being giant grouper, known as *hapuka* in this country. Sixty- to 100-pounders are quite likely, and even larger fish are caught. A 115-pounder that took 45 minutes to land on 50-pound tackle in 70 fathoms of water earned this writer the title of "hapuka king" on one offshore expedition to White Island.

Bay of Plenty waters provide a lot of other fishing as well. Striped, blue, and black marlin are all caught here, mostly from January through April when the currents are warmest, with special attention paid to these fish in the Mayor Island vicinity and further north at Mercury Bay. Unlike the marlin fishing in the Bay of Islands, until a decade ago there were no charter boats for billfishing in the eastern end of the Bay of Plenty, although local club anglers were fishing for marlin. This area is still under-exploited, as is the region to the east out to the sparsely populated stretch from Cape Runaway to East Cape.

Yellowfin and skipjack tuna are also caught in the Bay of Plenty. Skipjack and albacore are used for trolling baits, and many tuna are taken by trollers fishing their way out to White Island from Whakatane or to Mayor Island from Tauranga. Several types of sharks are quite abundant, with makos having most-favored status.

The most under-appreciated fishery in the Bay of Plenty, and perhaps in all of New Zealand, is kawahai. These remarkable fish are somewhat of a cross between a bonefish and bluefish in that they are voracious, run long and fight hard, and leap. Kawahai are one of the world's greatest gamefish and surprisingly are unknown in most of the world. In fact, they only recently received record recognition status from the International Game Fish Association. A few New Zealanders fish for kawahai for sport, but these fish are mainly sought for big-game trolling bait.

Found primarily inshore, and in schools, kawahai strike almost anything that is tossed their way, making them ideal for the light spinning tackle or fly rod user. It is thought that they will attain a size of between 10 and 12 pounds here, but common catches are in the 3- to 6-pound range. New Zealand has several world records for these fish.

When you combine the abundant angling opportunities here with the pleasing aesthetics of the countryside and the friendly disposition of the people, it is inevitable that you would rate the Bay of Plenty as one of the world's best saltwater fishing destinations. As Kiwis themselves say, she's a corker.

THE REST OF THE WORLD

From Europe through the continent of Africa in the Atlantic and Indian Oceans, the interest turns heavily to the bruisers of blue water. This is billfish, tuna, and shark country. Fish of large average size are the rule, with many record book entrants and some monstrous billfish that have been seen but never caught – the promise of things to come. Nevertheless, light-tackle angling, especially for sailfish, provides great sport in these waters, and there is ample opportunity to enjoy it. The locales that have been so far away to so many for so long are suddenly seeming closer and more inviting.

Although the premier fishing of these waters has been known to many European anglers, the word has not gotten out as well internationally, and thus, to many newcomers, these fisheries show not only great promise, but have an element of Old World atmosphere. Indeed, the full potential in some locales remains relatively unknown, and the excitement of developing frontiers exists.

THE AZORES
PORTUGAL

There is no dedicated big-game angler who doesn't dream of discovering new, unexploited grounds where lots of fish can be caught, where fish large enough to challenge existing records can be found, and where new heights in sportfishing can be attained. No less a pioneering angler than Ernest Hemingway, when congratulating famous saltwater angler Kip Farrington's wife Chisie for being the first woman to catch a swordfish in South America, said, "the real record is to take the first one, because if you catch the biggest fish, someone is eventually going to catch a bigger one".

Well the first swordfish, and the first blue marlin, and the first yellowfin tuna, and the first spearfish, and so

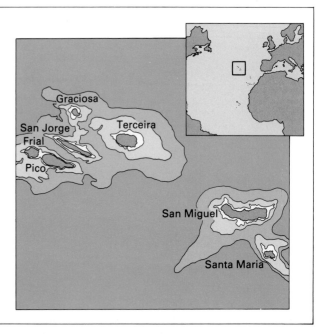

The nine islands in the Azores are spread over more than 100 miles, with Sao Miguel and Santa Maria easternmost, and a cluster of five islands in the center. Most of the sportfishing to date is done from three islands, Faial, Terceira, and Sao Miguel, although there are miles and miles of as yet unexplored waters in the area. A lot of effort has been concentrated on Condora Bank, which is off Faial. The water here drops off steeply fairly close to shore, and into the abyss a few miles away. When a big tuna wants to go deep here, you need more than muscle; you need a reel with lots and lots of line capacity.

The sun has barely begun to set on the angling potential in the Azores, where various species, including big blue marlin, have only been lightly exploited.

forth have all been caught in the Azores, but it has only been for the past five or six years that this has happened and with each season the reports glow brighter and brighter.

Despite the fact that only a few boats are fishing these waters, and that there are often heavy seas that create blow days when big-game trolling isn't feasible, the potential for angling here is outstanding. Clearly the full potential is unknown, and the outer limits of what may be possible remains to be defined.

Regarding marlin, this much is certain: when the water temperature is right, there are many marlin here, and they are big. The average size of the Atlantic blues being caught in the Azores far exceeds the average in other – and much better known – areas, being in the 500-pound category. And the stories of granders and much bigger fish being seen and lost are not mere stories.

In the mid-80s, first reports were mind-boggling. Commercial fishermen were said to see groups of marlin. One account had it that Azorean harpooners had snared a 1,144-pound blue marlin and a 1,188-pounder. Sportfishermen related losing monster blues, one estimated at 1,500 pounds.

In August 1988, an angler came just shy of catching the first grander in the Azores, taking a 980-pound blue on 130-pound line, establishing a European line class record. A report on this fish in an I.G.F.A. publication noted that in ten days of angling, 15 blues with an average weight of 600 pounds were caught, including an astounding double of 650 and 500 pounds. Then, that September, a 1,146-pound blue was caught to establish a new world record on 50-pound line. This is the second largest Atlantic blue ever caught on rod and reel. Is this the spot for the next all-tackle world record Atlantic blue marlin? Some think so, and return annually trying to prove it.

The Azores are a group of volcanic islands under Portuguese domain.

Billfish that are found in the Azores include blue marlin, white marlin, broadbill swordfish, and longbill spearfish; at least one blue over a thousand pounds has been taken on rod and reel.

There are nine islands in all, spread out over more than 100 miles. Separated from Europe by almost 1,000 miles, and from North America by 1,600 miles, they are volcanic mountains, rising from great ocean depths along the Mid-Atlantic Ridge. Fittingly, their shorelines are craggy and steep, but within a few miles of shore the ocean depths plunge to more than 2,000 feet.

Time has moved at a slow pace in these islands, which are a study in contrasts. The Azores is one of the few places left in the world where men in small boats challenge whales with hand-held harpoons. Yet, on Terceira Island, computers whir and hum as officials at the U.S. Air Force base at Lajes Field track submarines and re-supply fighters and transport planes.

One wonders if they see the blips of huge billfish on their radar as well as the hunks of metal.

One of the reasons why the marlin are here is because the Azores benefit climatically from a branch of the Gulf Stream, the North Atlantic Current, which protects against extreme warmth or cold on the islands. When the water temperature is warm enough, in the 75-degree range, the marlin abound. So far, the period from May to December produces blue marlin, with July through September best.

Other billfish that show up in these waters include white marlin, swordfish, and long-billed spearfish. Spearfish are still a bit of a mystery creature, with so few having being caught world-wide, yet quite a few have been boated in the Azores, especially off

Faial Island and off the coast of Sao Miguel from Ponta Delgada. White marlin show up frequently, arriving generally before the blue marlin. They are caught by tuna trollers more than by blue marlin fishermen, as the whites prefer more diminutive offerings, although offshore prospecting with baits that will attract either marlin is the way to go. Broadbill fishing is still unexplored, although some catches of swordfish of up to 350 pounds have been made here.

The Azores can offer sensational fishing for tuna. The primary target is yellowfins, and it is not uncommon to run across these fish by the acre. A lot of very big yellowfins, in the 200- to 300-pound class, are caught here, as well as some better than that, and possibilities for establishing new light-tackle world records look good.

Bluefin tuna are also found in the Azores, although not in the same abundance as yellowfins. Some giants have been caught. But bigeye tuna are here in great quantity and in large sizes, beginning in April, and there is excellent action for these fish into June, especially off Ponta Delgada. That is when yellowfin action picks

up. Yellowfin and bluefin action again heats up in September and October, although these fish are overshadowed by the billfish at that time.

One of the things that is still totally under-appreciated here is the opportunities for light tackle fishing, primarily the quest of big fish while trolling with light gear, but also the opportunity to cast to schools or to catch tuna using lighter gear while chumming with chunks or ground fish, as is done in the western Atlantic off Bermuda, Montauk, and so forth.

Making Wire Leaders

In billfish trolling there is a lot of debate over whether it is best to use a wire or nylon monofilament leader. Wire has tremendous abrasion resistance, unlike the best nylon monofilament line. But when trolling with bait, nylon mono bends easily enough to facilitate a billfish swallowing the bait head first without detecting the leader. Wire is stiffer and more detectable. When using bait, however, you can enhance the turning ability of wire leaders by cutting the wire ahead of the bait and rigging a barrel swivel to both ends of the cut wire. The swivel allows the wire to pivot when a fish attempts to swallow the bait, and there will be no kinking in the wire. With such a setup you won't lose natural bait rigs to some of the toothy creatures, like barracuda and wahoo, that often crash a natural bait.

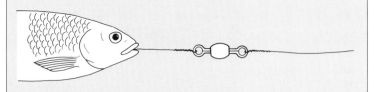

Right: Whether the Azores loom as the next big-game paradise remains to be determined, but it certainly holds diverse opportunity.

Yellowfins are the primary tuna species in the Azores; this 70-pounder is small compared to the 200- to 300-pounders that are found here.

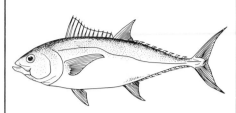

BIGEYE TUNA

Bigeye tuna were once thought to be a variation of yellowfin tuna, since they are similar in size and found in many of the same waters. Bigeyes are pelagic fish that undergo extensive migrations, and are found mainly in temperate waters. They are usually a deeper running fish than such surface wanderers as bluefins and yellowfins, but are also found on the surface. The all-tackle world record for the Atlantic variety is a 375-pound 8-ounce fish from Maryland, and the comparable fish in the Pacific variety is a 435-pounder from Peru. The latter is a 33-year-old record.

Besides all of this, there are also big mako sharks to be caught in Azorean waters, and some 500-pounders that have been trolled up have provided great excitement to people expecting other species. Blue sharks, threshers, and several others are here as well, and such species as dolphin, skipjack tuna, and bonito show up. Inshore fishing can produce barracuda, amberjack, grouper, bluefish (a 24-pounder here holds the 12-pound line-class world record), and a slew of bottom species. Certainly these aren't the target of expeditions to the Azores, but by bringing some extra gear along, on a blow day you can get into a leeward shore and still keep the lines wet and stretched.

By all accounts the Azores haven't yet got a heavy tourist trade like other western Atlantic islands, and the people are known to be warm and hospitable. If you've a yen to be part of the ongoing discovery process here, waste no time; the word is getting out, and some are even calling it the world's latest big game paradise.

THE MADEIRA ISLANDS
PORTUGAL

Located in the Eastern Atlantic about 500 miles from Lisbon, the five islands in the Madeiras are known more for their wine production, subtropical beauty, and place in early trade route navigational history than for their fishing, but this place is a sleeper.

As a sportfishing locale it appears to be similar in many ways to that of Portugal's other island group to the northwest, the Azores, although a decade behind in terms of serious big game effort. The boats and equipment available here for offshore fishing are few and not very impressive; most of what angling occurs is evidently geared toward the European tourist, focusing on barracuda, shark, bonito, mackerel, and some tuna.

There has been some big-game fishing, however, and monstrous blue marlin have been caught or seen by either sport or commercial fishermen in Madeira waters. The potential seems to be there for a developing frontier. As long ago as 1980 a near-grander was caught here on rod and reel, and sporadic reports through the eighties have filtered out about blues from 550 to 800 pounds.

Although little is known about the catch, and it didn't qualify for a

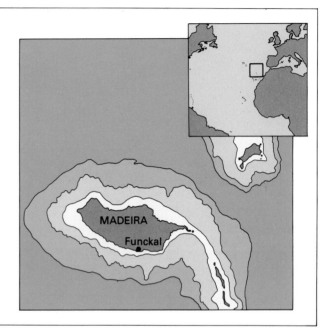

Madeira Island is the largest of the five islands in this group. Known big-game grounds exist at Deserta Island, 20 miles from Funchal on Madeira; Ponto de Pargo; Barlovento; and Porto Monic. Water depth in some spots crashes to 1,500 meters within 10 miles of the island, so clearly there is blue water closer to port, although, as in the Azores, the seas here can be very rough at times.

MADEIRA

Funckal

record, a 1,200-pound Atlantic blue was caught by a French angler two years ago in the Madeiras. Bigger fish have reportedly been registered by commercial fishermen, including a 1,320-pounder in 1986 and a 1,540-pounder in 1985.

In addition to the potential for blue marlin, there is an abundance of bigeye tuna, plus large bluefin and mako shark in these waters. Some broadbill have also been caught, as

well as a fair number of spearfish. The Madeiras hold world records for spearfish, including the a 90-pound 13-ounce fish that is the 50-pound line class and all-tackle record holder.

Formed from volcanic action, the Madeiras have extremely deep water near its cliff-like shores (the world's second-highest cliff is here by Cabo Girao). It can be argued that the sportfishing potential here is as limitless as the depths.

CANARY ISLANDS

SPAIN

When you consider that the Canary Islands in the eastern Atlantic Ocean are at about the same latitude as Daytona Beach, Florida, in the western Atlantic; that they aren't far geographically from the Madeiras and the Azores, which have produced some monster blue marlin, yellowfin tuna, and bigeye tuna, in recent years; and that they are situated on a shelf where the water drops off to awesome depths, you begin to wonder just what fishing opportunities could be possible here.

The Canaries, of course, are better known for their general sun, fun, and frolic activities than they are for fishing. Like the Madeiras, they do not have much in the way of modern sportfishing boats, equipment, and skills. Like other places in the eastern waters of the North and South Atlantic, where fishing is locally more a matter of inshore activities and sustenance owing to traditional commercial pursuits, there is seldom much effort devoted to rod-and-reel clashes with the big, speedy, powerful denizens of the deep. But occasionally there is a glimpse of what might be.

What might be in the Canaries is gigantic marlin and tuna. The record books show that the Canary Islands

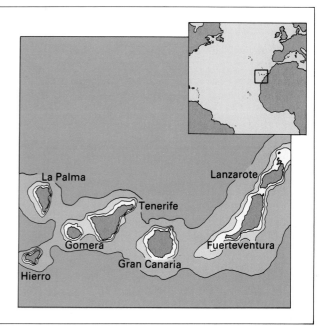

The Canary Islands are situated off the northwest coast of Africa in the Canary Basin of the Atlantic. There are seven islands in total, with Gran Canaria providing most of the fishing opportunities, and all having a deep dropoff not far from shore that creates an upwelling. The shelves and upwelling, coupled with the Canarian Current, attract pelagic species, with June through October being the preferred fishing period.

currently possess three line-class bigeye tuna records, the largest being a 363-pounder on 130-pound tackle; an 897-pound bluefin tuna record on 50-pound line; one Atlantic blue marlin line-class record; plus a few Atlantic bonito and albacore records (including the all-tackle record holding 88-pound albacore).

How big the marlin actually get is anyone's guess, but reports say that blues of 1,300 and 1,600 pounds have

been registered by commercial fishermen, as well as bluefin to 1,200 pounds and a broadbill swordfish of 691 pounds.

Sport fishermen do get yellowfin and bigeye tuna in the 200-pound class, sometimes in schools, and some success has been registered with smaller swordfish when fishing at night. In September of 1987, the Canaries produced its first 1,000-pound blue marlin on rod and reel.

THE WEST COUNTRY
UNITED KINGDOM

There seems to have been a direct correlation in the rising interest in shark fishing for sport with the release of the movie *Jaws* and its numerous sequels. However exaggerated the antics of the great white shark that was depicted in those movies, one thing that rang true was the depiction of the character Quint, the crusty and irrascible shark fishing expert, by British actor Robert Shaw.

Those movies weren't about angling, of course, but the formidable nature of sharks that was depicted brought out an urge in sportfishermen to have a go at them, and the pursuit of various species of sharks has intensified over the past 15 years.

In Europe, the decline of the North Seas tuna fishery also helped to refocus attention on other quarries, with the result being that the Cornwall area of the British Isles has emerged as *the* place to be in Europe for shark sportfishing activities.

While great whites are not the target, such game as blue, mako, thresher, and porbeagle sharks are, with the latter especially so. In fact, porbeagle are the most widely distributed shark in the British Isles, which may account for the fact that they dominate the world records. While the usual porbeagle catch is in the 80- to 120-pound range, bigger fish are taken, including some around 300 pounds every season. Twelve of the fourteen existing porbeagle world records are English fish, including the all-tackle mark of 465 pounds, which was caught from the rocky Cornwall coast off Padstow. Padstow can claim eight of those record fish, incidentally, with the others coming from Looe, Hartland Point at Devon, Gosport, and the Isle of Wight.

For porbeagle shark, most angling attention is centered around Hampshire and the Isle of Wight, the south and west coasts of Devon and Cornwall, the mid-Wales coast, and the west coast of Scotland, as well as much of the Irish coastline. For blue shark, the main fishery ranges from the south of Devon to the southwest coast of Ireland and beyond, with many boats based at Looe in Cornwall and Kinsdale in southern Ireland.

Porbeagle shark, such as this nice specimen caught off North Cornwall, are widely found in area waters.

Hi-Tech Positioning

Offshore anglers know that finding the proper places to fish, be that a seamount, wreck, depth change, or other important underwater feature, can be critical to success. In order to find and return to proven grounds, anglers are not only using sonar, but loran instruments that give them a precise fix on their location. These electronic navigational instruments indicate how far a boater is from a predetermined spot (called a "waypoint"), and how long it will take at a given speed to arrive there. Like a road map it will direct the boater on a course so he knows how to get from place to place unerringly, a factor that has merit for navigation under all conditions, as well as for fishing.

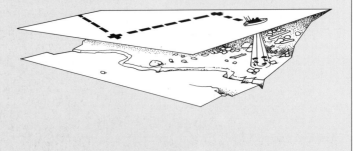

In the 70s, the Isle of Wight was seen as the porbeagle hotspot, being fished by boats from the ports of Lymington and Portsmouth, but that fishery has declined a bit in recent times. Prolific stocks of porbeagle are said to exist in the inhospitable waters off the northwest coast, and many anglers believe that those fish can be tapped when suitable boats become available for fishing those areas.

The blue shark may be the most abundant of British sharks, although it is not as widely distributed as the porbeagle. It is an extremely popular fish for anglers based out of Cornwall, with 40- to 60-pounders common. For whatever reason (some suggest that these are nursery waters), the largest blues are not caught here, with fish over 150 pounds being rare; the U.K. record for blue shark is 218 pounds. Blues are usually found from June onward in southwestern waters, seldom within 10 miles of land.

Although they are not as abundant as porbeagles and blues, mako and thresher sharks are occasional local catches, too. Threshers, which do not venture into the most popularly fished inshore waters very often, are a less likely catch, although they are fairly widespread in the area's offshore waters. The British record for this species stands at 323 pounds, but commercial fishermen have reportedly taken threshers to nearly a thousand pounds from the south of England. Most sporting action for these fish takes place around the Isle of Wight, Hampshire, and Sussex.

Makos are a bit more localized, with catches occurring between Start Point in south Devon and the Lizard in south Cornwall. Offshore reefs accessed from the Cornwall ports of Looe, Mevagissey, and Falmouth, are the principal locales. The British record for mako stands at 500 pounds, but much larger fish have been encountered.

With the exception of porbeagles, the generally cool waters of this area don't produce the largest specimens of the various shark species, and the biggest individuals are not the frenzied target catch as elsewhere in the world. In fact, smaller and more abundant relatives like tope attract a large following. Thus, the specialty boats for big game angling are generally lacking in this locale, with most emphasis on robust tackle and drift fishing with floats and dead baits.

CAPE VERDE

SENEGAL

For its size, the small West African country of Senegal lays claim to more than its share of line-class world records in the International Game Fish Association listings. These include two Atlantic bonito, three Atlantic blue marlin, eight Atlantic sailfish, and one yellowfin tuna, plus two sailfish tippet-class fly rod records. With the exception of the sailfish, most of these were caught by the same people, on light line, on the same day or trip. Nevertheless it says a few positive things about the coastal fishery here.

First, of course, that these (and other) desirable sportfish are present. Second, that there are enough fish to provide realistic line-class record opportunities. Records, especially light line records, seldom are set in locales where accidental catches of certain species occur. The best place to deliberately try to set light-line records is where there are ample opportunities, and where the fish grow large enough to make it feasible to put in time pursuing a record. Usually, the bigger the quarry, the more time and attempts it takes to achieve success.

Where sailfish are concerned, the records especially say a lot. Between Senegal and Angola further south, they

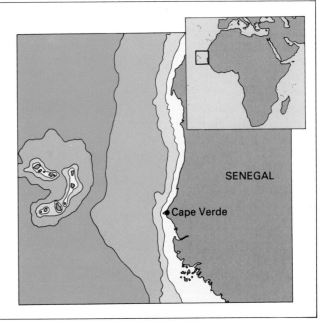

Cape Verde is the westernmost point in Africa. Heavy trade winds are experienced throughout this area and rough water is common. At the Cape Verde Islands, the blue water drops off into the abyss close to shore, and billfishing can be done within just a mile of the islands.

SENEGAL

Cape Verde

hold 13 of 18 total line-class categories. Angola's records were all set in the 70s, however, and most of the Senegal catches, including the largest (112 pounds 14 ounces), were established in 1987 or 1988. Good sailfishing reports from local tournaments support the fact that a lot of sailfish swim in the Senegal waters.

Frankly, not a great deal is known about the migrations of these and other billfish in this area, but there is

speculation that the region from Dakar, Senegal, to Abijdan on the Ivory Coast is a crossroads for both sailfish and marlin. Blue marlin, mostly ranging in the 200- to 400-pound class, are caught each year off the Senegal coast and further offshore at the Cape Verde Islands. A blue marlin in the 1,000-pound class was lost by an English angler at those islands off Ilha do Sal a few years ago. Swordfish and tuna are also caught in these waters.

The Kenyan coast is renowned for big-game fishing, and provides opportunities to catch black, blue, and striped marlin, as well as sailfish and tuna.

KENYA

Author Ernest Hemingway, who had a love affair with East Africa, discovered Kenyan coastal angling in the mid-30s fishing in Malindi out of a boat called *Xanadu*, which had to be jury-rigged by him and his companions for big-game fishing and which produced an assortment of species, including sailfish, on its first trip.

The son of the most famous mystery writer ever, Sir Arthur Conan-Doyle, reportedly took a 75-pound record dolphin off Mtwapa Creek south of Mombasa in the late 40s, which is when the big-game fishing off the Kenyan coast really started to attract attention.

Mostly, however, it only attracted the attention of expatriot anglers and some visiting Europeans. The international community of sport fishermen didn't really get clued in until about a decade ago, and only in recent years have the fires of big-game pursuit been stoked hard.

Today, the Kenyan coast is known as one of the world's premier sport-fishing destinations, and one of the very best places for Pacific sailfish action. In fact, the sailfishing has been so good that many have been content not to venture farther offshore more than occasionally to explore the marlin opportunities.

Originally, the most renowned Ken-

yan fishing spot was in the south-ernmost area, some 50 miles south from Mombasa in the Pemba Channel at Shimoni. That was, and still is, a hotspot for striped marlin, with blue and black marlin also caught, as well as sailfish. Unlike the northerly areas of the Kenyan coast, this locale is not a regular tourist stop and is enough off the beaten track to be still basic Africa.

The Pemba Channel is several miles offshore, with over 3,000 feet of water and a strong current. Fishing there is quite good, comparatively speaking. In a normal year about 230 billfish are caught in the Pemba Channel by less than a handful of boats. Although striped marlin have been taken up to 225 pounds, the average here is about a 100 pounds less. Blue marlin average about 250 pounds but have been taken twice that size. Blacks average about a 100 pounds more than blues, but have been caught on rod here to 800. Several accounts have been made of an estimated 1,500-pound black marlin that was sighted free jumping (not hooked to a lure or bait) here. Additionally, this locale has produced some swordfish, although the broadbills haven't really been targeted.

Up the coast at Mombasa, there is good inshore fishing for such species as wahoo, dolphin, yellowfin tuna, and sailfish. Fishing is concentrated out of Mtwapa Creek. Here, the water is stained inshore, becoming cleaner some 15 to 20 miles out, which is where the marlin activity picks up, although when the blue water is pushed inward occasionally by currents, the big bruisers can be caught closer in. Black and striped marlin are the major offshore billfish here.

Sixty miles to the north of Mombasa is Watamu, which has only recently become a fishing spot of renown. Another 20 miles above Watamu is Malindi. Both are true hotspots for sailfish as well as for all the other Indian Ocean species, and today they probably rate as highly overall as the long-respected Pemba Channel.

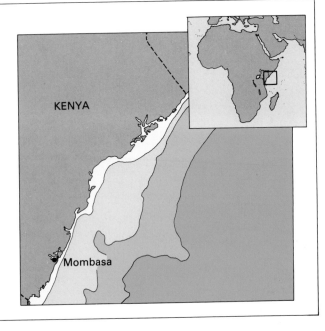

Sandwiched between Somalia and Tanzania, Kenya has the least amount of Indian Ocean shoreline (under 300 miles) of the East African countries. Just below the equator, Kenya benefits from the southerly movement of current along its coast, however, and the banks and dropoffs near its shoreline. Fishing is concentrated at the Pemba Channel, Mombasa, Watamu, and Malindi, with some fishing further north at Lamu Island.

The Haywire Twist

When fishing with single-strand wire or Monel wire the Haywire Twist should be used to prevent wraps from coming loose under severe pressure. To make the Haywire Twist, start by making a loop and crossing the strands (1). Hold the loop tightly with one hand or pliers, and with your free hand press down at point A (the upper strand) with forefinger and up at point B (the lower strand) with thumb. Check that the twist looks as illustrated in step 2, and make four more twists in the same manner. Then wrap the tag end of wire as snuggly as possible several times around the main strand to keep the entire rig from unwrapping (3). Bend the tag wire to form a crank (3); holding the loop tightly in one hand, crank the tag wire in a circle in the same direction as the wrap and parallel to the main strand until the wire parts neatly where the last wrap was made.

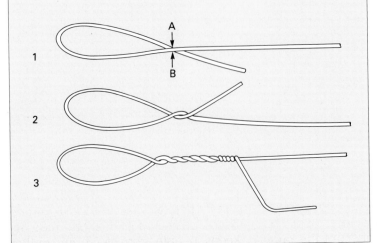

Sailfish are especially prominent off Kenya, particulalry at Malindi from November through April.

In some corners, Malindi is referred to as the "sailfish capital of the world". Considering that in recent years about a dozen boats have accounted for an average of 1,000 sailfish per season, that estimation may not be an unwarranted one.

The action focuses along the colored water line on the coast, which is produced by the outpouring of the Sabaki River. The sediment produced by the flowage has high silica content, which reportedly attracts a huge concentration of herring, which in turn bring the sailfish (and wahoo, dolphin, tuna, etc.) inshore.

Sailfish success is thought to be dependent upon the amount of flowage coming out of the Sabaki. The peak fishing period for sails is in November and December through to April, and that coincides with the onset (during November) of the rainy period in this part of Africa. Both lures and baits are fished for the sails, incidentally.

While small black marlin are sometimes caught closer to shore and mixed in with sailfish, the bigger black marlin, plus blues, are further offshore, and the striped marlin are still further yet.

The hotspot offshore from Watamu and Malindi is an area called the Rips, which is over 15 miles out. Here, upwellings caused by current flows over pinnacled seamounts concentrate marlin in pursuit of abundant baitfish. Blacks up to 800 pounds have been caught at Malindi and to 750 at Watamu, and blues to 540. Other species, including some large sailfish, plus tuna, wahoo, and dolphin are caught here as well, but the abundant action on the banks inshore routinely keeps people from venturing further out for the larger species. There are no existing I.G.F.A. records for the billfish species here (although Malindi claims the 2-pound yellowfin tuna line-class record), but some experts think that much larger blacks and blues, including the highly coveted granders, roam the Indian Ocean waters.

Inshore, there is some local fishing done with downriggers to catch black marlin, and live bait is popularly used. Yellowfin tuna are especially abundant. On the banks to the south, there is a sharp dropoff that often produces small billfish, and this is where live bait is slow-trolled.

Sailfish action picks up in September and October, with the peak season being from December through March. This is when a lot of European tourists are vacationing in the area as well, and space can be at a premium. The West Germans are especially fond of this area, and general tourists are taking in the sun and making game park excursions to view some of Kenya's famous East African wildlife.

The underwater creatures are just as diverse, of course, and someone who wanted to sample the entire variety in this region could have interesting

GIANT TREVALLY

Like other trevally, this species is distinguished by a blunt nose and deep body. Scientifically known as *Caranx ignobilis*, the giant trevally was inaccurately known as "lowly trevally" until about a decade ago, and was frequently misidentified. It is a coral and rock reef dweller found in warm waters of the Indian and Pacific Oceans, and has been caught on rod and reel up to 137 pounds (an Hawaiian fish). Giant trevally are caught with a variety of techniques, and their strong, stubborn fight never fails to impress an angler catching them for the first time.

fishing close to shore as well as far offshore. Obviously with the abundance of sailfish, the Kenyan coast presents a great opportunity for light-tackle fishing, which is beginning to be of more interest to visitors here.

In addition to the species already mentioned, such fish as giant trevally, mako shark, spinner shark, and tanguigue provide some excitement in Kenyan waters. The tanguigue, as well as wahoo, can be more of a nuisance at times, but the spinner (known here as a long-nosed gray shark) is a leaping, determined fighter. Giant trevally, which are called *karambesi* here, reach record proportions. Malindi is especially noted for these fish, and holds the 30-pound line-class world record with a 91-pound 7-ounce specimen.

Large black marlin have been caught off the Rips, accessed from Malindi and Watamu, as well as good-sized blue marlin.

MAURITIUS

It is probably safe to say that in this modern era of geographically illiterate people, many folks are more acquainted with the dodo bird than with the Indian Ocean island of Mauritius. In some ways, that is appropriate. The dodo is the most famous "nonexistent" bird that ever was; *Alice in Wonderland* brought it to the attention of millions of children.

But that large, goofy-looking, nonflying bird with the hooked bill did exist. It was one of many fascinating creatures and remarkable flora that Dutch explorers found on Mauritius when they arrived at the end of the 16th century. Mauritius was then uninhabited, which no doubt caused Mark Twain to comment that God had modelled heaven after this island.

Mauritius is inhabited now, of course, but it is still like a paradise to many visitors. And its fish are anything but extinct.

Although known to the jet set and to some of the European and South African big game fishing fraternity, the British Commonwealth state of Mauritius is virtually unknown to North American anglers, and a place that is often described as being a "new discovery" where angling is concerned. It is only new because it is so far away to so many. However, with efforts now being made to increase accommodation, and with more information being disseminated about its fisheries, Mauritius is poised to be fished more and to lay claim to being one of the best billfishing spots in the world.

Marlin are the main attraction in Mauritius, and some outstanding action can be had for either blue marlin or black marlin, which alone makes these waters unique. Blue marlin also grow especially big in these waters.

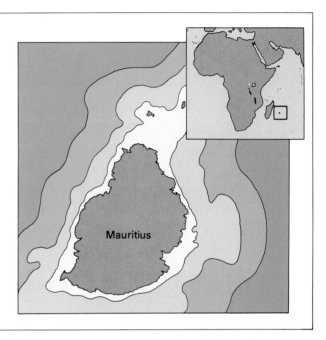

The 720-square-mile island of Mauritius is located east of Madagascar in the Indian Ocean, and is surrounded by an awful lot of water. It is roughly 1,120 miles from Mombasa, Kenya, 3,750 miles from Perth, Australia, and 1,250 miles from Durban, South Africa. This setting puts it in the migratory crossroads of many species of fish, and brings them close to the island itself. Most big game fishing is concentrated along the quick dropoff on the southwest corner of Mauritius.

Mauritius

At least a dozen Pacific blue marlin granders – fish over 1,000 pounds – have been caught in Mauritius waters since people took note of such things. A 1,100-pound blue caught off Le Morne in February 1966 was once an all-tackle world record. And in November 1984, a 1,430-pound blue marlin was taken on 130-pound tackle; unfortunately, it did not qualify for world record recognition because it struck two lines at the same time.

In 1989, a fish just under the 1,376-pound world record (Hawaiian) was taken. Naturally, many smaller blue marlin are caught in Mauritius, with 350 pounds being about the average size. So many big blues, however, fuels speculation that the next all-tackle world record, and possibly the first rod-and-reel blue marlin over 1,500 pounds, may come from the island of Mauritius.

As for black marlin, they run large on average, although no fish caught here yet contend with the granders of other locales. Nevertheless, fish up to 700 pounds have been landed, and black marlin here consistently average in the 300- to 500-pound range, which provides for plenty of excitement. A catch of a 300-pound blue and a 300-pound black on the same day is theoretically possible (though unlikely), and gives great fodder to the imagination.

The prime season for marlin is from December through March, and this is when most of the angling effort is directed. This is summertime here, and the peak of the European tourist trade. However, good catches have been made of both blues and blacks throughout the year. Most trolling is done with live bait, which is mainly bonito and skipjack tuna, but high-speed lures have been gaining in popularity. There is still room for a lot more exploration and experimentation here, and if fishing pressure

Had this blue marlin not struck two lines at the same time it might have been a world record on the tackle used. Clearly, some huge blue marlin swim in the waters off Mauritius.

BEACHCOMBER FISHING CLUB

BOAT	CHALLENGER 1
ANGLER	Louis Simonis
FISH	BLUE MARLIN
WEIGHT	1430 lbs
TACKLE	130 lbs
SKIPPER	ALAIN
DATE	23.11.84

increases, there will probably be a lot more learned about this area.

One of the most pleasant aspects of Mauritian big game trolling is that it can be done within minutes of shore. That is probably fitting, since the country is so far from most of the rest of the world. As a result, a nine-hour fishing day here involves little running and a lot of angling, meaning that one gets to cover a great deal of water.

Most of the Mauritius sportfishing fleet is harbored in Black River, on the southwestern corner of the island, and many marlin are caught a little to the south, offshore but in sight of the Le Morne peninsula. In this region the ocean floor drops off quickly from reef to great depths just a mile from shore. An upwelling here draws vast schools of bait to the surface, and the Black River provides a good fresh water runoff, especially after heavy rains, which may be an attractant as well. The bulk of marlin fishing is concentrated from the dropoff to about 7 miles offshore.

Closer inshore, one might encoun-

Upwellings

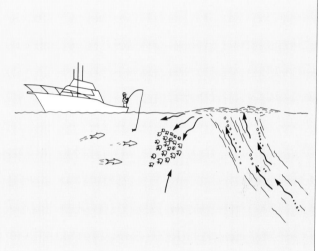

One of the keys to finding fish in open-water areas of the ocean is to find places where bait is attracted or pinned, or in some way disturbed so that larger game can find them easy prey. One such spot is an upwelling, which occurs when an underwater current is directed up toward the surface as the result of some geographic or (most likely) hydrographic phenomena or the existence of another current. Upwellings sometimes are visible because they produce a color change in the water. They often bring baitfish to the surface, which attracts large game. The outer edge of the upwelling, where bait is pushed, is more important to fish than the disturbed or "upwelled" water.

ter such other billfish as striped marlin and sailfish. Neither of these are considered abundant in Mauritian waters, but specimens to 240 and 80 pounds respectively have been recorded, and these two fish are taken from time to time each year. There is some suspicion that more could be caught if fishing effort was directed specifically at them.

Several species of tuna are abundant in this area of the Indian Ocean. Yellowfin tuna are found all year long, with the bigger fish, up to 200 pounds, caught in March and April. Skipjack tuna are especially prevalent in this

SKIPJACK TUNA

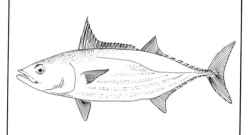

Skipjack tuna are a highly valued commercial fish and a good light tackle quarry for sportfishermen. These are a pelagic, migratory species, mostly found in temperate waters, but usually in substantial schools, sometimes in conjunction with other species, like yellowfin tuna. They feed primarily on small fish and squid and are caught in a variety of ways. Trolling with feathers and jigs is common, but when found in schools the opportunity exists for casting with flies, jigs, or spoons, and the action can be fast. These quick-swimming fish put up a great fight.

Most fishing in Mauritius is done close to shore, as there is a sharp dropoff to great depths within a mile of the island.

area all season. Mauritius holds the all-tackle world record for these species, which is shared by two 41-pound fish. An abundance of skipjack makes for light tackle and fly rod opportunities that are seldom explored here.

Dogtooth tuna are prevalent as well. The dogtooth, which is actually a bonito, is found in tropical reef waters and Mauritius holds the 50-pound line-class world record for this species with a 209-pounder caught off Le Morne in 1983. A 224-pounder was reportedly caught in 1988.

Wahoo, small dorado (dolphin), barracuda, and a variety of sharks, plus such reef fish as groupers, make up the other possibilities. The Mauritian record for wahoo is 125 pounds, but these fish are usually landed at one-third that size, with best action from September through January.

Sharks are fairly abundant, although they don't pose the big-game fighting problems (multilated billfish) that occur in some other marlin hotspots. Mako sharks grow quite large, and one over 1,000 pounds was reportedly taken in 1988. Hammerheads, tigers, and blues are also found, and a 400-pound blue from Mauritius holds an I.G.F.A. line-class world record.

Mauritius is roughly comparable in size to Maui in the Hawaiian Islands. It is ringed by a coral reef, and inshore the waters are calm, gorgeous, and conducive to all manner of water sports, with warm lagoons, soft powder-sand beaches, and tropical greenery. The interior landscape includes thick forests, waterfalls, gorges, mountains, lush vegetation, and all the things that Disney associated with tropical islands in its early movies. Combine the setting with some excellent fishing, and the superlatives for this island paradise flow naturally from all who have been there.

Striped, blue, and black marlin are on the menu at Mauritius, plus sailfish, assorted tuna, and a variety of other reef and offshore species.

SOUTH AFRICA

With 1,800 miles of shoreline, South Africa has plenty of Indian and Atlantic Ocean at its doorstep, and South Africans as a whole are ardent and enthusiastic sportfishermen. They have to be. Only the most enthusiastic would go through the rigors of launching 17- to 25-foot boats from the beach through pounding surf, as is done in many port-less coastal locations, then brave tumultuous seas, for opportunities to catch sundry fish on rod and reel.

And sundry those fish are. Such species as garrick, snoek, kon, stenbra, and leer fish, unknown to most of the world, are among the quarries here, as well as yellowtail, sailfish, bluefish, and various species of shark. South Africa has produced line-class world-record catches for such gamefish as Pacific bonito, tope, and bluefin trevally, pointing out the light-tackle possibilities here; better known, and most coveted by visiting sportfishermen, are its various billfishes and tunas.

It is the massive currents and countercurrents off the rugged east and west coasts of South Africa that bring the pelagic fish. Here at the tip of the African continent, the Agulhas Current of the Indian Ocean moves southerly from Mozambique down the eastern South African shore, then westerly; in the southern Atlantic Ocean, its Benguela Current moves northerly along the western South African shore. The Agulhas is a warmer current, so the Natal and Zululand regions of South Africa, from roughly Durban north, tend to be the most opportune spots for marlin. The colder Benguela brings tuna and swordfish to the Cape Town and north region. When warm drifts from the Agulhas spill over the Cape

South Africa's rugged and beautiful coast is largely devoid of rivers and ports. It becomes more barren as it nears Namibia on the northwest, and is known as the Wild Coast above East London. It is possible to come in from fishing at Cape Vidal in the northeast and see hippos and crocodiles in nearby Lake St. Lucia, which is not the kind of thing that most other hot saltwater fishing locations can offer. Deep shelf-like waters exist along the Indian Ocean shoreline, which is where most of the marlin fishing is concentrated, and this tapers off the Cape to the deep underwater Argulas Plateau.

MEASURING BILLFISH

In some locales, it is necessary to measure billfish that an angler wants to keep to be sure that they conform to minimum legal requirements. These measurements may apply to total length, lower jaw-fork length, and eye-fork length. The illustration depicts each of these measurements on a billfish.

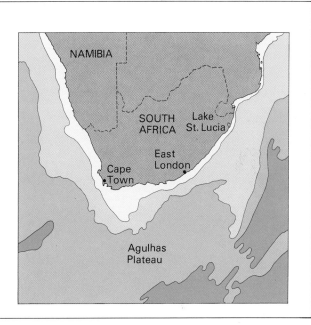

Eye-fork length
Lower jaw-fork length
Total length

Province, it may bring marlin further west, but the Indian Ocean proper has proven to be the most reliable location to date.

And some good-sized marlin there are. Black marlin up to 937 pounds have come from this area, chiefly off Cape St. Lucia. However, modern marlin trolling techniques are still in the early development stages here, and the thinking is that once the local anglers become more skillful, bigger and better results will be achieved, and more will be learned about the fisheries.

With so few ports along the east, the majority of boat fishing here is done by launching small craft, locally referred to as "ski" boats, on the sandy beach, a maneuver that can get dicey when the shore is taking a pounding. This isn't necessary at Durban and Richard's Bay, where there are natural ports. But elsewhere along the entire South African coast, there are only a few other natural ports, those being at East London, Port Elizabeth, Saldanha, and Cape Town.

The Cape Province, reaching from Cape Town to East London, is the departure point for the bulk of South Africa's commercial fleet, and also for tuna sportfishermen. Albacore, skipjack tuna, yellowfin tuna, and longtail tuna are the main pursuits, as these fish gather in good numbers here to feed on anchovy and herring.

Swordfish are present, too, but little effort is made for them, although commercial trawlers take many of these fish. The rough water off the Cape, and often unpredictable weather have made this an inhospitable place to be at night, when most broadbills are caught. Nonetheless, a 205-pounder was caught a few years ago off Cape Elizabeth, and reportedly some monsters have been taken by the longliners.

Tremendous currents mingle at the tip of South Africa, making this area conducive to black marlin, some of which are quite large, as well as tuna and swordfish.

NOT TO BE FORGOTTEN...

OTHER LOCALES THAT BEAR WATCHING

There are numerous places that have had some notable saltwater sport-fishing in the past, or may have in the future, and about which much is still unknown at the present time. Here are some places for the traveling angler to keep an eye on:

BAY OF ISLANDS
Honduras

Reports say that there are a lot of bonefish and permit that have not been fished over in this string of Caribbean islands and cays off the northcentral coast of Honduras, which is currently more well known for good diving. This appears to be a year-round fishery, although the rainy season, beginning in June, may diminish prospects, making winter and spring preferable. The bonefish are small but abundant, especially at Roatan, and some fish up to 8 pounds have reportedly been caught. Permit are plentiful, especially on the flats at Gaunaja Island, and offer a particularly good chance of catching one on a fly – which is one of the hardest of all saltwater feats to accomplish.

GUADELOUPE
French West Indies

Situated in the archipelago known as the Leeward Islands in between the Atlantic Ocean and the Caribbean Sea, Guadeloupe would seem to be a natural for good big-game fishing. Few people seem to be angling here, although blue marlin reportedly can be caught throughout the fall and winter. These fish are in the 200- to 300-pound class, with some larger. Wahoo, dolphin, and bonito are common. Few boats, little pressure, and excellent fishing to the northeast at the Virgin Islands, have combined to keep this area lightly explored.

FIJI

Marlin, tuna, sailfish, wahoo, dolphin, jacks, and an assortment of other typical Pacific fish are evidently abundant in Fiji waters, and if these islands ever become more developed (which probably they shouldn't), anglers may just find nirvana. Black marlin and sailfish (a 189-pound line-class world record came from here two decades ago) are sought from October through April; wahoo are plentiful, and so are yellowfin tuna, the latter from February through June. With all of the reefs here, reef fishing is probably exceptional. We've heard some good, but sketchy, reports about the angling opportunities east of here in the Tonga Islands, too.

BRAZIL

Brazil doesn't get a great deal of attention for its billfishing, but a check of the current record books shows that it holds one line-class blue marlin record (604 pounds, caught in 1986), and seven white marlin records, including a 181-pounder that is the all-tackle and 30-pound line-class holder. Vitoria, which is a good 300 miles north of Rio de Janeiro, is the hotspot for whites, with November through February prime. It also has sailfish and blue marlin. Offshore from Rio, sailfish predominate, and are abundant, especially in the peak months of December and January.

CHILE

Thanks to the course of the Humboldt current, and its upwelling nature near shore, Chile had world famous sword-fishing several decades ago. It still holds two women's line-class records and the all-tackle record of a monstrous 1,182-pounder. These were all established in the early 50s, and the fishery for broadbills and striped marlin there has been in decline for years as the result of commercial long-lining and netting. Fish of 533 and 650 pounds caught at Algarrobo in recent years established new line-class records, which says that big fish are still around. This coast still only has one or two recreational boats that are fishing and the swordfish population is not improved, but it's still better here for broadbills than anyplace else.

TRINIDAD AND TOBAGO

One of the world's mightiest rivers, the Orinoco, empties into the Atlantic about 100 miles southeast of Trinidad, and this silt-laden river, coupled with prevailing winds and currents, strongly influences the fishing opportunities here off the northeastern Venezuelan coast. Kingfish up to 70 pounds, wahoo, jack crevalle, and tarpon provide good inshore fishing around Tri-

There are still other places that have good angling potential, but about which much remains to be discerned.

nidad. Marlin and sailfish are more prevalent off the smaller island of Tobago, however, which is less affected by the Orinoco. Billfish and dolphin are winter quarries in the offshore environs here, with the Three Sisters Islands to the north being most productive. A good dropoff and minimal pressure make this an area that seems ripe for more intensive exploration.

TURKS AND CAICOS

This string of 30 islands is geologically, but not politically, part of the Bahamas, and virtually unknown. Situated off the southeastern tip of the Bahamas and north of Haiti, they are directly along the migration route of blue marlin, with a steep dropoff into the Atlantic within a few minutes of

shore. Only a minimal amount of trolling is done here throughout the season, but blue marlin are caught through the summer months, with most activities based from Providenciales. Sizes run from 150 to 250 pounds, but larger fish would seem possible. There is also some bonefishing on flats and sandy shores around various cays, as well as reef fishing for assorted species.